Proverbs

BIBLE STUDY COMMENTARY

A Topical Study

ELDON WOODCOCK

Wipf and Stock Publishers
150 West Broadway • Eugene OR 97401
2001

Proverbs
A Topical Study
By Woodcock, Eldon
Copyright©1988 by Woodcock, Eldon
ISBN: 1-57910-818-0

Reprinted by *Wipf and Stock Publishers*
150 West Broadway • Eugene OR 97401

Previously published by Zondervan Publishing House, 1988.

All Scripture quotations, unless otherwise noted, are taken from the HOLY BIBLE: NEW INTERNATIONAL VERSION (North American Edition). Copyright © 1973, 1978, 1984, by the International Bible Society. Used by permission of Zondervan Bible Publishers.

Contents

1. Introduction and Outline   7
2. Basic Terminology of Wisdom, Folly,
   Righteousness, and Wickedness   34
3. The Fear of the Lord   51
4. References to the Lord   60
5. The Two Ways: Wisdom and Folly   83
6. The Two Ways: Righteousness and Wickedness   123
7. Human Relationships   154
8. Business Principles   203
Subject Index   231
Scripture Index   233

Chapter 1
Introduction

The Book of Proverbs is a rich collection of God's wisdom for His people. Although not a theological work as such, there are many references to God and our relationship to Him as well as reliable guidelines for everyday living. The spiritual, ethical, psychological, intellectual, physical, marital, social, and professional areas of our lives are all addressed here.

Important segments of the New Testament present redemptive truth aimed at those who have received Jesus Christ as their Lord and Savior. Redemptive truth includes the solid foundation of salvation based upon Christ's redemptive, substitutionary, sacrificial death and the attitudes and actions in life derived from it. Many of these attitudes and actions make little or no sense to unbelievers who have rejected that redemptive foundation.

Although the spiritual element is an important part of the complete picture of wisdom presented in the Book of Proverbs, many principles of wisdom are effective even without that redemptive foundation. These principles for guiding people toward success in achieving their goals were established by God in the structure of His creation. Therefore, believer and unbeliever alike can apply them as part of God's creation truth.

Maxims in the Book of Proverbs are often general principles that should not be pressed into rigid absolutes. In fact, exceptions to these do not invalidate them because some relationships and situations are too complex to be covered adequately by a single principle. These principles, if followed, often increase the probability of success, but do not guarantee it.

Proverbs contains a powerful pragmatic emphasis. It includes astute observations about how things are without any moral evaluation so people can come to grips with them personally. Doing what is right is wise because it is more beneficial in the long run. Doing what is sinful is wrong because it produces more harm than any temporary benefit or pleasure.

In Proverbs, the way of wisdom is fearing God, doing right, and using common sense to develop life patterns that will bring harmony, happiness, and success in every area of life. Proverbs contains many earnest exhortations to follow that way and to avoid the alternative way of foolishness and wickedness.

A. Sections, Authorship, and Date

The Book of Proverbs is a collection of collections, so each of several sections is a collection of proverbs. Therefore, determining authorship becomes a complicated problem, since the authors of these materials functioned not only as originators but also as compilers, scribes, and editors.

Three sections (1–9; 10:1–22:16; 25–29) are attributed to Solomon (1:1; 10:1; 25:1), although some have plausibly understood 1:1 to attribute virtually the entire book to his authorship. The Solomonic proverbs of chapters 25–29 were compiled, edited, and transcribed by professional scribes financed by King Hezekiah's royal court (25:1). The total of about 800 proverbs in the 915 verses of the Book of Proverbs was only a portion of the 3,000 proverbs produced by Solomon (1 Kings 4:32). The content and literary features of these collections fit Solomon's time, around 950 B.C. The conclusion that the materials attributed to Solomon include proverbs that Solomon both wrote and collected is plausible.

Two sections (22:17–24:22; 24:23–34), called "the sayings of the wise" (22:17; 24:23), are not attributed to any individual, even though their content and literary features fit Solomon's time. Although not explicitly stated, it is entirely possible that these two collections may also have been compiled by Solomon. If so, then Proverbs 1–29 is Solomonic.

The numerous and close parallels between materials in this

collection and in the Egyptian *Teaching of Amenemope* are conspicuous. Consequently, one of these was the source of the other or both depended upon an earlier source.¹

The title "The Sayings of Agur son of Jakeh" (30:1) describes the collection in Proverbs 30. The title "The Sayings of King Lemuel" (31:1) refers clearly to 31:1-9 and possibly to the entire chapter. Nothing is known about Agur, Jakeh, and Lemuel. The content and style of these sayings suggest a late pre-exilic date, perhaps as early as the seventh century B.C. after the time of Hezekiah.²

Some have suggested that the word rendered "oracle" (30:1; 31:1) may refer to a place named Massa that was possibly in North Arabia. If so, then Lemuel may have been its king. These speculative conjectures are impossible to prove because currently there is no concrete information on the historical, geographical, or ethnic background of this material.

The acrostic of 31:10-31 (see discussion of Hebrew Poetic Techniques) about the prudent wife has no title. This could plausibly be explained by considering it part of the Lemuel material, but this conclusion has not been proven. So, the author may be anonymous. Perhaps it was added to Proverbs in the seventh century B.C.³

B. Ancient Wisdom

Ancient wisdom literature can be traced back to about 2500 B.C., well before the time of Abraham. From this time until after Jesus, wisdom literature continued to be produced. Its earliest sources were from Egypt and Babylonia, and others included Edom, Canaan, Phoenicia, and Israel. Wise men, such as Joseph, Moses, Solomon, and Daniel, are mentioned throughout Israel's history. Elements and literary features of wisdom are

---

¹For details, see Andrew K. Helmbold, "The Relationship of Proverbs and Amenemope," *The Law and the Prophets*, ed. John H. Skilton (Phillipsburg, New Jersey: Presbyterian and Reformed, 1974), 348-59; John Ruffle, "The Teaching of Amenemope and its Connection with the Book of Proverbs" (Wheaton: *Tyndale Bulletin* 28, 1977), 29-68.
²Kenneth Kitchen, "Proverbs and the Wisdom Books of the Near East" Wheaton: *Tyndale Bulletin* 28, (1977), 102.
³Ibid.

also found in the words of Amos, Isaiah, Jeremiah, Jesus, Paul, and James.

In ancient Israel there were three major categories of religious leaders: priests, prophets, and wise men. Although less prominent, the wise men were influential, especially after the time of Solomon. As with the priests and the prophets, there were both true and false teachers of wisdom. The latter group was sufficiently successful to be vehemently condemned by the prophets (Isa. 29:14–16; Jer. 8:8–12). Jeremiah rejected false priests, false prophets, and false wise men alike (Jer. 18:18–23). Of all the Hebrew wise men, none had a more outstanding reputation than did King Solomon (1 Kings 4:29–34).

The Book of Proverbs is the biblical example of prudential wisdom, which consists of practical instruction about how to attain a good, happy, and successful life. Assuming an orderliness based upon Yahweh's just workings, it includes many optimistic, straightforward, and perceptive observations about life.

C. Text

The Hebrew text has been transmitted in remarkably good condition; nevertheless, several readings pose difficulties for translators. Some of them involve words whose meanings have been lost; others involve words that occur only once in the Old Testament. For them we lack data to find out how these words were used. Obscure poetic expressions and structures pose other problems. Discoveries of ancient manuscripts in languages similar to Hebrew (e.g., Ugaritic) have made clear the meanings of several previously obscure words and phrases. Other currently obscure expressions may also be clarified by future discoveries of additional manuscripts.

D. Basic Literary Categories

The materials in the Book of Proverbs are diverse, ranging from two-liners to passages that develop a message or theme. Some of these categories are mentioned in Proverbs 1:6; however, they are not mutually exclusive, but overlap each other.

1. Proverb

The word rendered "proverb" comes from a root that means "represent," "compare," be "like." It is properly rendered "proverb"—a short, pithy statement conveying basic truth that is broadly applicable. Its striking imagery and ingenious wording help people to remember and repeat it. A proverb had such forms as direct statements and descriptive comparisons, yet it also designated extended wisdom poems (e.g., Ps. 78), parables, straightforward observations, and popular cliches. So it may refer to any material in the Book of Proverbs, as well as certain wisdom psalms. Its purpose was to picture reality. Literary techniques used in the Book of Proverbs include illustrations from the natural world based upon careful observation, similes, metaphors, hyperbole, rhetorical questions, exclamations, and puns.

2. Parable and Riddle

The Hebrew word dubiously rendered "parable" is parallel to "riddle" and similar in meaning (see Parallelism below). Like the "puzzling statement" (as Beck correctly renders "parable"), a riddle is an enigmatic saying, question, or story that the hearer interprets. Since it contained mysteries or problems that were difficult to understand, a hearer's ability to solve riddles displayed God-given intellectual capacity. Wise men were skilled in this area.

E. Hebrew Poetic Techniques

Much of the Book of Proverbs is poetry. Since Hebrew poetry has distinctive qualities that are important for interpretation, a few of those qualities should be briefly surveyed.

1. Parallelism

The most characteristic feature of Hebrew poetry is parallelism. A unit of Hebrew poetry is a pair of parallel lines in which the thoughts and words of one line are partially or completely balanced by corresponding thoughts and words in the next line. The thought in the first line may be repeated, contrasted, or advanced in the second line. Although parallelism usually occurs between lines, occasionally it involves phrases within a line or even groups of lines.

a. Synonymous Parallelism. A synonymous parallelism consists of two lines that are equivalent to each other. Each line expresses the same idea, but in different words. Easy to recognize, synonymous parallelism is most often used. Here is an example in Proverbs 8:1: "Does not wisdom call out? Does not understanding raise her voice?" Wisdom/understanding and call out/raise her voice are equivalent pairs, so each element in the first line is paralleled by a corresponding element in the second line. This is a complete correspondence.

Most examples of synonymous parallelism are incomplete. Although still expressing the same idea in two successive lines, they lack a complete word-for-word correspondence. There is an example in Proverbs 9:10: "The fear of the LORD is the beginning of wisdom, and knowledge of the Holy One is understanding." "Fear of the LORD" corresponds to "knowledge of the Holy One" and "wisdom" to "understanding." But nothing in the second line corresponds to "beginning." By recognizing the poetic structure of synonymous parallelism, the reader will not be tempted to find distinctions in thought between the two lines that do not exist.

b. Antithetic Parallelism. In antithetic parallelisms, which occur often in Proverbs, the second line conveys an opposite or contrasting idea to that conveyed by the first line. In Proverbs 10:1: "A wise man brings joy to his father, but a foolish son grief to his mother," the contrasting elements are wise/foolish and joy/grief.

c. Synthetic Parallelism. In a synthetic parallelism, the second line advances the thought of the first line. Since the poet expands his thought in the second line, he has produced a parallelism of form and rhythm rather than of thought. Here is an example in Proverbs 4:18: "The path of the righteous is like the first gleam of dawn, shining ever brighter till the full light of day." In other examples of synthetic parallelism, the thought is completed by means of a comparison (25:11) or an explanation (23:9).

d. Step Parallelism. Step parallelism involves both the repetition and the advance of thought in successive lines.

INTRODUCTION 13

Combining the elements of synonymous and synthetic parallelism, one word or phrase in the first line is repeated in the second line and then made the starting point for a fresh step. The second line extends or completes the thought. In Proverbs 2:12: "Wisdom will save you from the ways of wicked men, from men whose words are perverse." The repeated word is "men," the thought continuing from there.

e. Emblematic Parallelism. In emblematic parallelism, one line makes a statement in literal terms; the other line repeats it in figurative terms. Therefore, one line provides an emblem or figurative illustration of the other. An example is in Proverbs 25:25: "Like cold water to a weary soul is good news from a distant land."

2. Numerical Sayings

Numerical sayings are often found in synonymous parallelism. In a numerical saying, the first line (or member) of a verse mentions a number. The second line (or member) mentions the next higher number. This forms an $x/x+1$ pattern. Then follows a list of items that correspond to the latter number and that illustrate the point made. An example is in Proverbs 30:15-16: "'The leech has two daughters. "Give! Give!" they cry. There are three things that are never satisfied, four that never say, "Enough!": the grave, the barren womb, land, which is never satisfied with water, and fire, which never says, 'Enough!'" Since a whole number cannot have a parallel, it is paired with the whole number next to it. Variations of this form occur including different numbers (6:16-19) and only one number (30:24-28). This technique was also adopted by certain prophets (e.g., Amos 1:3-2:8).

It has been plausibly suggested that the numerical sayings may have developed from the riddle.[4] They were probably found to be useful at a later time to help the process of memorization and retention.

---
[4] Georg Fohrer, *Introduction to the Old Testament* (Nashville: Abingdon, 1968), 312.

3. Acrostic

Another form of Hebrew poetry was the acrostic, which has been described as an alphabetical poem (e.g., 31:10–31). In this form each line begins with a different letter of the alphabet. The first line begins with the first letter of the Hebrew alphabet; the second line, with the second letter; the third line, with the third letter. This pattern continues through the entire twenty-two letters of the Hebrew alphabet.

Although easily observable in the Hebrew text, this ancient Oriental structure is almost always lost in translation. The only English translation to preserve this feature was by the Roman Catholic scholar Monsignor Ronald Knox, whose innovative effort produced an English acrostic by starting each line with A, B, C, etc.[5]

F. Topical Approach

The material in the Book of Proverbs has been arranged according to topical categories to treat it systematically. Considering identical and similar texts together will also be efficient. The Scripture index will help those who want to consult the commentary only for individual verses.

The chapter on Basic Terminology summarizes the meanings and nuances of similar terms that occur relatively often in the treatment of wisdom, folly, righteousness, and wickedness. Chapters about the fear of the Lord and references to the Lord cover the materials that explicitly mention the Lord. The next section treats the themes of wisdom and folly with their associated characteristics; righteousness and wickedness are moral expressions of wisdom and folly. Principles from these sections are then applied to the areas of human relationships and business or professional practices.

These are not the only categories that could be used, nor is this classification of each text the only plausible one. Rather this is an effort to help the beginning Bible reader to grasp easily and quickly the main emphases of the diverse elements in the Book of Proverbs.

---

[5]*The Holy Bible, a Translation From the Latin Vulgate in the Light of the Hebrew and Greek Originals* by Ronald Knox (Kansas City: Sheed & Ward, Inc., 1956).

G. Abbreviations and Symbols

OT	Old Testament
NT	New Testament
Beck	*The Holy Bible, an American Translation* by William Beck (New Haven, Mo.: Leader Publishing Co., 1976)
JB	Jerusalem Bible
KJV	King James Version
NIV	New International Version
RSV	Revised Standard Version
TEV	Today's English Version
TWOT	*Theological Wordbook of the Old Testament*, edited by R. Laird Harris et al. (Chicago: Moody Press, 1980).

References to terms discussed in chapter 2, Basic Terminology of Wisdom, Folly, Righteousness, and Wickedness, include the following four categories:

VWm	Vocabulary of Wisdom
VF	Vocabulary of Folly
VR	Vocabulary of Righteousness
VWs	Vocabulary of Wickedness

Here is one final note about the arrangement of this commentary. Verses (NIV) precede each section of commentary, where they are explained. The references being explained are printed in boldface type; the cross references are printed in regular type. This should be helpful to the reader who consults the commentary only for specific verses.

H. For Further Study

1. Why are some non-Christians happier, better achievers, and more prosperous than some Christians? What difference should salvation make? Does it? What challenges do these issues give to Christians?

2. Read the article about Wisdom by H. L. Drumright, Jr., *The Zondervan Pictorial Encyclopedia of the Bible* (Grand Rapids: Zondervan Publishing House, 1975), 5:939–45.

3. For more details about the literary techniques (including parallelism) used by the ancient Hebrew wise men, read the helpful treatment by William E. Mouser, Jr., *Walking in*

Wisdom: Studying the Proverbs of Solomon (Downer's Grove, Ill.: InterVarsity, 1983).

4. What is the significance of Hebrew poetic parallelism for interpreting Proverbs (and other biblical Hebrew poetry)? What interpretive errors can be avoided by an awareness of this technique?

Outline

    I. Introduction
        A. Sections, Authorship, and Date
        B. Ancient Wisdom
        C. Text
        D. Basic Literary Categories
            1. Proverb
            2. Parable and Riddle
        E. Hebrew Poetic Techniques
            1. Parallelism
                a. Synonymous Parallelism
                b. Antithetic Parallelism
                c. Synthetic Parallelism
                d. Step Parallelism
                e. Emblematic Parallelism
            2. Numerical Sayings
            3. Acrostic
        F. Topical Approach
        G. Abbreviations and Symbols
        H. For Further Study
        I. Outline for the Book
   II. Basic Terminology of Wisdom, Folly, Righteousness, and Wickedness
        A. The Vocabulary of Wisdom
            1. Wisdom
            2. Understanding or Discernment
            3. Knowledge
            4. Discretion
            5. Prudence
            6. Advice
            7. Discipline
            8. Rebuke

9. Teaching
10. Command
B. The Vocabulary of Folly
   1. Fool or Foolish (*kᵉsîl*)
   2. Folly, Fool, Foolish (*'ĕwîl*)
   3. Fool (*nābāl*)
   4. Simple
   5. Mocker
   6. Sluggard
   7. Deceitful
C. The Vocabulary of Righteousness
   1. Righteous
   2. Justice
   3. Integrity
   4. Upright
   5. Good
D. The Vocabulary of Wickedness
   1. Wicked
   2. Evil
   3. Sin
   4. Transgression
   5. Perverse
E. For Further Study
III. The Fear of the Lord
   A. What the Fear of the Lord Involves
   B. Statements about Fearing the Lord
      1. Contrasting the Wise and the Foolish
         1:7; 14:2; 14:16
      2. Avoiding Evil
         8:12–13; 16:6
      3. Results of Rejecting Wisdom
         1:29–31; 24:21–22; 28:14
      4. Acquiring the Benefits of Wisdom
         3:7–8; 9:10–11; 10:27
      5. Cultivating the Qualities of Wisdom
         15:33; 19:23; 22:4; 23:17–18
      6. Appreciating the Values
         of God-fearing Wisdom
         2:1–5; 14:26; 14:27; 15:16

C. For Further Study
IV. References to the Lord
  A. God's Qualities
    1. God's Sovereignty
       16:1; 16:4; 16:9; 16:33; 19:21; 20:24; 21:1; 21:30; 21:31
    2. God's Providence
       18:22; 19:14; 20:12
    3. God's Wisdom
       25:2; 30:2–4; 30:5–6
    4. God's Wisdom in Creation
       3:19–20; 8:22–31
  B. Wisdom
    1. Values and Benefits of Wisdom
       2:5–8; 3:3–4; 8:35–36; 16:20
    2. Results of Rejecting Wisdom
       19:3
    3. Exhortation to Follow Wisdom
       22:17–21
    4. Result of Following Wisdom
       16:3
  C. Our Relationship to God
    1. God's Protection of the Righteous
       3:25–26; 10:3; 10:29; 16:7; 18:10
    2. Our Trust in God
       3:5–6; 29:25
    3. God's Discipline
       3:11–12
  D. Ethical Contrasts
    1. Righteous and Wicked
       3:31–32; 3:33–35; 11:20; 12:2; 15:8; 15:9; 15:26; 15:29; 22:12; 28:5; 28:25
    2. Truth and Lying
       12:22
    3. Honesty and Dishonesty in Business (Weights)
       11:1; 16:11; 20:10; 20:23
  E. God's Judgment
    1. What God Hates
       6:16–19; 17:15

INTRODUCTION

  2. Religious Practices
     21:3
  3. God's Knowledge of Man
     5:21; 15:3; 15:11; 16:2; 17:3; 20:27; 21:2; 24:11–12
  4. The Lord's Judgment of the Wicked
     16:5; 21:12; 29:26
  5. Exhortations Against Vengeance
     20:22; 24:17–18; 25:21–22
 F. Financial Concepts and Principles
  1. The Rich and the Poor
     22:2; 29:13
  2. Attitude Toward and Treatment of the Poor
     14:31; 15:25; 17:5; 19:17; 22:22–23; 22:28; 23:10–11
  3. Finances
     3:9–10; 10:22; 30:7–9
 G. For Further Study
V. The Two Ways: Wisdom and Folly
 A. Exhortations to Obtain Wisdom
  1. Wisdom's Invitation
     1:20–21; 8:1–7; 9:1–6; 24:3–4
  2. Commands to Acquire Wisdom
     1:1–6; 4:1–5; 18:15; 19:20; 23:22–23
  3. Commands to Keep Wisdom
     7:1–4; 8:32–34; 23:12; 23:19; 23:26
 B. Characteristics of Wisdom
  1. The Wise Listen to Wisdom.
     5:1–2; 16:21
  2. The Wise Benefit from Good Advice.
     11:14; 15:22; 20:18; 24:6
  3. The Wise Accept and Value Rebukes.
     15:31; 25:12
  4. The Wise Use Self-Control to Appease Anger and to Avoid Danger.
     16:14; 19:11; 23:1–3; 25:28
  5. The Wise Are Righteous and Just.
     2:20–22; 8:8–9

6. The Wise Have Power.
   16:32; 21:22; 24:5
7. The Wise Are Protected by Wisdom.
   2:9–11; 2:12–15; 4:6
8. The Wise Find Wisdom Attractive and Pleasant.
   1:8–9; 3:21–26; 4:8–9; 4:10–13; 24:13–14; 27:9
9. The Wise Value Wisdom Highly.
   3:1–2; 3:13–18; 4:7; 8:10–11; 8:12–21; 16:16; 19:8; 20:15

C. Benefits of Wisdom
   1. Life and Health
      4:20–23; 6:20–23; 11:30; 13:14; 15:24
   2. Rejoicing Parents
      23:15–16; 23:24–25; 27:11

D. Results of Rejecting Wisdom
   1:20–33; 15:10; 19:27; 21:16

E. Characteristics of Foolishness
   1. The Foolish Repeat Their Foolishness.
      26:11
   2. The Foolish Have Zeal without Knowledge.
      19:2
   3. The Foolish Reject the Knowledge That They Lack.
      14:7; 18:2; 23:9; 26:4; 26:5
   4. The Foolish Detest Turning from the Evil They Plot.
      13:19; 24:8–9
   5. The Foolish Are Quick-Tempered.
      14:17
   6. The Foolish Are Dangerous, Quarrelsome, Vexing, and Arouse Hostilities.
      17:12; 22:10; 27:3; 30:32–33
   7. The Foolish Are Arrogant.
      17:7; 21:24; 26:12
   8. The Foolish Are Slanderous.
      10:18
   9. The Foolish Are Useless to Others.
      a. As a Messenger (26:6)
      b. As an Employee (26:10)

10. The Foolish Find Certain Items Useless.
   a. Money (17:16)
   b. Luxury (19:10)
   c. Honor (26:1, 8)
   d. Proverbs (26:7, 9)
F. Results of Foolishness
   1. The Foolish Receive Penalties, Beatings, and Death.
      19:29; 20:30; 26:3; 27:22
   2. The Foolish Bring Ruin.
      10:10
   3. The Foolish Bring Grief to Their Parents.
      17:21; 17:25; 19:13a
G. Contrasts Between Wise and Foolish
   1. The Wise and the Foolish Do Not Acquire Wisdom with the Same Ease.
      14:6; 14:33; 24:7
   2. The Wise Enjoy and Keep Wisdom; the Foolish Enjoy Evil and Wander.
      10:23; 17:24
   3. The Wise Do Not Trust in Themselves; the Foolish Do.
      26:16; 28:26
   4. The Wise Acquire and Follow Knowledge; the Foolish Display Their Foolishness.
      12:23; 13:16; 14:18; 15:14; 15:21
   5. The Wise Are Thoughtful; the Foolish Are Naive and Misguided.
      14:8; 14:15
   6. The Wise Listen to Advice; the Foolish Prefer Their Ways and Quarrel.
      12:15; 13:10
   7. The Wise Are Humble; the Proud Are Brought Down.
      11:2; 16:18; 18:12; 25:6–7; 29:23
   8. The Wise Have Self-Control, Patience, and Good Will; the Foolish Are Quick-Tempered, Express Anger, and Arouse Tensions and Hostilities.
      12:16; 14:9; 14:29; 14:35; 20:3; 29:8; 29:9; 29:11

9. The Wise Build; the Foolish Tear Down.
   14:1
10. The Wise Learn, Grow, Obey, and Avoid Danger; the Foolish Experience Danger, Harm, Ruin, and Death.
    10:8; 10:14; 10:21; 13:20; 22:3; 27:12
11. The Wise Are Rewarded; the Foolish Suffer.
    9:12; 10:13; 13:15; 16:22
12. The Wise Receive and Appreciate Discipline, Correction, and Rebuke; the Foolish Reject and Resent Them and Are Punished and Beaten.
    9:7–9; 10:17; 12:1; 13:1; 13:13; 13:18; 15:5; 15:12; 15:32; 17:10; 19:16; 19:25; 21:11; 29:1
13. The Wise Are Praised; Warped (Foolish) Minds Are Despised.
    12:8
14. The Wise Become Wealthy; the Foolish Experience Folly and Poverty.
    14:24; 21:5; 21:20
15. The Wise Bring Joy; the Foolish Bring Grief to Their Parents.
    10:1; 15:20; 28:7; 29:3

H. For Further Study

VI. The Two Ways: Righteousness and Wickedness
   A. Qualities of the Righteous and the Wicked
      1. The Righteous Walk Straight Paths of Integrity and Uprightness.
         a. The Path of the Upright (11:3; 15:19; 21:8; 25:19)
         b. The Path of Integrity (4:25–27; 11:5; 13:6; 16:17; 20:7)
         c. The Path of the Wicked (4:14–17; 17:11; 21:10)
         d. The Brightly Shining Path of the Righteous (4:18–19; 13:9)
      2. The Righteous Devise Just Plans.
         12:5
      3. The Wicked Plot Violent Plans.
         1:10–19; 16:27; 16:29; 16:30; 21:7; 30:11–14

4. The Righteous Care About Justice.
   29:7
5. Justice Requires Both Sides to Be Heard.
   18:17
6. The Wicked Pervert Justice; the Righteous Impart Justice.
   17:23; 17:26; 18:5; 19:28; 24:23–25; 24:26; 28:21
7. The Righteous Are Generous; Man Is Never Satisfied.
   12:10; 21:25–26; 27:20; 30:15–16
8. The Righteous Are Careful.
   12:26; 21:29
9. The Wicked Are Arrogant.
   21:4
10. The Righteous Keep the Law.
    29:18
11. The Righteous Hate What is False and Dishonest.
    13:5; 29:27
12. The Wicked Bring Shame, Disgrace, and Hostility.
    18:3; 19:26; 29:10
13. The Righteous Are Bold and Resist the Wicked.
    28:1; 28:4
14. The Righteous Bounce Back from Adversity.
    24:15–16

B. Evaluation of the Righteous and Wicked
   1. Conduct Indicates Character.
      20:11
   2. The Righteous Are Polluted by Giving Way to the Wicked.
      25:26
   3. Better to Be Righteous and Poor Than to Be Unjust, Arrogant, or Perverse.
      16:8; 16:19; 19:1; 28:6
   4. People Rejoice When the Righteous Prosper, but Hide from the Powerful Wicked.
      11:10; 28:12; 28:28; 29:2

5. The Wicked's Religious Practices Are Detestable.
21:27; 28:9
C. Results of Being Righteous or Wicked
 1. Deliverance for the Righteous; Trouble for the Wicked.
    a. The Righteous Are Delivered; There Is Trouble for the Wicked (11:21).
    b. The Righteous Are Delivered from Trouble; the Wicked Encounter Trouble (11:8; 12:21; 13:17; 22:5).
    c. The Wicked Have Trouble (22:8; 24:1–2).
    d. Righteousness Delivers the Righteous; Evil Desires Trap the Unfaithful (11:6).
    e. Righteousness Delivers from Death; Ill-Gotten Wealth Is Worthless (10:2; 11:4).
 2. The Righteous Are Secure; the Wicked Fall.
    6:12–15; 10:9; 10:25; 10:30; 12:3; 12:7; 14:11; 14:32; 28:18
 3. The Righteous Attain Life; the Wicked, Punishment and Death.
    a. The Wicked Have No Future Hope (11:7; 24:19–20).
    b. Mistreatment of Parents Is Wrong and Often Fatal (20:20; 28:24; 30:17).
    c. The Apparently Right Way Leads to Death (14:12; 16:25).
    d. The Righteous Live Long (16:31; 28:15–16).
    e. The Righteous Attain Life; the Wicked Are Punished and Die (10:11; 10:16; 11:19; 12:28; 21:21).
    f. You Get What You Seek (11:27; 14:22; 17:13).
 4. The Righteous Get What They Want; the Wicked, What They Dread.
    10:24; 11:23
 5. The Righteous Are Blessed; the Wicked Are Punished.
    10:6; 10:7; 28:20

INTRODUCTION

  6. The Righteous Are Rewarded; the Wicked Get What They Deserve.
   11:18; 11:31; 14:14
  7. The Righteous Prosper; the Wicked Fail and Fall.
   11:28; 12:12; 13:21; 13:22; 13:25; 15:6; 28:10
  8. The Wicked Are Victimized by Their Evil Schemes and Deeds.
   5:22–23; 26:27
  9. The Righteous Experience Joy; the Wicked Encounter Deceit, Traps, Terror, and Futility.
   10:28; 12:20; 21:15; 29:6
  10. The Wicked Are Hampered and Tormented by Their Guilt.
   28:17; 29:24
  11. Righteousness Exalts and Establishes a Nation; Wickedness Is Detested and Disgraceful.
   14:34; 16:12; 20:28; 25:4–5; 29:4; 29:14
  12. The Righteous Benefit at the Expense of the Wicked.
   14:19; 21:18; 29:16
  13. Sins Are Universal, but Are to Be Confessed and Renounced.
   20:9; 28:13
 D. For Further Study
VII. Human Relationships
 A. The Adulterous Woman
  1. Descriptions of the Adulteress and Her Deadly Path
   2:16–19; 5:3–6; 6:23–29; 6:30–35; 7:4–27; 9:13–18
  2. Warnings to Avoid the Adulteress
   5:7–20; 31:1–3
  3. Negative Qualities of an Adulteress
   11:22; 22:14; 23:26–28; 29:3b; 30:20
 B. The Wife
  1. Unbearable Situations
   30:21–23

PROVERBS

    2. A Quarrelsome Wife
       19:13b; 21:9; 21:19; 25:24; 27:15–16
    3. Noble Character; Disgraceful Character
       12:4
    4. Beautiful Qualities of a Prudent Wife
       31:10–31
    5. Amazing Romantic Love
       30:18–19
C. Family Relationships and Practices
  1. General Observations
    a. A Man Who Strays from Home Is Lost (27:8).
    b. A Man Who Troubles His Family Forfeits His Future (11:29; 15:27; 17:2).
    c. There Is Misery in Family Hostilities (15:17; 17:1).
    d. There Is Glory in Youth, Respect in Age (20:29).
  2. Children
    a. The Value of Training Children (22:6)
    b. The Importance of Disciplining Children (13:24; 19:18; 22:15; 23:13–14; 29:15; 29:17)
    c. Relationships Between Generations (17:6)
  3. The Importance of Disciplining Servants
    29:19; 29:21
D. Friends
  1. Unfriendliness Is Selfish and Unsound.
    18:1
  2. A Friend Is Faithful.
    17:17; 18:24; 20:6; 27:6
  3. Do Not Forsake Your Friend.
    27:10
  4. Love Covers Wrongs.
    10:12; 17:9; 27:5
E. Neighbor
  1. Do Not Visit Your Neighbor Too Often.
    25:17
  2. Do Not Put Off Your Neighbor.
    3:27–28

3. Sharpen One Another.
   27:17
F. Kindness or Ruthlessness
   1. Kindness Brings Respect; Ruthlessness, Only Wealth.
      11:16
   2. Kindness Is Beneficial; Cruelty, Harmful.
      11:17
   3. Kindness to the Needy Is Blessed; Hatred Is Sinful.
      14:21
G. Encouragement; Discouragement
   1. Joy; Bitterness
      14:10
   2. Deceptive Appearances
      14:13
   3. Expressive Appearances
      15:13; 27:19
   4. Good Attitude; Poor Attitude
      14:30; 17:22; 18:14
   5. Fulfilled Desires; Deferred Desires
      13:12
   6. Kind Words; Anxious Hearts
      12:25
   7. Cheerfulness; Oppression
      15:15; 15:30; 25:13; 25:25
H. Conversation
   1. Human Words Are Deep Waters.
      18:4; 20:5
   2. The Wise Limit What They Say; the Foolish Talk Too Much.
      10:19; 11:12; 17:27; 17:28
   3. A Wise Man's Conversation Increases Knowledge; a Foolish Man's Talk Gushes Folly and Evil.
      10:31; 15:2; 15:7; 15:28; 16:23; 18:13; 29:20
   4. The Wise Speak What Is Fitting; the Foolish, What Is Perverse.
      4:24; 10:32

5. Wise Conversation Is Valuable; Wicked Talk Is Not.
   10:20
6. Apt Words Are Delightful.
   15:23; 25:11
7. Gracious, Gentle Speech Is Powerful and Influential.
   15:1; 22:11; 25:15
8. Speech Is Powerful in Affecting Life Quality.
   18:21
9. Beneficial Talk Brings Good.
   12:14; 13:2; 18:20
10. Righteous Talk Benefits; Wicked Talk Brings Conflict and Destruction.
    11:9; 11:11
11. The Righteous Escape Trouble; the Wicked Talk Themselves into Trouble.
    12:6; 12:13; 13:3; 14:3; 18:6; 18:7; 21:23
12. A Man Is Trapped by Rash Vows.
    20:25
13. An Undeserved Curse Is Futile.
    26:2
14. Wise Conversation Heals; Reckless Deceptive Words Hurt and Demoralize.
    12:18; 15:4; 16:24
15. Wicked Talk Is Deceptive, Malevolent, and Produces Anger.
    25:23; 26:23–26
16. A Blessing Can Be a Curse.
    25:20; 27:14
17. Boasting Is Futile.
    25:14; 27:1; 27:2
18. Flattery Is Harmful, Threatening, and Brings No Favor.
    26:28; 28:23; 29:5
19. The Sins of Lying and Perjury
    a. Liars Listen to Malice (17:4).
    b. Riches Gained by Lies Are Brief (21:6).
    c. Poverty Is Better Than Lying (19:22).

d. Liars Get into Trouble (17:20).
e. Lying Lasts Briefly (12:19).
f. A Deceptive Joker Is Dangerously Reckless (26:18–19).
g. False Testimony Is Malicious and Dangerous (25:18).
h. False Accusation and Betraying a Confidence Are Prohibited (3:29–30; 24:28–29; 25:8–10).
i. A False Witness Lies (12:17; 14:5; 14:25).
j. A False Witness Will Be Punished (19:5; 19:9; 21:28).
20. The Sins of Gossip and Slander
    a. Gossip Penetrates Deeply (18:8; 26:22).
    b. Gossip Betrays Confidence (11:13; 20:19).
    c. Gossip Separates Close Friends (16:28).
    d. Gossip Fuels Quarrels (26:20).
    e. Slander Provokes Curses and Punishment (30:10).
21. Quarrels
    a. Quarrelsome Men Stir Up Conflicts (15:18; 26:21; 29:22).
    b. Quarreling Involves Sin (17:19).
    c. It Is Dangerous to Meddle in Another's Quarrel (26:17).
    d. Quarrels Are Difficult to End (17:14).
    e. Quarrelers Do Not Back Down (18:19).
    f. Avoid Quarrelsome People (19:19; 22:24–25).
    g. Disputes May Be Settled by Lot (18:18).
22. Intolerable Jealousy
    27:4
I. For Further Study
VIII. Business Principles
    A. Working Hard Contrasted with Being Lazy
        1. Work in Season Produces Food and Income; Excessive Sleep Produces Inadequate Work, Food, and Income.
        10:5; 20:4; 20:13

2. The Sluggard Is Rebuked for His Disastrous Excessive Sleep.
    6:9–11; 19:15; 24:30–34; 26:14
3. The Sluggard Is Too Lazy to Eat.
    19:24; 26:15
4. The Sluggard Has Wild Excuses.
    22:13; 26:13
5. Working the Land Produces Food; Chasing Fantasies Leads to Poverty.
    12:11; 28:19
6. Diligent, Productive Work Produces Profit, Wealth, and Authority; Laziness Breeds Poverty and Slavery.
    10:4; 12:24; 12:27; 13:4; 14:23
7. The Sluggard Brings Misery to Those Who Send Him.
    10:26
8. Laziness Is Destructive.
    18:9
9. Slackening Under Pressure Displays Weakness.
    24:10
10. The Ant Works.
    6:6–8; 30:24–28
11. The Worker Is Motivated by His Appetite.
    16:26
12. There Are Priorities in Work.
    24:27
13. The Worker's Equipment Is Essential.
    14:4
14. Good Stewardship Is Important.
    27:23–27
15. There Are Benefits in Hard, Effective Work.
    22:29; 27:18

B. Administration
1. A King Needs Many Subjects.
    14:28; 30:29–31
2. The King's Mind Is Unsearchable.
    25:3

3. An Understanding King Maintains Order.
   28:2
4. A Wise King Eliminates Evil and Destroys the Wicked.
   16:10; 20:8; 20:26
5. The King's Favor Brings Benefits and Life; His Wrath Brings Danger and Death.
   16:15; 19:12; 20:2
6. A King Can Have Destructive Tendencies.
   28:3; 29:12

C. Rich and Poor
   1. The Bitter Tastes Sweet to the Hungry.
      27:7
   2. The Rich Are Popular; the Poor Are Shunned.
      14:20; 19:4; 19:6; 19:7
   3. The Poor Are Ripped Off by Injustice and by Harsh Responses.
      13:23; 18:23
   4. The Rights of the Poor Are to Be Defended, Not Ignored.
      21:13; 28:27; 31:8–9
   5. The Rich Dominate the Poor.
      22:7
   6. The Rich Consider Themselves Wise; the Discerning Poor Know Better.
      28:11
   7. Wealth Is Considered a Fortress; Poverty, Ruin.
      10:15; 18:11
   8. Riches May Be Temporary and Are Easily Lost.
      20:21; 21:17; 23:4–5; 28:22
   9. Those Who Get Rich by Wronging the Poor Will Become Poor.
      22:16; 28:8
   10. A Rich Man Ransoms His Life; a Poor Man Is Not Threatened.
       13:8
   11. Some Are Not As They Seem.
       13:7

12. Better to Be Poor with Something Than Pretend to Be Rich with Nothing.
   12:9
D. Generous and Stingy
   1. Gifts Open Doors.
      18:16
   2. The Generous Prosper; the Stingy Become Poor.
      11:24; 11:25; 11:26; 22:9
   3. Avoid a Stingy Man.
      23:6–8
E. Honest and Dishonest
   1. Gains from Fraud Produce Misery.
      20:17
   2. Dishonestly Acquired Money Dwindles, but Gradual Financial Growth Works.
      13:11
   3. Bribes Contribute to Success and Avert Anger.
      17:8; 21:14
   4. Kings Appreciate Honesty and Truth.
      16:13
   5. A Good Reputation Is More Valuable Than Wealth.
      22:1; 27:21
F. Physical Excesses: Gluttony and Drinking
   1. Too Much Honey Is Bad.
      25:16; 25:27
   2. Drunkenness and Gluttony Breed Poverty.
      23:19–21
   3. Drinking and Forgetting Go Together.
      31:4–7
   4. The Dangers of Drinking Are Great.
      20:1; 23:29–35
G. Buying
   20:14
H. Putting Up Security for Another
   1. Its Undesirable Implications
      11:15; 17:18; 20:16; 27:13

2. Exhortations to Avoid or to Escape from Putting Up Security for Another
6:1–5; 22:26–27
I. For Further Study

Chapter 2

Basic Terminology of Wisdom, Folly, Righteousness, and Wickedness

A major purpose of the Book of Proverbs is to motivate its readers to apply the ways and principles of wisdom to every dimension of their lives. Several terms describe different aspects of wisdom, folly, righteousness, and wickedness. Overlapping in meaning, some terms within each category are at times virtually synonymous. We shall examine for each word its basic range of meanings, distinctive nuances, and usage in Proverbs.

A. The Vocabulary of Wisdom (VWm)

1. *Wisdom*

Several Hebrew words, *ḥākām* and cognates, describe being "wise," "skillful," "prudent." These words occur 101 times in Proverbs and define the central theme—wisdom.

Wisdom involves a right attitude and approach to all areas of life. In spiritual life, it includes a commitment to follow the teachings of the holy and righteous God who expects His people to reflect His qualities, and a moral commitment to do what is right and to avoid what is wrong. In secular life, wisdom involves prudence, skills in the arts and various types of work, administrative ability, and development of strong personal relationships. In all of these areas, wisdom enables us to adapt what we know so we can do effectively what we do.

Readers are often commanded to obtain wisdom as their top priority (4:7). One obtains wisdom by observing (6:6), associating with the wise (13:20), accepting instruction (19:20) and commands (10:8), being corrected by rebukes (15:31) and, if necessary, the rod of correction (29:15).

The Lord who used His wisdom in creation (3:19) gives wisdom, knowledge, and understanding (2:6). The fear of the Lord is the beginning of wisdom (9:10), teaches wisdom (15:33), and motivates one to wisely avoid evil (14:16). In fact, there is no mere human wisdom or plan that can succeed against the Lord (21:30).

The wise maintain a right attitude (23:19), seek knowledge (18:15), store it (10:14), commend it (15:2), and spread it (15:7). They are discerning (16:21), prudent (14:8), righteous (10:31), humble (11:2), understanding (10:23), and accept advice (13:10).

Wisdom is rewarding (9:12) and a fountain of life (13:14). It provides guidance (4:11), protection (28:26), and healing (12:18). It enables people to speak wisely (31:26) and to appease anger by keeping themselves under control (29:8, 11). The wise win people (11:30), obtain honor (3:35), wealth (14:24), and power (24:5). There is no material benefit or monetary value that can even begin to be comparable to the tremendous privilege of possessing wisdom (8:11; 16:16).

Virtually synonymous to these words for wisdom are the Hebrew words (*śekel*) and cognates. They picture a thorough understanding of how to integrate the relevant thoughts and facts to generate a wise, prudent, and successful course of action.

2. Understanding or Discernment

Several Hebrew words, *bîn* and cognates, include the ideas of "understanding," "discernment," "perception," and "insight." These words occur sixty-six times in Proverbs. Their key idea is to come to an understanding by discerning and choosing between such alternatives as good and evil, right and wrong, true and false. Understanding is received as a gift from God, yet it is to be diligently sought by those who would be discerning.

The Book of Proverbs was designed to motivate and to enable its readers to attain wisdom (1:2). Wisdom exhorts us to gain (understand) prudence (8:5), to obtain understanding (4:7), and to follow its ways (9:6).

Understanding or discernment is very closely related to wisdom. These terms overlap each other, at times being almost equivalent in meaning. The wise are called discerning (16:21). The discerning person perceives that the teachings of wisdom are right (8:9) and delights in them (10:23). He keeps wisdom in view (17:24), possesses it (14:33), expresses it in his conversation (10:13), and discerns human purposes (20:5). The discerning are urged to get guidance (1:5) and acquire knowledge when rebuked (19:25). Knowledge comes easily to the discerning who seek it (14:6).

Understanding has an important role in the spiritual, ethical, and social realms. Knowledge of God is understanding (9:10) which the Lord gives (2:6). By wisdom and understanding, the Lord created the heavens and the earth (3:19). There is no human wisdom or insight that can succeed against the Lord (21:30). Thus we are to trust in the Lord and not lean on our own understanding (3:5). The discerning understand the fear of the Lord (2:5).

The discerning keep the law (28:7) and understand justice (28:5b). Understanding involves a straight course (15:21), patience (14:29), and appropriate restraint (11:12). God discerns (or "weighs") the inner thoughts and motivations of a person (24:12). People with understanding are blessed (3:13) and protected (2:11). Understanding is far more valuable than vast riches (16:16). For he who cherishes understanding prospers (19:8).

3. Knowledge

The Hebrew words, *yāda'* and cognates, occur over eighty times in Proverbs. They primarily mean "knowledge" but include "perception," "discernment," "wisdom," and "knowing people." They cover many facets of knowledge, especially those obtained through the physical senses and experience.

These words describe both knowledge by God and about God. The Lord used His knowledge in creation (3:20) and knows people's thoughts (24:12). The Lord gives knowledge to man (2:6). Fearing the Lord is the beginning of knowledge (1:7) and is equivalent to knowing the Lord (2:5). Those who know

Him are to acknowledge Him (3:6). In some cases the verb may mean "cause to know"; for example, to "teach" (22:19).

Knowledge is often associated with similar and overlapping terms. Those who would be wise are urged to gain (know) understanding (4:1). Discerning people seek knowledge (15:14) and acquire it (18:15) easily (14:6), even occasionally from a rebuke (19:25). Wise men gain knowledge through instruction (21:11), store that knowledge (10:14), commend it (15:2), and spread it (15:7). The converse is also true. For knowledgeable people discern words of wisdom to be faultless (8:9). The Book of Proverbs enables people to attain (know) wisdom and discipline (1:2). Closely associated with knowledge are discretion (1:4), wisdom (8:12), discipline (12:1), and counsel (22:20). The prudent man possesses and uses knowledge (13:16). A righteous man learns when taught (made to know, 9:9). He uses his knowledge to avoid the destructive talk of the godless (11:9). He knows what is fitting (10:32). He cares (knows) about justice for the poor (29:7).

A man of knowledge increases his strength (24:5) and uses his words with restraint (17:27). A knowledgeable ruler maintains order (28:2). Zeal is undesirable without knowledge (19:2). Knowledge is pleasant (2:10) and more valuable than huge quantities of money (8:10) and rubies (20:15). Thus, knowledge is to be preserved (5:2). The ideas of wisdom and knowledge overlap because both concepts involve a person's effective functioning in relationships with God, family, and other people. In Proverbs, what a person knows generally produces knowledgeable behavior; what he does reflects what he knows.

4. Discretion

The Hebrew words, *m^ezimmâ* and cognates, describe making plans—both good and evil. They often picture people with evil plans (30:32), evil intent (21:27), foolish schemes (24:9), and evil conduct, perhaps as a result of evil plans (10:23). They describe crafty men as condemned by the Lord (12:2), hated (14:17), and plotting evil (24:8).

The singular form of *m^ezimmâ* pictures discretion, that is, being careful about what a person says and does, as a result of perceptive planning that lies behind wise actions. It is a quality of wisdom (8:12) that a person should maintain (5:2), since it provides protection (2:11).

5. Prudence

The Hebrew words, '*ārum* and cognates, picture being prudent—using common sense and sound judgment. Prudence is closely associated with wisdom (8:12). A prudent man keeps his knowledge to himself (12:23) and is crowned with knowledge (14:18), which he uses (13:16). Giving thought to his ways (14:8), he takes refuge when he perceives danger (22:3). He overlooks an insult (12:16) and heeds correction (15:5). The words rendered "prudence" and "discretion" overlap in their meanings and are, at times, virtually synonymous.

6. Advice

The Hebrew words, '*ēṣâ* and cognates, convey the ideas of "advice" or "counsel" based upon a carefully developed plan. The Lord's purpose or plan must succeed (19:21). The earnest counsel of a friend is pleasant and valuable (27:9). Counsel is a property of wisdom (8:14). The wise listen to advice (13:10) on which they base their plans (20:18). Promoters of peace experience joy (12:20). Sound advice produces victory in battle (11:14) and success in other enterprises (15:22). That is why it is foolish to ignore wise counsel (1:30–31).

7. Discipline

The Hebrew words, *mûsār* and cognates, picture "corrective discipline" that results in instruction. This correction may include chastisement. They describe God's disciplining His children in their covenant relationship to Him and parents' disciplining their children. Discipline lays the foundation for developing wisdom, knowledge, and understanding.

The fear of the Lord produces the disciplined instruction that leads a person to wisdom (15:33). Those who love discipline love knowledge (12:1). Readers are urged to listen to instruction (4:1), to accept it (19:20), and to apply themselves to learning through it (23:12). For following discipline is the way to life (6:23). The Book of Proverbs was written to enable people to acquire discipline (1:2–3). People need to acquire discipline

(23:23) by giving it top priority, to hold on to it (4:13), and then to be sure to discipline their children (13:24). For the rod of discipline will remove folly from a child's heart (22:15).

The dangers of ignoring discipline include despising oneself (15:32), leaving the path of knowledge (19:27), and being led astray by one's folly (5:23), producing the results of poverty and shame (13:18). The wise do not despise the Lord's discipline (3:11).

8. Rebuke

The Hebrew words, *tôkaḥat* and cognates, mean "rebuke," "reproof," "correction." The purposes of a rebuke are to expose a person's sin, to bring that person to repentance, and to correct his ethical or social behavior to conform to the standards of wisdom and righteousness.

The wise teacher urges his readers not to resent the Lord's rebuke (3:11–12). One who heeds correction has honor (13:18), prudence (15:5), and understanding (15:32). For the rod of correction imparts wisdom (29:15) and makes wise those who listen (15:31). That is why the wise man loves the one who rebukes him (9:8) and the discerning man gains knowledge by it (19:25). Thus, it is valuable (25:12). An open rebuke is better than hidden love (27:5), for the corrections of discipline are the way to life (6:23).

9. Teaching

The Hebrew noun *tôrâ* means "teaching" or "instruction." God's revealed instruction for the lives of his people Israel governs every area—spiritual, moral, social, civil, political, financial—and is called the Law, which is recorded in Exodus through Deuteronomy. But in its broader sense of teaching, the *tôrâ* comprises the entire OT. Therefore, it includes not only the Law, but also history, illustrations, prophecy, and the sort of advice that is recorded in Proverbs. In the Book of Proverbs, *tôrâ* refers to the teachings of wisdom. It makes no specific reference to the law of Moses, although it may include it in such references as 29:18.

Wise teachings are described as a light (6:23) and as a fountain of life (13:14). The wise wife (31:26) consistently presents them. Readers are urged to guard wise teachings as their most valuable possession (7:2). Those who follow wise teachings are blessed (29:18), discerning (28:7a), and resist the wicked (28:4b). Readers are commanded neither to forget (3:1) nor to forsake (4:2) wise parental teachings. Those who do forsake them find even their prayers to be detestable to the Lord (28:9).

10. Command

The Hebrew noun, *miṣwâ,* means command. Although often used in the OT to refer to the commandments revealed by God to define Israel's covenant obligations, in Proverbs it involved the instruction given by the teachers of wisdom. It indicates the authority behind the command, whether that of God, parent, or teacher. The wise teacher urges his students to absorb and obey his commands (2:1; 6:20), which are a lamp (6:23). He who respects a command is rewarded (13:13); he who accepts commands is wise (10:8). He who obeys instructions is guarding his life (19:16).

B. The Vocabulary of Folly (VF)

Three Hebrew words are rendered "fool." We have distinguished among them by indicating in parenthesis the Hebrew root from which "fool" comes.

1. Fool or Foolish (kᵉsîl)

The Hebrew word *kᵉsîl* pictures one who is foolish, stupid, and inclined to make wrong choices. His decisions move him in a direction that may provide immediate pleasure, but will eventually lead to ruin and destruction. He is mentally dull, morally insensitive, arrogant, disrespectful, deceitful, and untrustworthy.

Fools lack knowledge (14:7), prudence, and understanding (8:5). They reject wisdom, knowledge, and discernment (1:22; 18:2; 23:9). Fools express their folly (12:23) repeatedly (26:11). Complacent (1:32), they trust in themselves (28:26). Money (17:16) and provisions (21:20) are useless to fools who consume them rapidly. Luxury (19:10) and honor (26:1, 8) are also inappropriate. Fools are useless as messengers (26:6) and are

BASIC TERMINOLOGY   41

generally unemployable (26:10). Fools enjoy evil (10:23) and hate to turn away from it (13:19). Their folly is deception (14:8). Speaking in haste (29:20), they spread slander (10:18), speak perversely (19:1), express uncontrolled anger (29:11), and are hotheaded and reckless (14:16). Such talk is their undoing (18:7). It produces strife (18:6) and makes them dangerous (17:12). Fools are shamed (3:35) and suffer harm (13:20), including beatings (19:29) and destruction (1:32).

2. *Folly, Fool, Foolish ('ĕwîl)*

The Hebrew words, 'ĕwîl and cognates, also convey the idea of being a fool or foolish. These words overlap $k^e sîl$ in meaning. The 'ĕwîl seems somewhat worse than the $k^e sîl$, for it stresses spiritual and moral deficiency, even moral insolence more than stupidity. However, this distinction is a matter of emphasis rather than a major difference, since both terms include these qualities.

Fools are considered wise and discerning if they remain silent (17:28). But in reality wisdom is too high and unattainable for a fool (24:7), so he becomes a servant to the wise (11:29) because fools despise and reject wisdom and discipline (1:7). The way of a fool seems right to him (12:15). Lacking judgment, he delights in folly (15:21).

Folly is bound up in a child's heart (22:15). It is extremely difficult to remove from fools (27:22). Instead, fools feed on folly (15:14), produce it (14:24), expose it (13:16), gush it (15:2), and repeat their foolish acts (26:11). Fools are often quarrelsome (20:3), quick tempered (14:17, 29), and very burdensome (27:3). They answer before listening (18:13). The folly of fools is deception (14:8) that leads them astray (5:23). They develop sinful schemes (24:9) and mock at making amends for sin (14:9). Fools die as a result of their poor judgment (10:21). They are punished (16:22), ruined (19:3), and bring disaster (17:12).

3. *Fool (nābāl)*

The Hebrew words, nābāl and cognates, mean to "be foolish," "stupid," "senseless," and "disgraceful." They include the ideas of insensitivity to the Lord, moral apathy, and rejecting what is reasonable. They overlap the other Hebrew words for fool, 'ĕwîl and kᵉsîl. But the nābāl words emphasize strongly the disgraceful, boorish, and domineering aspects of the fool's behavior. Observe Nabal's behavior (1 Sam. 25). Arrogance is unsuitable to a fool (17:7). A fool exalts himself (30:32) and, when stuffed with food, is intolerable (30:22).

4. Simple

The Hebrew word, petî, means "simple" or "naïve." It describes one who is immature, foolish, naïve, inexperienced, excessively open, and thus easily enticed to do wrong. A simple person lacks the discernment needed to distinguish between right and wrong or wise and foolish behavior. He is often thoughtless and impulsive.

Gullible (14:15), the simple are easily led astray from what is right and into serious danger (1:32), which they neither detect nor avoid (22:3). For example, they are enticed into adultery (7:7ff.). The simple need wisdom (9:4) and prudence (8:5) to motivate them to leave their simple ways (9:6), which they naïvely love (1:22).

5. Mocker

The Hebrew words, lîṣ and cognates, convey the ideas of mocking, scorning, deriding. They express an attitude of arrogance combined with an open contempt for what is good and righteous. They describe stubborn people who adamantly refuse to change their ways, aggressive free thinkers who scornfully push their ways on others.

Proud and arrogant (21:24), mockers delight in mockery (1:22b). A corrupt witness mocks at justice (19:28). Fools mock at making amends for sin (14:9). No wonder that mockers produce strife and tensions (22:10). Since mockers reject rebukes (13:1) and correction (15:12), they do not find wisdom (14:6). The Lord mocks mockers (3:34). They are detested (24:9), will suffer (9:12), be punished (21:11) and flogged (19:25).

A synonym is la'ag. It describes a fool who mocks the poor (17:5) and his father (30:17) just as wisdom mocks the foolish in their disaster (1:26).

6. Sluggard

The Hebrew words, '*āṣēl* and cognates, mean to be "sluggish" or "lazy." They describe people who have no ambitions and who avoid work. The sluggard does not satisfy his desires because he is unwilling to do the necessary work (21:25). He claims to be afraid to go outside to work because of a lion that may be prowling in the area (26:13). As a result, his way is blocked with thorns (15:19). Inclined to excessive sleep (6:9), he is intolerable to send on an errand (10:26).

Another Hebrew word, *rᵉmiyâ*, is a synonym. It pictures the results of laziness as not eating (12:27), hunger (19:15), poverty (10:4), and slave labor (12:24).

7. Deceitful

Three groups of virtually synonymous Hebrew words involve the ideas of lying and deceit. They picture a deliberate presentation of what is false or misleading for purposes of deception, fraud, dishonesty, or treachery.

For the Hebrew words, *mirmâ* and cognates: The folly of fools is deception (14:8). False witnesses (14:25) and malicious people who plot evil are deceitful (12:20). The Lord detests dishonest (or deceitful) scales (20:23). Deceitful behavior shrugged off as a joke is deplorable and potentially dangerous (26:18–19).

For the Hebrew words, *kāzāb* and cognates: God will rebuke and establish as a liar anyone who adds to His words (30:6). A person is not to crave a ruler's food because it is deceptive (23:3). Rather it is better to be poor than a liar (19:22b). Agur asked the Lord to keep falsehood and lies far from him (30:8a). A false witness in court deceives (14:25) and lies (14:5b). False witnesses will be punished by not going free (19:5b) and perishing (19:9b).

For the Hebrew words, *sheqer* and cognates: Lies and hatred are closely related (26:28). A liar pays attention to malicious talk (17:4). The Lord detests lying (12:22), especially from false witnesses (6:19). The righteous also hate what is false (13:5). Both lying (17:7) and listening to lies (29:12) are inappropriate and disastrous to a ruler. Gains obtained by fraud are temporary and unpleasant, whether food (20:17) or money (21:6). The wicked earn deceptive wages (11:18). For liars will not go unpunished (19:9a). Deceptive boasting is futile (25:14); charm, deceptive (31:30).

C. The Vocabulary of Righteousness (VR)

1. Righteous

The Hebrew words, *ṣedeq* and cognates, mean "righteous," "just," "correct," and "innocent." The Lord loves those who pursue righteousness (15:9). He considers righteousness to be better than sacrifice (21:3). He blesses and responds to the prayers of the righteous (10:6; 15:29).

Righteousness makes a straight path (11:5), guards integrity (13:6), and hates what is false or dishonest (13:5; 29:27). The righteous are committed to justice (29:7) and disapprove of any miscarriage of justice (18:5), as does the Lord (17:15). They give honest, accurate testimony (12:17). The wise speech (10:31) of the righteous is choice silver, nourishing many (10:20–21). They are generous (21:26), bold (28:1), and wise (8:20).

The righteous keep on getting up after falling (24:16). They display stability, standing firm (10:25) and not being uprooted (12:3). They are delivered from trouble (11:8). The righteous triumph over the wicked (29:16), experiencing great prosperity (13:21; 15:6). Their desires are fulfilled (10:24). Rewarded (11:18), they experience joy (10:28). The righteous attain life (11:19), living long and fruitful lives (16:31). Righteousness exalts a nation (14:34) and secures its government (16:12) through its commitment to justice (8:15).

2. Justice

The Hebrew words, *mishpāṭ* and cognates, indicate justice administered by all functions of government. The verb pictures going to court to obtain justice (29:9) and the importance of fairness in judging (29:14). In most of its occurrences in Proverbs, the noun means "justice" or "just." The Lord guards the course of the just (2:8) and provides justice in His judgment (29:26). It is important for kings to carefully maintain justice for their political stability (29:4). It is wrong to pervert justice

BASIC TERMINOLOGY 45

through bribes (17:23) or partiality (18:5). The righteous plan what is just (12:5) and rejoice in justice (21:15). The Lord is the source of just (i.e., accurate) scales and balances (16:11).

3. Integrity

The Hebrew words, *tōm* and cognates, convey the idea of completeness, ethical soundness, especially integrity and uprightness. Since these words also picture those who are innocent of charges against them, they are often rendered "blameless" and even "perfect." They do not, however, convey the idea of sinless perfection. For the best of people are excellent without being perfect, generally blameless without being absolutely blameless or sinless.

The Lord delights in (11:20) and protects the blameless (2:7b). Their protection (28:18) by righteousness (13:6) enables them to prosper (28:10). The righteous (11:5) and the upright (11:3) have integrity, which is better than riches (28:6).

4. Upright

The Hebrew words, *yāshār* and cognates, have the central idea of "straight," from which the ethical meanings "upright," "right," "fair" developed. The upright do what is morally proper.

At times the physical and ethical nuances of being or going straight merge in the same text. Such are the exhortation to look straight ahead (4:25) and the seductive invitations of the woman Folly to those who go straight on their way (9:15). The Lord and the righteousness of the upright make straight paths for them (3:6; 11:5). The wise lead along straight paths (4:11) that the understanding keep (15:21).

The upright have integrity, righteousness, and innocence (11:3, 6; 21:8). Their paths avoid evil (16:17) while the wicked leave the straight paths (2:13). The upright fear the Lord (14:2) who gives them victory (2:7). Their prayers please Him (15:8) as He takes them into His confidence (3:32). They express their upright ways in both their speech (8:6) and conduct (20:11). They prosper (14:11), express goodwill (14:9), and are appreciated by kings (16:13). The wicked detest them (29:27) and try to kill them (29:10). Thus, the words rendered "integrity" and "upright" overlap in meanings.

5. Good

The Hebrew words, *ṭōb* and cognates, designate many varieties of what is good.

They often convey an ethical sense of good. The Lord watches the good and the wicked (15:3). A good man obtains favor from the Lord (12:2). Evil men bow down in the presence of the good, who are righteous (14:19). Every good path involves what is right, just, and fair (2:9). To walk in the ways of good men is to follow the paths of the righteous (2:20).

They also picture what is beneficial. The wise secure a good reputation (3:4). He who seeks good finds good will (11:27). Those who plan what is good find love and faithfulness (14:22). A wise wife brings her husband good (18:22; 31:12), including profitability (31:18). Acquiring wisdom brings sound (good) learning (4:2) and good understanding (13:15). Those who follow instruction and cherish understanding prosper (literally, find good; 16:20; 19:8). And that prosperity produces affluence (13:21-22).

The words rendered "good" also portray a happy, positive, encouraging attitude. The cheerful (good) heart has a continual feast (15:15). Such a healthy attitude is good medicine (17:22). A good, encouraging word brings cheer (12:25), joy (15:23), health (15:30), and refreshment (25:25). Positive, encouraging talk produces good things (12:14). The wise use their knowledge competently (15:2). The generous (literally, with a "good eye") will be blessed (22:9). Honey is good to eat (24:13). "Good" is often used in comparisons that designate one thing as better than another (e.g., 15:16-17).

D. The Vocabulary of Wickedness (VWs)

1. Wicked

The Hebrew words, *rāshā'* and cognates, mean "wicked," "evil," "wrong," "guilty." They are general terms for all that is contrary to God's character, attitude, and will. Covering virtually all categories of sin, "wicked" refers to both sinful acts and sinful people. Wicked people are often hostile to God, neighbor, and community. They do not hesitate to violate the financial and social rights of others through dishonest business practices, false testimony in court, and even violence.

The most basic characteristic of the wicked is their craving for evil (21:10), which they absorb (4:17; 19:28) and discuss incessantly (15:28). They are sinful (21:4), cruel (12:10), desire plunder (12:12), and speak destructively (12:6). Apathetic to justice (29:7), they accept bribes to pervert justice (17:23). When in power, their rule is irresponsible, often disastrous (28:15), and promotes sin (29:16). Giving deceitful advice (12:5), they lead people astray (12:26). They detest the upright (29:27) and abuse those who rebuke them (9:7).

The Lord detests the way of the wicked (15:9), especially their perversion of justice (17:15) and their hypocritical sacrifices (15:8). Thus, He remains far from them, rejecting their prayers (15:29). God's negative response is mirrored in the human realm where wickedness brings contempt (18:3). People groan (29:2) and become inconspicuous when the wicked rise to power (28:12).

The future for the wicked is bleak. For their wages are deceptive (11:18), bringing treasures without value (10:2). Their hopes come to nothing (10:28). What they dread will occur (10:24). The Lord thwarts their craving (10:3) and allows them to be hungry (13:25). He curses the wicked (3:33), who are ensnared by their evil deeds (5:22). They are humbled before the righteous (14:19), punished (10:16), overthrown (12:7), brought down by calamity (14:32). They experience trouble (11:8), ruin (3:25), disaster (16:4), violence (10:6), and premature death (10:27). As a result, they perish (11:10), being swept away (10:25), destroyed (14:11), snuffed out (24:20).

2. *Evil*

Two groups of Hebrew words, *ra'*, *'āwen* and their cognates, picture both what is morally evil and what is naturally bad without any moral connotation. In their moral sense, they are similar to "wicked." In their nonmoral sense, they mean "bad," "wrong," "poor quality," "trouble," "harm," "calamity," "ruin." The trouble may, at times, result from one's evil behavior. However, these are general terms that describe any sort of badness.

For the Hebrew words, *ra'* and cognates: The wicked crave evil (*ra'*; 21:10). Evil people listen to evil talk (17:4), plot evil (16:27), rush into evil (6:18), delight in doing evil (2:14), and gush evil (15:28). They do not understand justice (28:5).

It is inappropriate to sing to a heavy (*ra'*) heart (25:20). The oppressed are continually wretched (*ra'*; 15:15). The buyer complains that the merchandise is bad before he boasts about his purchase (20:14). The stingy (literally with an "evil eye") are eager to get rich (28:22).

The wise avoid the ways of evil men (2:12) and immoral (*ra'*) women (6:24). This enables them to avoid danger (22:3), harm (1:33), trouble (19:23). The wise hate (8:13) and shun evil (14:16; 16:17). They are ordered not to avenge wrong (20:22) and not to envy wicked men (24:1). For the Lord detests the wicked's thoughts (15:26) and disapproves of gloating over one's enemy (24:17–18).

Those who search for evil will find it (11:27). Evil men are trapped by their sinful talk (12:13) and ensnared by their own sin (29:6). Their wickedness will be exposed (26:26) and not go unpunished (11:21).

A companion of fools suffers harm (13:20). For fools detest turning from evil (13:19). The wicked experience trouble (12:21), misfortune (13:21), stern discipline (15:10), ruin (21:12), calamity (24:16). Pursuing evil leads to death (11:19). The evil have no future hope (24:20).

For the Hebrew words, *'āwen* and cognates: The wicked gulp down evil (19:28). Evil people listen to evil talk (17:4) and devise wicked schemes (6:18). Nevertheless, an adulteress claims to have done nothing wrong (30:20). Justice brings terror to evildoers (21:15). The wicked (*ra'*) encounter trouble (22:8), but no harm comes to the righteous (12:21).

3. Sin

The word often rendered "sin" is a standard term for sin that means to "miss the mark or way" (19:2). More often it refers to sin as falling short of the standard set by the Law or by wisdom.

No one can make a valid claim to be without sin (20:9). Sinners entice (1:10) others to participate in foolish, evil schemes (24:9). Sin includes despising one's neighbor (14:21) and being haughty and arrogant (21:4). It is a disgrace (14:34) that will be punished (10:16). The cords of a man's sin hold him fast (5:22). Misfortune pursues the sinner (13:21). Wickedness overthrows the sinner (13:6) whose wealth is stored up for the righteous (13:22). Those who would be wise are urged not to envy sinners (23:17).

4. Transgression

The Hebrew words, *pesha‛* and cognates, mean "transgression," "rebellion," "sin," "offense." They picture a deliberate act of sin that expresses a person's rebellion against God. Such a person has rejected God's authority by doing what He has rightly prohibited. They also describe the breaking down of human relationships by disregarding the principles that define them.

Much talk includes sinful elements (10:19). It is wrong to conceal one's sins (28:13) and sinful to deny one's wrongs (28:24). Quarreling (17:19) and uncontrolled temper (29:22) produce sin. Sin or transgression thrives when the wicked thrive (29:16). An evil man is trapped by his sinful talk (12:13) and snared by his sin (29:6). An offended brother is more unyielding than a fortress (18:19). Love covers all wrongs (10:12). Overlooking an offense promotes love (17:9) and brings honor (19:11).

5. Perverse

Two synonymous Hebrew words, *tahpūkâ* and *‛iqqēsh*, picture a turning away from what is straight to what is crooked. Whether referring to attitudes, speech, or deeds, they portray them as crooked, twisted, distorted, perverted, deceptive.

For *tahpūkâ:* The wicked rejoice in the perversity of evil (*ra‛* ; 2:14). They produce perverse talk (10:32), which the Lord hates (8:13). They plot perversity (16:30) and are deceptive (6:14). The wicked are overthrown and are no more (12:7). When drunk, men become confused and imagine confused things (23:33).

For *‛iqqēsh:* The Lord hates perverse hearts (11:20), talk

(6:12), and ways (28:6). The perverse may expect exposure (10:9), obstacles (22:5), trouble (*ra'*; 17:20), and a sudden fall (28:18).

E. For Further Study

1. This chapter discusses the vocabulary on the basis of their usage in Proverbs. Read discussions of these words in *The Zondervan Pictorial Encyclopedia of the Bible* for a broad, biblical perspective.

2. What are the relationships among wisdom, understanding, knowledge, discretion, and prudence? In what ways are these qualities important and desirable?

3. For acquiring wisdom, what is the significance of discipline and rebukes? Why should a person appreciate them?

4. What are the relationships among righteousness, justice, uprightness, and integrity? Why are these qualities important elements in biblical wisdom? How important are they to Christians?

Chapter 3
The Fear of the Lord

A. What the Fear of the Lord Involves

"The fear of the LORD is the beginning of knowledge" (1:7a). This statement is a central tenet of biblical wisdom (1:7; 9:10; Job 28:28; Ps. 111:10; Eccl. 12:13).

The term "fear" pictures being afraid, anticipating evil, failure, or other undesirable, disastrous, frightening developments. It also involves a profound reverence, a deeply respectful awe. The references to fearing God in Proverbs primarily portray this latter meaning. Yet the above elements are not entirely absent.

God-fearing believers honor God by their worship and by their profound respect for Him. This attitude overflows into their lives as they seek the Lord's will and obey His laws and precepts, thereby developing righteous lifestyles. Worship and life are inextricably interconnected. The term "God-fearing," was derived from this and similar texts.

The word "beginning" refers to a starting point. Developing a reverential awe for the Lord is the first step in developing godly wisdom. "Beginning" also refers to what is important, so the fear of the Lord is the first, foundational, and controlling principle of godly knowledge. Knowing God, acknowledging His absolute lordship, and fearing Him are essential for acquiring and applying knowledge of the truth. This God-centered perspective saturates the intellectual, moral, and practical elements of the wisdom taught in Proverbs. Apart from that perspective, knowledge may delete God and become futile and destructive.

B. Statements about Fearing the Lord

1. *Contrasting the Wise and the Foolish*

1:7 "The fear of the LORD is the beginning of knowledge, but fools despise wisdom and discipline."

14:2 "He whose walk is upright fears the LORD, but he whose ways are devious despises him."

14:16 "A wise man fears the LORD and shuns evil, but a fool is hotheaded and reckless."

The wise (see VWm) build their knowledge upon a spiritual foundation that involves fearing God and accepting His discipline (**1:7**). The prominent moral element in their wisdom is made conspicuous by their righteous (see "Upright" in VR) lifestyle (**14:2**) that avoids evil (**14:16**). This expresses their love and respect for God, who demands righteousness.

In contrast, the foolish despise any wisdom and discipline that is rooted in a spiritual commitment to God (**1:7**). Although these fools may be intellectually brilliant (!), they are spiritually and morally defective because they fail to perceive the value of the spiritual realm. Derived from a word that means "turn aside," the word rendered "devious" (**14:2**) means "crooked," "deceptive," "perverse." The devious prefer their ignorance and defective perspective to God's infinite wisdom and comprehensive, balanced perspective for making life decisions. Their evil deeds, perhaps subconsciously, express their hatred of God (**14:2**). Their intense anger and their presumptuous actions (**14:16**) reflect the absence of the Lord's discipline, which produces caution. The word rendered "hotheaded" (**14:16**) pictures someone whose insolence easily provokes anger and who is quick to display extreme anger and evil.

2. *Avoiding Evil*

8:12–13 "'I, wisdom, dwell together with prudence; I possess knowledge and discretion. To fear the LORD is to hate evil; I hate pride and arrogance, evil behavior and perverse speech.'"

16:6 "Through love and faithfulness sin is atoned for; through the fear of the LORD a man avoids evil."

For "wisdom," "prudence," "knowledge," and "discretion," (see VWm). To fear the Lord is equivalent to hating evil (**8:12–13**). Especially intolerable are pride, arrogance, evil behavior, and perverse speech (see VWs). The cognate words rendered "pride" and "arrogance" picture an insolence that is excessively self-conscious and cynically apathetic to human needs.

In **16:6** the word rendered "atoned for" means "to cover" sin. It pictures deliverance from God's wrath by means of a substitutionary sacrifice and anticipates the basic principle on which the gospel of salvation rests.

The Hebrew word, *ḥesed*, rendered "love" covers a broad array of ideas, including love, grace, mercy, kindness, loyalty, faithfulness. It designates God's covenant loyalty to the promises that He made to His people, but it is not necessarily limited to covenant obligations.[1] Although God expressed these qualities in establishing His covenants and in providing atonement, here it refers to human expressions of these qualities that are to be patterned after God's.

What is the relationship between obtaining atonement and the qualities of love and faithfulness? Do these qualities expressed in good works provide atonement? Redemption by works contradicts NT teaching (e.g., Rom. 3:19–20; Gal. 2:15–16; 3:10–11). Actually our text removes neither the roles of grace nor of substitutionary sacrifices from redemption. Rather, it presents the qualities of love and faithfulness as results of atonement. Their presence in those who fear God shows the reality of their redemption.

3. Results of Rejecting Wisdom

1:29–31 " 'Since they hated knowledge and did not choose to fear the LORD, since they would not accept my advice and spurned my rebuke, they will eat the fruit of their ways and be filled with the fruit of their schemes.' "

24:21–22 "Fear the LORD and the king, my son, and do not

---

[1] See Harris, R. Laird, "(*ḥsd*)," TWOT (Chicago: Moody Press, 1980), 1:305–7 for a thorough and perceptive discussion of *ḥesed*.

join with the rebellious, for those two will send sudden destruction upon them, and who knows what calamities they can bring?"

28:14 "Blessed is the man who always fears the LORD, but he who hardens his heart falls into trouble."

For the godly Hebrew wise man, to have knowledge (see VWm) involved fearing the Lord; hating knowledge involved not fearing the Lord (**1:29**). To hate and to spurn is to despise, abhor, resent, and reject what a person finds repugnant. The decision not to fear the Lord included rejection of the advice and rebukes provided by godly wisdom (**1:30**). "Fruit" is an agricultural metaphor describing the result of something (**1:31**). Foolish behavior will produce its own results: People will reap what they sow and be stuffed with it.

To fear God and king means respecting their authority and conforming to their will (**24:21**). In describing government as God's agency for maintaining justice and order, both Peter and Paul alluded to our text: Peter, to **24:21** (1 Peter 2:17); Paul, to **24:22** (Rom. 13:4). The wise will not support the political agitators and radical revolutionaries who rebel against the laws of God and king (**24:21**) because their intrigues will come to a sudden and disastrous end (**24:22**). Then they will face the judgment and wrath of both God and king.

In contrast to fearing God is hardening one's heart (**28:14**). It involves an utter disrespect for God, which removes the inhibitions against sin that the fear of God produces. As a result of their evil deeds, God will bring upon them the trouble (see "evil" in VWs) or calamity that is appropriate for the sins committed.

4. Acquiring the Benefits of Wisdom

3:7–8 "Do not be wise in your own eyes; fear the LORD and shun evil. This will bring health to your body and nourishment to your bones."

9:10–11 " 'The fear of the LORD is the beginning of wisdom, and knowledge of the Holy One is understanding. For through me your days will be many, and years will be added to your life.' "

10:27 "The fear of the LORD adds length to life, but the years of the wicked are cut short."

Those who fear the Lord will not develop the sort of self-confidence that prompts one to ignore God and His ways (3:7–8). Fearing the Lord brings the physical benefits of vigor and refreshment, strengthening one's overall health. It is what McKane pictures as "beneficial therapy."[2]

The fear of the Lord is coupled with knowledge of the Holy One (9:10). This attitude is the very essence of wisdom, which lengthens one's life (9:11; 10:27). The NT expectation of eternal life goes far beyond these statements.

5. Cultivating the Qualities of Wisdom

15:33 "The fear of the LORD teaches a man wisdom, and humility comes before honor."

19:23 "The fear of the LORD leads to life: Then one rests content, untouched by trouble."

22:4 "Humility and the fear of the LORD bring wealth and honor and life."

23:17–18 "Do not let your heart envy sinners, but always be zealous for the fear of the LORD. There is surely a future hope for you, and your hope will not be cut off."

The statement in **15:33** is a variation of 1:7, "'the fear of the Lord is the beginning of knowledge.'" Here it provides the perspective and attitude that are essential to a properly balanced godly wisdom.

The word rendered "humility" (**15:33; 22:4**) pictures the condition of the afflicted and oppressed. Humility avoids self-exaltation and self-centeredness; nevertheless, it does not involve considering ourselves worthless and incompetent. Rather we recognize our human limitations and our dependence upon God. We confess and repent for our sins and guilt in the presence of our perfectly holy God. To be humble, we evaluate ourselves in a way that neither minimizes our accomplishments nor overemphasizes our failures. The fear of the Lord saturates our self-evaluation. For "humility," see additional discussion under **18:12**. Identical to **15:33b** is **18:12b**. The development of

---

[2] McKane, William, *Proverbs: A New Approach* (Philadelphia: Westminster, 1970), p. 293.

humility preceding honor is a general principle that pictures a natural sequence, not a magical formula that covers every case.

The closely associated attitudes of humility and fearing God produce material riches, social prestige, life, and contentment. Life (19:23; 22:4), more than mere existence, involves a good healthy quality of life in the spiritual, moral, psychological, marital, social, and material realms. Ideally, it involves developing and applying one's abilities to function effectively in all areas, including the nourishment, health, satisfaction, happiness, prosperity, and success that contribute much to the quality of life. Life, in Proverbs, focuses primarily on the quality of life here and now, rarely life after death. The word rendered "content" means "full," "satisfied" (19:23). Often picturing sufficient nourishment, it also describes financial affluence, personal satisfaction, and spiritual and psychological fullness. Occasionally, it indicates too much of a good thing (e.g., 25:17; 30:9). These benefits of humility and fearing God picture a natural pattern and are not automatic results of a success formula.

Those who fear God are not to envy sinners (23:17), who use evil methods to acquire wealth. They are not to make the improvement of their financial position their top priority. The spiritually wise are to be characterized by continuous (literally, "all the day") fear of the Lord. A person with that attitude has no reason to envy sinners. For those who fear the Lord do have a future hope (23:18). The word rendered "hope" indicates an eager, confident expectation that here expresses faith in the Lord. In Proverbs "future" and "hope" generally picture future prospects in this life, but may occasionally point to a future life.[3]

Here the main emphasis is on the present life, but the future life is not excluded. That hope will not be cut off or destroyed, that is, one's life will not be prematurely terminated by some divinely arranged disaster as punishment. Rather, a person can expect to have a well-rounded life that will include well-being and honor. Identical are 23:18b and 24:14c.

---

[3] Harris, R. L., " ('aḥar)," TWOT (Chicago: Moody Press, 1980), 1: 33–34; Hartley, J.E.H., " (qāwâ)," TWOT (Chicago: Moody Press, 1980), 2:791–92.

6. Values of God-Fearing Wisdom

2:1–5 "My son, if you accept my words and store up my commands within you, turning your ear to wisdom and applying your heart to understanding, and if you call out for insight and cry aloud for understanding, and if you look for it as for silver and search for it as for hidden treasure, then you will understand the fear of the LORD and find the knowledge of God."

14:26 "He who fears the LORD has a secure fortress, and for his children it will be a refuge."

14:27 "The fear of the LORD is a fountain of life, turning a man from the snares of death."

15:16 "Better a little with the fear of the LORD than great wealth with turmoil."

"My son" was a standard way for the ancient wise man to address his disciple (2:1) and does not necessarily indicate a biological relationship.

The wise teacher presented three conditions for acquiring wisdom. He used synonymous parallelisms (see the introduction) to state each condition twice in different words (2:1–2, 3, 4).

The first condition is described by four equivalent clauses (2:1–2): "accept my words," "store up my commands within you," "turn your ear to wisdom," and "apply your heart to understanding." These involve absorbing the principles of wisdom so thoroughly that a person's personality and life automatically express them. The second condition is to express verbally one's desire to obtain wisdom (2:3). The third condition is to "look for it as for silver," which is equivalent to "search for it as for hidden treasure" (2:4). To "look for" is to hunger for, to have a powerful desire to obtain, to exert a strong effort to acquire. People's searching for wisdom includes persistent inquiries, attentive listening, and diligent looking for the purpose of acquiring it. Wisdom is far more valuable than all of the material wealth in the world.

To "understand the fear of the LORD" is to "find the knowledge of God" (2:5). Fulfilling the above conditions produces the central spiritual element in biblical wisdom.

Those who fear the Lord have a secure fortress (**14:26**).

Derived from a verb rendered "trust," "be confident," the word rendered "secure" means "safety," "security," "confidence." God-fearers are assured of their spiritual inheritance that God has lovingly provided. Security based upon God's promises in his Word provides a solid basis for their confidence. The word rendered "fortress" means "strength." It refers to physical strength, military prowess, and impregnable fortifications. A powerful person, army, or fortress will not be easily defeated. To saturate our homes with the principles of wisdom that begin with fearing God is to develop a refuge for our children that will protect them from sinful foolishness and encourage them to make these principles their own. The word rendered "refuge" refers literally to shelter from rain and storm (Isa. 4:6) and safety in the hills from danger (Ps. 104:18). It is often used figuratively to depict taking refuge by confidently trusting a stronger power for protection. The Lord is a marvelous refuge when we face danger and even imminent death (Ps. 31:1–5).

To have the fear of the Lord is to have "a fountain of life" (**14:27**). "Fountain of life" is a metaphor picturing a refreshing source of vitality from which a high quality of life flows (see 10:11; 13:14; 16:22). Those who drink from that fountain will be refreshed and experience health and vitality. (For "life," see the comments about 19:23.) To fear God provides a perspective that protects one from "the snares of death," which are dangers that may produce premature death. The "snare," a "trap" for animals, often figuratively describes manipulating people to harm or destroy them. "Death" includes physical death, which the lack of wisdom may induce prematurely. It may also involve a low quality of living that includes illnesses, disasters, sins, and dissatisfying superficiality. Statements about the fear of the Lord in **14:27** and "the teaching of the wise" in 13:14 are identical.

The statement in **15:16** was not intended to promote poverty as a virtue and suggest wealth as undesirable. Rather, its point is that although people would prefer not to be poor, wealth is not a necessary element in a full life. For those who are materialistic can never acquire enough things or money to satisfy them. The trouble and distress that can accompany wealth may more than offset the pleasures that wealth brings. If a person should acquire wealth through unethical means, his guilt and the hostility of his victims will prevent it from providing satisfaction. But there is no incompatibility between wisdom and wealth as long as his lifestyle reflects the principles of wisdom. For wealth can be a great asset when a person desires to serve God on a massive scale. Even though the affluent can contribute far more financially than the poor, far more valuable than great wealth is the fear of the Lord. That is why it is much better to fear God without being wealthy than to be wealthy without fearing God.

For the final text mentioning the fear of the Lord, see the comments about 31:30.

C. For Further Study

1. Read the article about fear by G. B. Funderburk in *The Zondervan Pictorial Encyclopedia of the Bible* (Grand Rapids: Zondervan Publishing House, 1975), 2:518–21. For a more thorough and somewhat technical treatment, read "The Fear of the Lord as the 'Principle' of Wisdom" by Henri Blocher in *Tyndale Bulletin*, 28 (1977): 3–28.

2. Why is the fear of the Lord an important element in your relationship to Him? How does it relate to loving Him? How does it affect your attitude and behavior?

3. What is the difference between humility and humiliation? Why is the former desirable and the latter undesirable? How can you be humble and avoid the extremes of self-exaltation and self-deprecation?

4. What is the relationship between "life" in Proverbs and "life" in the NT? Read "Life" by W. B. Wallis in *The Zondervan Pictorial Encyclopedia of the Bible* (Grand Rapids: Zondervan Publishing House, 1975), 3:927–32.

Chapter 4

References to the Lord

Although the Book of Proverbs has been understood as a compilation of ancient, secular, pragmatic wisdom, its materials refer to the Lord over ninety times, excluding the references to the fear of the Lord. These statements describe some of God's qualities, functions, and ethical principles.

A. God's Qualities

1. God's Sovereignty

16:1 "To man belong the plans of the heart, but from the LORD comes the reply of the tongue."

16:4 "The LORD works out everything for his own ends—even the wicked for a day of disaster."

16:9 "In his heart a man plans his course, but the LORD determines his steps."

16:33 "The lot is cast into the lap, but its every decision is from the LORD."

19:21 "Many are the plans in a man's heart, but it is the LORD's purpose that prevails."

20:24 "A man's steps are directed by the LORD. How then can anyone understand his own way?"

21:1 "The king's heart is in the hand of the LORD; he directs it like a watercourse wherever he pleases."

21:30 "There is no wisdom, no insight, no plan that can succeed against the LORD."

21:31 "The horse is made ready for the day of battle, but victory rests with the LORD."

Several proverbs stress human limitations by contrasting divine and human capabilities (**16:1, 9; 19:21**). People can plan, make decisions, and work. Regardless of their efforts, it is God who determines the ultimate results. "Man proposes, God disposes." The Lord's reply (**16:1**) is His creative word that fulfills His purpose (Isa. 55:10–11). God determines (establishes, directs) human steps without destroying human liberty or disrupting human responsibility (**16:9; 20:24**). He exerts His influence in such a way—even periodically overruling human endeavors—that He guarantees the ultimate achievement of His purposes, whether through or in spite of human intentions (**19:21**; see Jer. 10:23). This principle even applies to exalted kings within whom God's influence is like that of a man's building a watercourse to be used for irrigation (**21:1**; see Isa. 10:5–7; Ezra 7:21, 27). God can cut it in any direction that He wants the water to go.

The Lord exercises His sovereignty by using everything to accomplish His purpose (**16:4**). Thus, nothing is useless, however trivial it may seem. Even the wicked are included in His comprehensive plan, and no sins by the wicked will motivate Him to deviate from His plan. God's plan includes the wicked's facing temporal calamity and ultimately an awesome day of judgment when His perfect handling of justice will involve the pouring out of His wrath.

No human mind completely understands how God works out His purposes in human life (**20:24**). Thus, no one understands fully the meaning and significance of what he experiences. This drastically limits our ability to avoid moving in the wrong direction, so it is necessary for us to seek God's guidance to accomplish what He has planned for us to do (Eph. 2:10).

Lots (**16:33**) were used in ancient Israel to answer questions that could be handled by a simple yes or no. Although the OT does not describe how the procedure worked, several techniques were probably used. One method may have been to place two distinguishable stones into a fold or pocket in the priest's garment. Whichever stone was chosen would provide the answer. They believed that by controlling which stone was chosen, God would reveal His will concerning the decision to be made (**16:33**; see Josh. 7:14ff; Acts 1:24–26). The basis for using lots was their confidence in the Lord's control over the selection procedure.

The sages did not disapprove of the preparation and use of standard military equipment, such as horses in ancient armies (**21:31**). But they perceived that even exceptional military power could not guarantee victory (Ps. 33:16–17; 1 Sam. 17:47). For the outcome of a battle or a war depends upon the Lord's involvement (**21:31**; see Ps. 20:7–8). Therefore, it is futile to fight without relying upon the Lord. The word rendered "victory" means "salvation," "deliverance." In the OT, it usually pictures a deliverance from one's enemies that produces victory and the safety and security that deliver from fear. It points toward a spiritual salvation, involving forgiveness of sins.

The emphasis in **21:30** is that the most brilliant human wisdom, analysis, and plans are futile when contrary to God's purposes (see Ps. 33:10–11; Job 5:12–13; for a classic biblical example, see 2 Sam. 15:31; 16:23; 17:14). God is in control. He will accomplish His purposes and succeed in His plans, no matter how universal human opposition or apathy may be.

2. God's Providence

18:22 "He who finds a wife finds what is good and receives favor from the LORD."

19:14 "Houses and wealth are inherited from parents, but a prudent wife is from the LORD."

20:12 "Ears that hear and eyes that see—the LORD has made them both."

God's providence involves His meeting the needs of His creatures by equipping and benefiting them. For example, God provides our eyes and ears that function in generally reliable ways to enable us to acquire knowledge (**20:12**). God also provides spiritual perception to those who know Him. Another example is a prudent wife (**19:14**) or good wife (**18:22**), the sort of woman described in 31:10–31. She is intelligent, thrifty, industrious, spiritual, wise, and the joy of her husband. Her pleasing personality promotes domestic peace and comfort. She helps her husband in his spiritual, moral, and material progress.

A wise man with a prudent wife appreciates her as a precious gift from God.

3. God's Wisdom

25:2 "It is the glory of God to conceal a matter; to search out a matter is the glory of kings."

30:2-4 "'I am the most ignorant of men; I do not have a man's understanding. I have not learned wisdom, nor have I knowledge of the Holy One. Who has gone up to heaven and come down? Who has gathered up the wind in the hollow of his hands? Who has wrapped up the waters in his cloak? Who has established all the ends of the earth? What is his name, and the name of his son? Tell me if you know!'"

30:5-6 "'Every word of God is flawless; he is a shield to those who take refuge in him. Do not add to his words, or he will rebuke you and prove you a liar.'"

The workings of God are mysterious and inscrutable, often baffling (**25:2**). Finite human minds can never completely comprehend God's infinite wisdom. In contrast, kings, whose knowledge is finite, need to investigate thoroughly to learn what they can about any situation concerning which they develop governmental policies.

Although he studied wisdom, Agur did not believe that he had mastered it (**30:2-3**). He described his inadequacies by four equivalent statements. Behind these statements lurks an undertone of irony that is perhaps directed toward people who, like Job's friends, claimed to understand God and to explain what He does. In spite of his disclaimers, Agur had a good grasp of wisdom. For a similar ironic contrast between Paul's "stupid" wisdom and the Corinthian "wise" stupidity, see 1 Corinthians 4:8-13.

This series of rhetorical questions (**30:4**) shows the impossibility of any human being's duplicating God's achievements (see Job 38). The final questions in **30:4** sarcastically challenge his readers to identify the man who could achieve so much. They make it clear that Agur's readers did not know and that he knew it.

In its immediate context the "word of God" (**30:5**) consists of what God has revealed through Moses and the prophets for man's spiritual and moral guidance. In principle, it applies to God's message or instruction as revealed through all of Scripture. The Word of God is our primary source of truth that is to affect our attitudes and behavior (Ps. 18:30; 2 Sam. 22:31).

The word rendered "flawless" describes the process of smelting metal, of purification by removing the impurities. When a metal is tested by fire, either its impurities will be removed or it will be shown to be pure, usually the former. When the Word of God is thoroughly tested, it is found to be morally perfect, completely reliable, inerrant. The military image of a shield that protects a soldier in battle dramatically pictures the Lord's erecting an impenetrable barrier that protects His people and keeps them safe (**30:5**). For "refuge," see the comments about 14:26.

Since God's Word is as complete as He intended, we are not to supplement God's words (**30:6**, see Deut. 4:2; 12:32) and credit the additions to Him. We are to accept God's words as they are in Scripture and obey them. Whoever adds to God's words will experience His rebuke and disciplinary punishment, which will expose him as a liar and deceiver who has presented his opinions as if they were God's Word.

4. God's Wisdom in Creation

3:19–20 "By wisdom the LORD laid the earth's foundations, by understanding he set the heavens in place; by his knowledge the deeps were divided, and the clouds let drop the dew."

8:22–31 " 'The LORD brought me forth as the first of his works, before his deeds of old; I was appointed from eternity, from the beginning, before the world began. When there were no oceans, I was given birth, when there were no springs abounding with water; before the mountains were settled in place, before the hills, I was given birth, before he made the earth or its fields or any of the dust of the world. I was there when he set the heavens in place, when he marked out the horizon on the face of the deep, when he established the clouds above and fixed securely the fountains of the deep, when he gave the sea its boundary so the waters would not overstep his command, and when he marked out the foundations of the earth. Then I was the craftsman at his side. I was filled with delight day after day, rejoicing always in his presence, rejoicing in his whole world and delighting in mankind.'"

God used wisdom in His creation of the universe to change chaos to order (**3:19**). It is prominently displayed in both God's creation and in His providential care for the physical world (cf. Job 38–39; Ps. 104; Isa. 40:12–14; Jer. 10:12). His creative activities included His establishing the proper relationships and places for water, land, and air on the earth. He divided the waters (**3:20**) among rain, dew, streams, rivers, lakes, and seas to make it readily available for supporting plant, animal, and human life.

In **8:22–31**, the poetic portrayal of wisdom's role in creation was a vivid personification, but not an hypostasis (the description of an attribute or activity of God as if it had a personal identity). This very description of wisdom may have influenced the NT writers who described Christ's role in creation (John 1:1–14; Col. 1:15–16; Heb. 1:2–3).

Wisdom originated with God who possessed it even before He displayed it in His creative activity (**8:22**). The rendering "eternity" (**8:23**) is too strong to accurately convey the idea, since it refers to the distant past or future. Here it refers to a time before the creation. For wisdom came into being (pictured by birth imagery) before the earth (**8:24–26**). God created and established the waters, mountains, earth, skies, clouds, and the foundations of the earth (**8:27–29**).

Yahweh's personified wisdom as displayed in His creation was described by a Hebrew word (*'āmôn*) whose meaning is unclear (**8:30**). Suggested interpretations include "craftsman" (NIV), "little child," "guardian," "binding" or "uniting," and "faithful." No conclusive evidence favors any of these. The meaning that best fits the context is "binding," the idea being that wisdom was at Yahweh's side as a vital bond or link between Yahweh and His creation.[1] Personified wisdom was continually delighted with Yahweh's presence and creation, especially mankind (**8:31**).

---

[1] For thorough exegetical support for this interpretation, see R. B. Y. Scott's "Wisdom in Creation: the *'āmôn* of Proverbs 8:30" in *Vetus Testamentum*, New York: E. J. Brill, Inc. (April, 1960), 213–23.

B. Wisdom

1. Values and Benefits of Wisdom

2:5–8 "Then you will understand the fear of the LORD and find the knowledge of God. For the LORD gives wisdom, and from his mouth come knowledge and understanding. He holds victory in store for the upright, he is a shield to those whose walk is blameless, for he guards the course of the just and protects the way of his faithful ones."

3:3–4 "Let love and faithfulness never leave you; bind them around your neck, write them on the tablet of your heart. Then you will win favor and a good name in the sight of God and man."

8:35–36 "'For whoever finds me finds life and receives favor from the LORD. But whoever fails to find me harms himself; all who hate me love death.'"

16:20 "Whoever gives heed to instruction prospers, and blessed is he who trusts in the LORD."

For similar texts, see Benefits of Wisdom in chapter five.

Seeking and striving diligently brings a person to understand the fear of the Lord, which involves knowing Him (2:1–5), for he finds what the Lord provides (**2:6**). The Lord's wisdom, knowledge, and understanding that come from His mouth as His Word produce continuing success (**2:7**; see "upright" and "blameless" [integrity] in VR).

The theme of God's protection for the just who are faithful to Him continues in **2:8**. The similar words rendered "guard" and "protect" describe the careful observation and precautions taken in guarding important military installations or even immensely valuable treasure. They also picture people as guarding themselves in an ethical sense by obedience to God's law (Exod. 20:6), parental commands (6:20), and the teachings of wisdom (3:1, 21; 4:13). The most competent human guards may need help against a major danger, but the Lord needs no aid in handling even the most difficult and dangerous threats. With Him we are safe.

In **3:3–4**, for "love," see comment about 16:6. The images of wearing a signet attached to a cord around one's neck and of recording on the tablet on one's heart (3:3) picture a close attachment. The idea is to saturate one's personality with love and faithfulness that will be constantly expressed (see 7:3; 2 Cor. 3:3). The person with these qualities rooted in him will get along well with people, be highly regarded, and have a good reputation with both God and man (3:4).

In **8:35-36**, wisdom is personified. Whoever finds her finds life (see the comments about 19:23). Those who reject or fail to find wisdom will harm themselves (**8:36**) by forfeiting wisdom's benefits. For "death," see the comments about 14:27.

In **16:20**, "instruction" may also refer to the Word of God. Following "instruction" is equivalent to trusting in the Lord who is its source. To trust in the Lord is to have a sense of well-being and security based upon confidence in Him, to count upon Him to fulfill His purposes in us. The words rendered "prosper" literally mean "find good" (see "good" in VR); in other words, to do well in all areas of life.

2. *Results of Rejecting Wisdom*

19:3 "A man's own folly ruins his life, yet his heart rages against the LORD."

A man's sinful foolishness twists, distorts, and perverts his perspective so that he blames the Lord for his troubles and rages against Him. Actually he brought his troubles and failures upon himself.

3. *Exhortation to Follow Wisdom*

22:17-21 "Pay attention and listen to the sayings of the wise; apply your heart to what I teach, for it is pleasing when you keep them in your heart and have all of them ready on your lips. So that your trust may be in the LORD, I teach you today, even you. Have I not written thirty sayings for you, sayings of counsel and knowledge, teaching you true and reliable words, so that you can give sound answers to him who sent you?"

For similar texts, see Exhortations to Obtain Wisdom in chapter five.

This section is a prologue to the collection of proverbs in 22:17-24:22. For "wise," "teach," "knowledge," see "wisdom," "knowledge" under VWm. To "apply your heart" (**22:17**) is to set your mind to concentrate upon what you have learned and to have the principles of wisdom saturate your attitude and behavior. For "keep" (**22:18**), see the comments about "protect" in 2:8.

These principles, when absorbed (**22:17**) and shared (**22:18**), promote faith in Yahweh (**22:19**). The word rendered "thirty" is difficult (**22:20**). It may mean "thirty" (NIV) or "excellent" (NIV footnote). By acquiring this reliable knowledge, one can handle competently the questions, tasks, and reports assigned (**22:21**).

4. Result of Following Wisdom

16:3 "Commit to the LORD whatever you do, and your plans will succeed."

To commit to the Lord is to turn contemplated actions over to Him for His disposal or to turn troubles over to Him for resolution. It includes both trusting Him to lead and yielding to His will.

C. Our Relationship to God

1. God's Protection of the Righteous

3:25–26 "Have no fear of sudden disaster or of the ruin that overtakes the wicked; for the LORD will be your confidence and will keep your foot from being snared."

10:3 "The LORD does not let the righteous go hungry, but he thwarts the craving of the wicked."

10:29 "The way of the LORD is a refuge for the righteous, but it is the ruin of those who do evil."

16:7 "When a man's ways are pleasing to the LORD, he makes even his enemies live at peace with him."

18:10 "The name of the LORD is a strong tower; the righteous run to it and are safe."

The refuge (**10:29**) is a stronghold for protection against enemies. Often part of a wall surrounding a fortified city, the tower (**18:10**) was also a refuge. The "way of the LORD" (**10:29**) is an ideological refuge for the righteous who come to His protection (**18:10**) from traps (**3:26**). These images encourage the righteous to follow the Lord's way, trusting Him for His protection. They need not fear the sudden ruin that falls upon the wicked (**3:25; 10:29**).

The Lord provides the righteous with their basic nourishment (**10:3**). In contrast, He frustrates (pushes aside, expels) the evil desires of the wicked, who, even if they get what they want, will not be satisfied. The most striking picture of the Lord's protective influence is His enabling the righteous to maintain peace with their enemies (**16:7**). This is so unusual that it implies a special working of God.

These pictures of the Lord's protection are not to be understood as either absolute or universal. Job was one of many exceptions to this description. Rather, these proverbs indicate a general tendency. The Lord does provide His protection for the righteous, but not always totally. However, righteous and considerate behavior does make it easier for our enemies to act in a similar way toward us.

2. Our Trust in God

3:5–6 "Trust in the LORD with all your heart and lean not on your own understanding; in all your ways acknowledge him, and he will make your paths straight."

29:25 "Fear of man will prove to be a snare, but whoever trusts in the LORD is kept safe."

In **3:5**, for "trust" and "heart," see the comments about "trust" in 16:20 and "heart" in 4:23.

The way of wisdom is to rely upon the Lord as the source of our wisdom and guide for our behavior (**3:5**). We are to use our minds, but we are not to rely entirely upon them, since they are fallible and vulnerable because of our prejudices and temptations. Our minds are skilled in rationalizing what we want to do, which may be contrary to God's will. Our limited perspective may even prevent us from knowing the best direction to take. Thus, we need to acknowledge the Lord (**3:6**). This involves an attitude of respect, dependence, and submission. The metaphor of making paths straight describes the Lord's enabling us to discern and follow His will. Just as the preparation of a road requires smoothing rough spots and removing obstacles, so also the Lord straightens our paths when we seek His guidance.

In **29:25**, fear of man includes fear of how others will react to a person's behavior. The desire to avoid such reactions as hostility and scorn may paralyze our efforts to do what is right, or what reflects our convictions. It powerfully inhibits productivity by reducing the intensity of our efforts. Trust in the Lord replaces such fears with faith in Him. "Fear knocked at the door, faith answered, and no one was there."[2]

3. God's Discipline

3:11–12 "My son, do not despise the LORD's discipline and do not resent his rebuke, because the LORD disciplines those he loves, as a father the son he delights in."

This text balances the false impression that God's people who trust Him should expect automatic prosperity with no obstacles. Such problems may include the Lord's disciplinary action, which is designed to produce repentance and behavioral change. Although not a complete explanation, it comprises part of our understanding of why the righteous suffer from time to time.

The attitude of loathing and consequently rejecting God's discipline is prohibited. For He disciplines those whom He loves, thereby expressing His love by His effort to return them to the path He has chosen for them. This text was later quoted during a thorough NT treatment of the Lord's discipline (Heb. 12:6; see also Prov. 12:1; 13:18; 15:32).

D. Ethical Contrasts

1. Righteous and Wicked

3:31–32 "Do not envy a violent man or choose any of his ways, for the LORD detests a perverse man but takes the upright into his confidence."

3:33–35 "The LORD's curse is on the house of the wicked, but he blesses the home of the righteous. He mocks proud mockers but gives grace to the humble. The wise inherit honor, but fools he holds up to shame."

11:20 "The LORD detests men of perverse heart but he delights in those whose ways are blameless."

---

[2]Cited by Skip Ross, *Say Yes to Your Potential* (Waco: Word, 1983), 30.

12:2 "A good man obtains favor from the LORD, but the LORD condemns a crafty man."

15:8 "The LORD detests the sacrifice of the wicked, but the prayer of the upright pleases him."

15:9 "The LORD detests the way of the wicked, but he loves those who pursue righteousness."

15:26 "The LORD detests the thoughts of the wicked, but those of the pure are pleasing to him."

15:29 "The LORD is far from the wicked but he hears the prayer of the righteous."

22:12 "The eyes of the LORD keep watch over knowledge, but he frustrates the words of the unfaithful."

28:5 "Evil men do not understand justice, but those who seek the LORD understand it fully."

28:25 "A greedy man stirs up dissension, but he who trusts in the LORD will prosper."

See also 10:3, 29 and chapter five.

In 3:31, the word rendered "envy" pictures an intense desire that motivates a person to take action. It may picture positively the zeal that inspires us to work hard, long, and effectively to achieve a legitimate goal or to support a worthy cause. It often refers negatively to a strong desire for another's quality, condition, or property, which prompts us to use sinful means to obtain it. Or it may picture the intense anger or jealousy aroused by marital unfaithfulness. Nevertheless, the apparent prosperity and success of the wicked, who obtain wealth and power by violent and other illegal means, should never produce envy in the righteous. For in spite of appearances, they are not better off (see 23:17–18; 24:1, 19–20).

Evil men do not distinguish clearly between justice and injustice (**28:5**). The greedy (**28:25**) are selfish, inconsiderate, and have an insatiable appetite for fulfilling their desires. They can never get enough. No wonder that greedy people often stir up dissensions!

These proverbs describe the Lord's attitudes and actions toward the wicked. He abhors the perverse (**3:32; 11:20**), the sacrifices, thoughts, and ways of the wicked (**15:8, 9, 26**). Their thoughts and deeds express their rebellion against God and their apathy toward others. This is why the Lord is far from the unrepentant wicked (**15:29**), unresponsive to their futile religious practices. He rejects their sacrifices and tunes out their prayers (**15:8**).

God condemns the crafty (**12:2**) as devious and unscrupulous in their contriving evil schemes against others. The Lord will not allow such guilty people to escape their just punishment. He turns aside the words (**22:12**) of the unfaithful (disloyal, treacherous, deceptive) and destroys their credibility. God's curse upon the house of the wicked (**3:33**) prevents them from enjoying what they have acquired through unethical and illegal means, including perhaps the disrupting thoughts of their consciences. He mocks the proud mockers (**3:34**; see VF), sometimes by bringing upon them what they have brought upon others. He shames fools who reject the way of the wise (**3:35**). The disgrace produced by their misdeeds makes conspicuous the shameful results of their sinful foolishness.

The Lord's favor (**12:2**) involves His protection and help. God loves those who aggressively and persistently work to be righteous (**15:9**). Whether or not associated with their sacrifices, their sincere and reverent prayers please the Lord (**15:8**). The benevolent intent of the pure pleases Him (**15:26**). He delights in those whose ways are blameless (**11:20**; see "integrity" in VWm). He hears the prayer of the righteous and is accessible and responsive to them (**15:29**). He takes them into His confidence as He would a close friend (**3:32**). He blesses the home of the righteous (**3:33**), both spiritually and materially. To "bless" means to invoke or bestow power for success, prosperity, happiness, long life, and other good things. He bestows His favor upon the humble (**3:34**). He honors the wise (**3:35**), often blessing them with a good reputation, happy and stable family life, and success in their endeavors. He preserves knowledge for the benefit of His people (**22:12**).

Those who seek (see comment about "look for" in 2:4) the Lord and discern His will as revealed in His Word distinguish accurately between right and wrong (**28:5**). Those who trust in the Lord will prosper (**28:25**). The word rendered "prosper" means literally, "be fat." In ancient times, fat animals were regarded as the healthiest and most valuable, so it was natural for the derived metaphorical meanings "prosperous," "rich," "fully satisfied" to develop. It pictures the abundant satisfaction of having more than enough as a result of great prosperity.

2. *Truth and Lying*

12:22 "The LORD detests lying lips, but he delights in men who are truthful."

The Lord abhors anything that distorts the truth and leads people astray. He thoroughly enjoys those with such integrity that their word can be trusted (see 14:25; 15:4; 19:22).

3. *Honesty and Dishonesty in Business (Weights)*

11:1 "The LORD abhors dishonest scales, but accurate weights are his delight."

16:11 "Honest scales and balances are from the LORD; all the weights in the bag are of his making."

20:10 "Differing weights and differing measures—the LORD detests them both."

20:23 "The LORD detests differing weights, and dishonest scales do not please him."

Ancient scales were based upon the principle of balancing what was being weighed against standard stone weights, so a quantity of grain or a lump of silver would be weighed accurately only if the stone weights were accurate. Archaeologists have discovered the two sets of weights that were used in this way. When buying grain, dishonest merchants used heavy weights to buy extra grain without paying for it. When selling the grain to customers, they used the light weights to increase their profit. Needless to say, these weights varied considerably from official standards.

The Lord loathes such unethical and dishonest business practices (**11:1; 20:10, 23**; see also Lev. 19:35–36; Deut. 25:13–16; Mic. 6:10–11). He delighted in the honest merchants who used accurate weights in both their buying and selling (**11:1; 16:11**). He intends for us to be honest in our business practices. For similar themes, see Honest and Dishonest in chapter eight.

E. God's Judgment

1. What God Hates

6:16–19 "There are six things the LORD hates, seven that are detestable to him: haughty eyes, a lying tongue, hands that shed innocent blood, a heart that devises wicked schemes, feet that are quick to rush into evil, a false witness who pours out lies and a man who stirs up dissension among brothers."

17:15 "Acquitting the guilty and condemning the innocent—the LORD detests them both."

In this numerical proverb (see introduction), the two lines of **6:16** state the common quality of the examples: The Lord despises them. The hated qualities are disruptive, malevolent, and destructive of good neighborly relationships. These sins include the categories of attitude (**17a**), thought (**18a**), speech (**17b, 19a**), action (**17c, 18b**), and influence (**19b**). As in the OT texts cited in Romans 3:13–16, parts of the body are mentioned to picture the whole person's involvement in sin.

"Haughty eyes" (**6:17a**) picture an arrogant, conceited person who often has no respect for spiritual and moral principles, as well as no concern for the rights of others. Other sins mentioned include lying (**17b**), perjury (**19a**), murder (**17c**), plotting evil (**18a**), and eagerness to activate the evil plans (**18b**).

"A man who stirs up dissension among brothers" (**19b**) disrupts the normal amicable relations within family and among friends; love is replaced with hostility. To "stir up" involves both initiating hostilities and conflicts and fueling them so that they intensify and expand.

The Lord despises the corruption of the courts that administer "justice" on the basis of profit rather than integrity and righteousness (**17:15**; see Exod. 23:6–8). For the wicked to buy a favorable verdict at the expense of the innocent who cannot afford it is despicable.

2. Religious Practices

21:3 "To do what is right and just is more acceptable to the LORD than sacrifice."

Although not critical of the sacrificial rituals, the wise men did not understand them to replace one's moral responsibility and obedience to the Lord. For them, as with the prophets, the latter was far more important than careful attention to ritualistic details (see also 15:8, 29; Isa. 1:10–17).

3. God's Knowledge of Man

5:21 "For a man's ways are in full view of the LORD, and he examines all his paths."

15:3 "The eyes of the LORD are everywhere, keeping watch on the wicked and the good."

15:11 "Death and Destruction lie open before the LORD— how much more the hearts of men!"

16:2 "All a man's ways seem innocent to him, but motives are weighed by the LORD."

17:3 "The crucible for silver and the furnace for gold, but the LORD tests the heart."

20:27 "The lamp of the LORD searches the spirit of a man; it searches out his inmost being."

21:2 "All a man's ways seem right to him, but the LORD weighs the heart."

24:11–12 "Rescue those being led away to death; hold back those staggering toward slaughter. If you say, 'But we knew nothing about this,' does not he who weighs the heart perceive it? Does not he who guards your life know it? Will he not repay each person according to what he has done?"

God's omniscience, which includes His exhaustive observation and examination of all that people do (5:21; 15:3), is the basis for His just and accurate evaluation.

The Hebrew words sh^e'$ôl$ and '$ăbaddôn$ (rendered "death" and "destruction"), are synonymous terms that refer to the mysterious, shadowy realm of the dead that lies beyond the scope of human knowledge (15:11). They describe in a general way the category of the dead without getting into the NT issue of heaven and hell. God, who knows sh^e'$ôl$ completely, knows human minds fully (15:11).

Man tests silver and gold for their purity by heating them in the process of refining (17:3). The Lord rigorously examines the whole person to detect such moral qualities as integrity. Only God can expose every flaw and impurity by His spiritual refining techniques. The imagery of scales and balances (16:2;

21:2; 24:12) pictures God using perfect "weights" to "weigh" what has no weight—human attitudes and motives. Even a man with distorted judgment who expertly rationalizes his behavior, considering all that he does to be innocent and right, cannot mislead Him. For the Lord penetrates through the smoke screen of human rationalizations to expose the actual motives and attitudes that lie behind human actions. Like a lamp that sheds its light into the darkest corners of a room, the Lord probes a man's innermost being and examines his attitudes and motivations (**20:27**).

The idea conveyed by the parallel exhortations to rescue those being led away or staggering toward death (**24:11**) is not entirely clear. It may involve rescuing people from physical violence or, more likely, from the "legal" violence of a death penalty, such as an unjust verdict by a corrupt court.

To plead ignorance was inexcusable and unacceptable (**24:12**). For God, who knows all of the inner workings of human minds, will not be conned by human rationalizations. He will discern the real motivation behind our action or inaction and dispense His perfect justice, which gives each person exactly what he deserves.

4. *The Lord's Judgment of the Wicked*

16:5 "The LORD detests all the proud of heart. Be sure of this: They will not go unpunished."

21:12 "The Righteous One takes note of the house of the wicked and brings the wicked to ruin."

29:26 "Many seek an audience with a ruler, but it is from the LORD that man gets justice."

See also 16:4 and 24:11–12 with comments.

The Lord despises the proud of heart (**16:5**). For they are haughty, arrogant, insensitive, and indifferent to Yahweh's will as revealed in His Word.

"Be sure of this" could be literally rendered "hand upon hand" (see 6:1; 11:15). It was an emphatic statement derived from a bargaining procedure when the parties clasped hands to cement their agreement. This imagery of shaking or striking hands with another confirmed and guaranteed what had been promised. It was like saying, "You have my Word on it! You may count on it." We have God's Word that the arrogant will certainly be punished; He guarantees it.

"The Righteous One" (**21:12**) is an indirect reference to Yahweh, who observes attentively the wicked and brings deserved calamity and ruin upon them. For "wicked" and "ruin," see "wicked" and "evil" under VWs.

The effort to obtain preferential treatment from governmental officials (**29:26**), even though it may be at the expense of others who lack the necessary contacts, is common. Corrupt officials may be bribed to bestow requested favors. Deficiencies in the working out of justice through human institutions do not occur with God, who is the ultimate source of perfect justice.

5. Exhortations Against Vengeance

20:22 "Do not say, 'I'll pay you back for this wrong!' Wait for the LORD, and he will deliver you."

24:17–18 "Do not gloat when your enemy falls; when he stumbles, do not let your heart rejoice, or the LORD will see and disapprove and turn his wrath away from him."

25:21–22 "If your enemy is hungry, give him food to eat; if he is thirsty, give him water to drink. In doing this, you will heap burning coals on his head, and the LORD will reward you."

We need to avoid a hostile or vengeful attitude toward those who wrong us. This means no promise of vengeance (**20:22**) and no rejoicing when our enemy encounters trouble or even ruin (**24:17–18**). Such rejoicing might prompt Yahweh to give relief to the enemy, while He disciplines us for our sinful attitude, since vengeance assumes that we are always right in our judgment. Rather, we are to provide the enemy with food and water whenever needed (**25:21**).

The heaping of burning coals on his head (**25:22**) is a difficult expression to understand because the imagery is obscure in our context. The burning pain may picture the burning shame and remorse produced by the unexpected and undeserved act of friendship, which may even lead to a reconciliation. Or it may refer to an ancient Egyptian penitential ritual in which the penitent endured hot coals on his head as an act of contrition.³ Although the details of the imagery are obscure, it is evidently either a reconciliation or at least an easing of the hostility. Either would be the Lord's reward for such exemplary behavior.

The principle in **25:21–22**, to want good for and do good to your enemies, is also taught by the Law (Exod. 23:4–5), by the Lord Jesus Christ (Luke 6:27–36), by Paul, who quoted this text (Rom. 12:19–20), and by Peter (1 Peter 3:9). This unusual attitude is based upon trusting Yahweh for His deliverance and justice, then loving and caring for others, even enemies.

F. Financial Concepts and Principles

1. The Rich and the Poor

22:2 "Rich and poor have this in common: The LORD is the Maker of them all."

29:13 "The poor man and the oppressor have this in common: The LORD gives sight to the eyes of both."

The "oppressor" (**29:13**) refers to the rich who had often developed or increased their wealth at the expense of the poor. Far more significant than the financial differences between rich and poor is what they have in common. Both were created by God (**22:2**); both share the benefits of God's providence, including sight (**29:13**). Under God, personal worth is more important than personal wealth and is not measured by material or financial criteria.

2. Attitude Toward and Treatment of the Poor

14:31 "He who oppresses the poor shows contempt for their Maker, but whoever is kind to the needy honors God."

15:25 "The LORD tears down the proud man's house but he keeps the widow's boundaries intact."

17:5 "He who mocks the poor shows contempt for their Maker; whoever gloats over disaster will not go unpunished."

19:17 "He who is kind to the poor lends to the LORD, and he will reward him for what he has done."

22:22–23 "Do not exploit the poor because they are poor

---

³William Klassen, "Coals of Fire; Sign of Repentance or Revenge?", *New Testament Studies*, 9 (1963), 337–50; William McKane, *Proverbs: A New Approach* (Philadelphia: Westminster, 1970), 592.

and do not crush the needy in court, for the LORD will take up their case and will plunder those who plunder them."

22:28 "Do not move an ancient boundary stone set up by your forefathers."

23:10–11 "Do not move an ancient boundary stone or encroach on the fields of the fatherless, for their Defender is strong; he will take up their case against you."

For related themes, see Rich and Poor in chapter eight.

Underlying these proverbs is the Lord's creation of and care for both rich and poor (22:2). Therefore, to gloat (17:5) over another's calamity (especially if it produces poverty), to mock (17:5; see VF) the poor, and to oppress (crush or defraud) the poor (14:31) are to invite God's wrath. Such despicable attitudes and actions display a gross disrespect for God and blasphemously scorn Him (14:31; 17:5). For they defy God's will that we should be kind to the poor and help them.

Those who are gracious to the poor thereby honor God by sharing His attitude (14:31). Kind acts, whether financial assistance or other help, are equivalent to lending to the Lord, who will pay back with His reward (19:17). These proverbs doubtless provide the basis for the Lord Jesus Christ's teaching that whatever we do for those in need, we do for Him (Matt. 25:31–46).

One unethical strategy was for a person to change illegally (Deut. 19:14) the boundary markers of another's property to expand his own property (22:28; 23:10). Identical are 22:28a and 23:10a. Other tactics were to quietly encroach upon another's land (23:10) by using it for one's own benefit and to exploit (rob) and to crush the poor in court (22:22). Widows were most vulnerable to the operations of the unscrupulous (15:25). The helplessness of the widows, orphans, and other poor victims of these forms of robbery made the injustices especially contemptible, but more tempting to the unethical. Nevertheless, such attitudes and policies will not produce prolonged prosperity.

For the Lord will function as the redeemer-relative (gō'ēl) of the victims of such crimes (23:11), defending, protecting, and avenging them. A redeemer (gō'ēl) accepted social and even financial responsibility for his closest relative who had severe difficulties. He would defend him and even avenge him if severely wronged. If there should be no human redeemer (*gō'ēl*), then God will be the redeemer who provides the justice that he would otherwise be denied. He defends him against those who would remove his boundaries or encroach upon his land (**15:25**). He undertakes his case and fights his cause (**22:23**). He judges and punishes those who violate the rights of the poor. He will demolish the house of the proud (**15:25**), including both his status and his wealth. See comments about "pride" in 8:13. God will press the life out of those who oppress the poor, which will result in their premature deaths (**22:23**).[4]

3. Finances

3:9–10 "Honor the LORD with your wealth, with the firstfruits of all your crops; then your barns will be filled to overflowing, and your vats will brim over with new wine."

10:22 "The blessing of the LORD brings wealth, and he adds no trouble to it."

30:7–9 " 'Two things I ask of you, O LORD; do not refuse me before I die: Keep falsehood and lies far from me; give me neither poverty nor riches, but give me only my daily bread. Otherwise, I may have too much and disown you and say, "Who is the LORD?" or I may become poor and steal, and so dishonor the name of my God.' "

To honor the Lord with your wealth (**3:9**) involves giving top financial priority to Him and His work. The parallel line emphasizes this point with agricultural imagery. This may involve various tithes (Lev. 27:30–33; Num. 18:21–32; Deut. 12:5–18) and sacrificial giving (Mark 12:41–44; 1 Cor. 16:1–4; 2 Cor. 8:1–7).

Those who honor God with their wealth will experience great financial prosperity, which is described here as an abundance of their standard crops (**3:9–10**). This is a general principle that Job and his friends misunderstood as an absolute truth. It is also why Job was baffled by his misfortunes while his friends were critical of his spirituality and character. If this were an absolute truth, then giving to the Lord would not be a way of

---

[4] Aelred Cody, "Notes on Proverbs 22:21 and 22:23b," *Biblica*, 61 (Rome, Italy: Biblical Institute Press, 1980): 426; see also William McKane, *Proverbs: A New Approach* (Philadelphia: Westminster 1970), 378.

honoring Him; rather, it would be an investment that was guaranteed to make a person rich! Honoring the Lord involves giving Him priority, regardless of financial circumstances.

Prosperity depends upon the Lord's blessing (**10:22**; see the comment on "bless" in 3:33). Even hard work by talented people may be futile apart from Him. The wise combine their honoring and depending upon the Lord with their consistent hard work. Those who follow the Lord's principles will not experience the anxieties and problems that those who acquire wealth by unethical means may encounter.

Agur, evidently a spiritual, God-fearing man, asked the Lord to keep from him (1) anything false or deceptive and (2) any financial extreme (**30:7–8**). Excessive wealth may create the illusion of complete self-sufficiency that leads a person to ignore or even to reject God by expressing ignorance of Him (**30:9**). Poverty makes people especially materialistic. The miserable conditions associated with poverty may even drive them to sinful acts that dishonor God, just to obtain the necessities of life. Or desperation may give way to such despair that they express disrespectful anger against God for their misery. To avoid these character-threatening dangers, Agur requested that God provide him only with his basic needs. He wanted sufficient income to enable him to live in God's will without facing the temptations of either poverty or great affluence.

G. For Further Study

1. What is the relationship between God's sovereign control of events to assure the fulfillment of His purposes and the human will's ability to make decisions and to take actions? Between God's sovereignty and human responsibility?

2. What is the relationship between what God does and what you do in achieving your goals? In developing a fruitful ministry? In obtaining protection from danger? In winning a battle? In developing a prosperous business? In building strong personal relationships?

3. Why are the statements about God's protection of the righteous and His punishment of the wicked to be regarded as general principles with some exceptions rather than as absolute

promises with universal application? What are the dangers of the latter view?

4. Use a concordance to trace the biblical references to parts of the human body as pictures of the whole person; for example, eyes, ears, nose, mouth, lips, tongue, face, hands, arms, heart, stomach, bowels, legs, feet. Observe how frequently this usage occurs.

5. What is the proper relationship between worship and behavior? How do they interrelate?

6. How should awareness of God's attitude toward various qualities and types of behavior affect your attitudes and actions? Does it?

Chapter 5

The Two Ways: Wisdom and Folly

A. Exhortations to Obtain Wisdom

The Book of Proverbs is saturated with varied and repetitive exhortations to obtain wisdom. They contain a broad diversity of words and images, which urge readers to absorb and to express in their lives the qualities of wisdom.

1. Wisdom's Invitation

1:20-21 "Wisdom calls aloud in the street, she raises her voice in the public squares; at the head of the noisy streets she cries out, in the gateways of the city she makes her speech."

8:1-7 "Does not wisdom call out? Does not understanding raise her voice? On the heights along the way, where the paths meet, she takes her stand; beside the gates leading into the city, at the entrances, she cries aloud: 'To you, O men, I call out; I raise my voice to all mankind. You who are simple, gain prudence; you who are foolish, gain understanding. Listen, for I have worthy things to say; I open my lips to speak what is right. My mouth speaks what is true, for my lips detest wickedness.'"

9:1-6 "Wisdom has built her house; she has hewn out its seven pillars. She has prepared her meat and mixed her wine; she has also set her table. She has sent out her maids, and she calls from the highest point of the city. 'Let all who are simple come in here!' she says to those who lack judgment. 'Come, eat my food and drink the wine I have mixed. Leave your simple ways and you will live; walk in the way of understanding.'"

24:3-4 "By wisdom a house is built, and through understanding it is established; through knowledge its rooms are filled with rare and beautiful treasures."

For "wisdom" (1:20; 8:1; 9:1; 24:3), "understanding" (8:1, 5; 9:6; 24:3), "prudence" (8:5), and "knowledge" (24:4), see the comments under VWm. For "simple" (8:5; 9:4, 6) and "foolish" (*kᵉsîl*; 8:5), see the comments under VF.

In both 1:20-21 and 8:1-7, wisdom is personified as a woman who publically offers wisdom to any who want to improve their ways. The repetition emphasizes the urgency of her invitation.

Wisdom's approach was to present honestly and publicly her message to all who would hear (8:4). The wise teachers went to the streets, especially the public squares, city gates, and busy intersections (8:2) to reach many people. People entered walled cities through the city gates. Often providing shade, a gateway (1:21; 8:3) was a natural location for the city elders to conduct local political and legal affairs. Nearby were the public squares, which were open areas where people gathered to conduct business, socialize, and hear public speeches. Opposing wickedness by teaching what was right and true (8:6-7), they urged the naive and foolish to become prudent and discerning (8:5).

In 9:1-6, wisdom is personified as a woman who has built a large elegant house (9:1) designed for her to function continuously as a hostess at a sumptuous feast (9:2). She issued a public invitation to the naive who lacked judgment (9:3-4) to eat her food and to drink her mixed wine (9:5; see the comment about "wine" in 31:4). This appetizing image of a delicious dinner was drawn to picture food for thought. For the imagery of food and drink portrayed the instruction of wisdom as the real nourishment to be digested by her guests. In 9:6, she dropped the image of gracious hospitality and dining and urged them directly to stop being naive and to become discerning.

In 24:3-4, the imagery of house construction pictures the building up of wisdom. Both involve time, effort, and work. When done properly, the structure is solidly built and firmly established, furnished with the exquisite valuables that accompany success. This metaphor applies to building character, relationships, and business. The picture is similar to Jesus' parable of houses built upon rock and sand (Luke 6:46–49).

2. *Commands to Acquire Wisdom*

1:1–6 "The proverbs of Solomon son of David, king of Israel: for attaining wisdom and discipline; for understanding words of insight; for acquiring a disciplined and prudent life, doing what is just and right and fair; for giving prudence to the simple, knowledge and discretion to the young—let the wise listen and add to their learning, and let the discerning get guidance—for understanding proverbs and parables, the sayings and riddles of the wise."

4:1–5 "Listen, my sons, to a father's instruction; pay attention and gain understanding. I give you sound learning, so do not forsake my teaching. When I was a boy in my father's house, still tender, and an only child of my mother, he taught me and said, 'Lay hold of my words with all your heart; keep my commands and you will live. Get wisdom, get understanding; do not forget my words or swerve from them.'"

18:15 "The heart of the discerning acquires knowledge; the ears of the wise seek it out."

19:20 "Listen to advice and accept instruction, and in the end you will be wise."

23:22–23 "Listen to your father, who gave you life, and do not despise your mother when she is old. Buy the truth and do not sell it; get wisdom, discipline and understanding."

For "wisdom" (1:2, 5; 4:5; 18:15; 19:20; 23:23), "understanding," "discernment," "insight" (1:2, 5; 4:1, 5; 18:15; 23:23), "knowledge" (1:4; 18:15), see VWm. For "simple" (1:4), see VF.

The wise seek (see "look for" in 2:4) and acquire knowledge **(18:15)**. The parallel (see introduction) Hebrew word rendered "acquire" **(18:15)**, "get" **(4:5)**, and "buy" **(23:23)** is a marketing term that describes purchasing merchandise. Here it pictures doing whatever is necessary in terms of effort, learning, hard work, and integration to acquire the desired knowledge. The discerning eagerly pay that price for knowledge. Perhaps that is why they are discerning!

The Book of Proverbs begins with a prologue that consists of its official title **(1:1)** and a statement of its purpose **(1:2–6)**, which is to equip readers to acquire the key quality of wisdom that produces right, just, and fair behavior (1:3). A person acquires these qualities by reading, studying, learning, and assimilating the principles of wisdom that are taught in Proverbs. The wise expand their knowledge in the same way. For the more we learn, the more we realize our need to learn more.

Readers of Proverbs are often urged to listen (1:5; 4:1; 19:20; 23:22) and to pay attention (4:1). Not a mechanical routine, active listening includes hearing, paying attention, understanding, assimilating, and, when appropriate, obeying. This response to wisdom will make us wise (19:20) and show respect for the wisdom and experience of our parents (4:1; 23:22). To refuse to listen to them is equivalent to despising them (23:22).

The exhortations in 4:1–5 are presented in the imagery of parental instruction. These and other similar passages may reflect actual parental instruction preserved in writing, or a manual for parental instruction assembled by the wise men, or a wise teacher's use of parental imagery to instruct his disciples affectionately.

To gain understanding means literally to know it through what a person has experienced (4:1). The sound (reliable) teaching is not to be rejected (4:2). The writer fondly recalled that in his early childhood when he was very impressionable (4:3), his father urged him to lay hold of his teachings and commands (4:4). To lay hold is to grasp firmly, retaining and applying them rigorously.

3. Commands to Keep Wisdom

7:1–4 "My son, keep my words and store up my commands within you. Keep my commands and you will live; guard my teachings as the apple of your eye. Bind them on your fingers; write them on the tablet of your heart. Say to wisdom, 'You are my sister,' and call understanding your kinsman."

8:32–34 "'Now then, my sons, listen to me; blessed are those who keep my ways. Listen to my instruction and be wise; do not ignore it. Blessed is the man who listens to me, watching daily at my doors, waiting at my doorway.'"

23:12 "Apply your heart to instruction and your ears to words of knowledge."

23:19 "Listen, my son, and be wise, and keep your heart on the right path."

23:26 "My son, give me your heart and let your eyes keep to my ways."

These texts use vivid images to emphasize the need to maintain, preserve, and use wisdom. For "keep" (7:1-2; 8:32), see "protect" in 2:8. Wisdom has no less value than the apple (literally, pupil) of a person's eye (7:2), which he instinctively protects. To "watch" (8:34) for wisdom is to be constantly alert for any opportunity to absorb more of it.

The images in 7:3 of attaching to fingers and writing on the tablet of one's heart are almost identical to those in 3:3 (see the comments there). References to fingers (7:3), heart (7:3; 23:12, 19, 26), ears (23:12), and eyes (23:26) are a common biblical technique for referring to a part of the human body as a figurative representation of the entire person. To call wisdom your sister or kinsman (7:4) indicates an intimate family relationship with her.

These images picture internalizing the principles of wisdom to the extent that they saturate our minds, form our attitudes, and control our behavior. They are to become such an integral part of us that we subconsciously follow them.

B. Characteristics of Wisdom

1. The Wise Listen to Wisdom.

5:1-2 "My son, pay attention to my wisdom, listen well to my words of insight, that you may maintain discretion and your lips may preserve knowledge."

16:21 "The wise in heart are called discerning, and pleasant words promote instruction."

Pleasant words, literally sweetness of the lips, picture a gracious, attractive, enjoyable style of teaching (16:21). They enhance instruction by enabling students to enjoy it, want more of it, and be more open to it. The teacher who can make wisdom more productive for others by successfully motivating them to implement its principles is even more valuable than the one who is wise. The most effective teaching involves both making clear what is presented and selling its value to the students. Motivated students will "pay attention" (**5:1**; see note about **4:1**), maintain and preserve (see note about "protect" and "guard" in **2:8**) what they learn.

2. The Wise Benefit from Good Advice.

11:14 "For lack of guidance a nation falls, but many advisers make victory sure."

15:22 " Plans fail for lack of counsel, but with many advisers they succeed."

20:18 "Make plans by seeking advice; if you wage war, obtain guidance."

24:6 "For waging war you need guidance, and for victory many advisers."

The statements in **11:14a** and **15:22a** are variants with the same point. The sayings of **11:14b** and **24:6b** are identical in the Hebrew text, while **15:22b** is a variant with the same point. The sayings of **11:14; 15:22; 24:6** may be used as an inspired mini-commentary on **20:18**. The main idea of these texts is that competent advisers make success more likely, but lack of such counsel contributes to failure.

3. The Wise Accept and Value Rebukes.

15:31 "He who listens to a life-giving rebuke will be at home among the wise."

25:12 "Like an earring of gold or an ornament of fine gold is a wise man's rebuke to a listening ear."

There is benefit and value in a perceptive rebuke to an open recipient who admits its validity and takes corrective action.

4. The Wise Use Self-Control to Appease Anger and to Avoid Danger.

16:14 "A king's wrath is a messenger of death, but a wise man will appease it."

19:11 "A man's wisdom gives him patience; it is to his glory to overlook an offense."

23:1–3 "When you sit to dine with a ruler, note well what is before you, and put a knife to your throat if you are given to gluttony. Do not crave his delicacies, for that food is deceptive."

25:28 "Like a city whose walls are broken down is a man who lacks self-control."

The wise possess the self-control to shrug off insults and offenses and to avoid heated responses. They are slow to anger ("patient" in NIV; see "patient" in 14:29). Their restraint from anger and forgiving attitude (**19:11**) promote harmony and bring honor to them.

When with a king who has the authority to harm or even to kill (**16:14**), the wise are cautious, eating only moderate portions of his food (**23:1**). "To put a knife to your throat" (**23:2**) is an Oriental expression for practicing self-restraint. Here it refers to a restrained appetite, since the king's food may involve more than calories. It may be a means for the king to lay heavy obligations upon a person or to involve him in an evil plan. Using self-control, a wise man appeases a king's deadly anger (**16:14**) and earns honor for his forgiving attitude.

A man who "lacks self-control" (**25:28**) has literally "no restraint to his spirit." Easily angered and frustrated, he is vulnerable to foolish, impulsive, dangerous statements and actions prompted by his uncontrolled emotions. It is as disastrous for a man to be without self-control as for a city to have its protective wall breached, leaving it defenseless. Self-control is part of the fruit of the Spirit (Gal. 5:22).

5. The Wise Are Righteous and Just.

2:20-22 "Thus you will walk in the ways of good men and keep to the paths of the righteous. For the upright will live in the land, and the blameless will remain in it; but the wicked will be cut off from the land, and the unfaithful will be torn from it."

8:8-9 " 'All the words of my mouth are just; none of them is crooked or perverse. To the discerning all of them are right; they are faultless to those who have knowledge.' "

The ethical and beneficial aspects of wisdom mentioned in **2:20-22** are in contrast to the warnings against sinful ways in **2:12-19**. For "blameless" (integrity; **2:21**), see VR. A menace to a smoothly and justly operating society, the wicked will be removed from the land of Israel that God had promised to Jacob's physical descendants (**2:22**). Their removal will occur through death or expulsion. The upright will remain in that land (**2:21**).

The correctness of wisdom is not always accepted. The morally discerning recognize the principles of wisdom as right and true (**8:8–9**). One encounters the same contrasting reactions to the gospel that seems strange and even foolish to many who reject it (see 1 Cor. 1:18–25).

6. *The Wise Have Power.*

16:32 "Better a patient man than a warrior, a man who controls his temper than one who takes a city."

21:22 "A wise man attacks the city of the mighty and pulls down the stronghold in which they trust."

24:5 "A wise man has great power, and a man of knowledge increases strength."

More significant than heroic exploits by powerful warriors is a patient (see comment about 14:29) man who is slow to anger. For he has self-control (**16:32**), that is, he literally "rules his spirit" (contrast with 25:28). Intelligent and moral strength is more powerful than military might (**21:22**). A wise man may detect the point of weakness in a fortified city and develop an effective strategy for an attack. The superiority of the wise over military might is established by their victories.

In **24:5**, the two synonymous parallel statements (see introduction) indicate the presence of strength in wisdom and the enhancing of strength by wisdom. Working hard may be ineffective, but working hard intelligently is more likely to produce success.

7. *The Wise Are Protected by Wisdom.*

2:9–11 "Then you will understand what is right and just and fair—every good path. For wisdom will enter your heart, and knowledge will be pleasant to your soul. Discretion will protect you, and understanding will guard you."

2:12–15 "Wisdom will save you from the ways of wicked men, from men whose words are perverse, who leave the straight paths to walk in dark ways, who delight in doing wrong and rejoice in the perverseness of evil, whose paths are crooked and who are devious in their ways."

4:6 "Do not forsake wisdom, and she will protect you; love her, and she will watch over you."

After fulfilling the conditions of 2:1–4 and receiving the benefits of God's working pictured in 2:5–8, we experience the benefits of 2:9ff. The piling up of similar positive moral terms—right, just, and fair—emphasizes the moral content of wisdom (2:9). Walking, the most common ancient method of moving from one place to another, pictured the activities of life. Thus, to walk is to live. "Ways" or "paths" (2:9, 12, 13, 15) on which people walked usually refer figuratively to qualities, patterns, and directions of a person's life, especially those reenforced by repetition. For wisdom to enter someone's heart (2:10) is for wisdom to live there, to be absorbed into his personality. Wisdom, which is almost personified here, in that context rescues a person from spiritual, moral, and physical dangers (2:11–12; 4:6). So the wise person loves and follows the good, straight path of wisdom (2:9, 13; 4:6) and enjoys the pleasures of true knowledge (2:10).

In contrast, the wicked follow "dark ways" (2:13) that picture figuratively the evil deeds often done in the privacy provided by the darkness of night. The wicked enjoy their perverse ways (2:14) and leave the straight, upright ways of the wise (2:13) to follow crooked paths (2:15).

8. The Wise Find Wisdom Attractive and Pleasant.

1:8–9 "Listen, my son, to your father's instruction and do not forsake your mother's teaching. They will be a garland to grace your head and a chain to adorn your neck."

3:21–26 "My son, preserve sound judgment and discernment; do not let them out of your sight; they will be life for you, an ornament to grace your neck. Then you will go on your way in safety, and your foot will not stumble; when you lie down, you will not be afraid; when you lie down, your sleep will be sweet. Have no fear of sudden disaster or of the ruin that overtakes the wicked, for the LORD will be your confidence and will keep your foot from being snared."

4:8–9 "Esteem her, and she will exalt you; embrace her,

and she will honor you. She will set a garland of grace on your head and present you with a crown of splendor."

4:10–13 "Listen, my son, accept what I say, and the years of your life will be many. I guide you in the way of wisdom and lead you among straight paths. When you walk, your steps will not be hampered; when you run, you will not stumble. Hold on to instruction, do not let it go; guard it well, for it is your life."

24:13–14 "Eat honey, my son, for it is good; honey from the comb is sweet to your taste. Know also that wisdom is sweet to your soul; if you find it, there is a future hope for you, and your hope will not be cut off."

27:9 "Perfume and incense bring joy to the heart, and the pleasantness of one's friend springs from his earnest counsel."

For the exhortations of 1:8, 3:21, 4:10, see the previous page.

Images picturing wisdom as beautiful, attractive, and pleasant include a chain (probably a necklace, 1:9), garland (likely a wreath, 1:9; 4:9), and crown (a head covering for ordinary people, perhaps a garland, which it parallels in 4:9). The wise teacher used decorative imagery to picture figuratively the beauty of wisdom, which clothes the wise with discernment (3:21–22), honor (4:8–9), and splendor (4:9).

The pleasure of wisdom is compared with the sweet scents of perfume and incense (27:9). These delightful scents were associated with having good health, honoring guests, and promoting joyful social fellowship. Although the relationship between 27:9a and 27:9b is not clear, the best of many suggestions is to see an analogy between these verse halves: Perfume and incense bring joy to a person; so does the pleasantness of a friend's earnest counsel.

The wise teacher urged his readers to eat honey (24:13). Raw honey (the only kind available in ancient times) and its synonymous parallel equivalent (see introduction), honey from the comb, are deliciously sweet and nutritious. Eating honey brightened Jonathan's eyes (1 Sam. 14:24–30) and renewed his strength (alternate readings for 1 Sam. 14:27, 29), indicating its nourishing effect. Like raw honey, wisdom is also sweet and nourishing (24:14) for all areas of life.

Walking in wisdom involves the easy progress that results

when the obstacles that hamper progress and cause stumbling are removed (3:23; 4:12). The wise person's confidence in the Lord enables him to follow paths with a sure footing (3:26). Such confidence and assurance enable us to relax with sleep that is restful, refreshing, and undisturbed (3:24).

Someone who values wisdom highly embraces her, holding her close (4:8). High esteem and tender embraces are clearly expressions of love. In response, Wisdom will exalt and honor you, causing others to respect you. In 4:13, "hold on" is to grasp firmly so as not to relax one's grip and let go. A person is to guard wisdom as carefully as a treasure whose value it exceeds, for it is the essence of quality living.

9. *The Wise Value Wisdom Highly.*

3:1–2 "My son, do not forget my teaching, but keep my commands in your heart, for they will prolong your life many years and bring you prosperity."

3:13–18 "Blessed is the man who finds wisdom, the man who gains understanding, for she is more profitable than silver and yields better returns than gold. She is more precious than rubies; nothing you desire can compare with her. Long life is in her right hand; in her left hand are riches and honor. Her ways are pleasant ways, and all her paths are peace. She is a tree of life to those who embrace her; those who lay hold of her will be blessed."

4:7 "Wisdom is supreme; therefore get wisdom. Though it cost all you have, get understanding."

8:10–11 "'Choose my instruction instead of silver, knowledge rather than choice gold, for wisdom is more precious than rubies, and nothing you desire can compare with her.'"

8:12–21 "'I, wisdom, dwell together with prudence; I possess knowledge and discretion. To fear the LORD is to hate evil; I hate pride and arrogance, evil behavior and perverse speech. Counsel and sound judgment are mine; I have understanding and power. By me kings reign and rulers make laws that are just; by me princes govern, and all nobles who rule on earth. I love those who love me, and those who seek me find me. With me are riches and honor, enduring wealth and prosperity. My fruit is better than fine gold; what I yield surpasses choice silver. I walk in the way of righteousness, along the paths of justice, bestowing wealth on those who love me and making their treasuries full.' "

16:16 "How much better to get wisdom than gold, to choose understanding rather than silver."

19:8 "He who gets wisdom loves his own soul; he who cherishes understanding prospers."

20:15 "Gold there is, and rubies in abundance, but lips that speak knowledge are a rare jewel."

These proverbs assert the supreme value of wisdom, which is scarcer and should be sought and treasured more than the finest gold and silver, rarest jewels, and most elegant possessions (3:14–15; 8:10–11, 19; 16:16; 20:15). These comparisons remind us of Jesus' parables about the hidden treasure and exquisite pearl (Matt. 13:44–46). Almost identical are **3:15** and **8:11**.

Wisdom's superiority to the most exquisite wealth is portrayed by both merchandising ("profitable" in 3:14 and "get" in 4:7; 16:16; see 18:15) and agricultural ("fruit" and "yield" in 8:19) imagery. This preference emphasizes the superior value of wisdom to material wealth, which is pictured throughout Proverbs as beneficial and desirable. That is why the reader is urged to perceive Wisdom's supreme value and to make her acquisition his top priority (**4:7; 16:16**), no matter what the cost.

Wisdom is personified as a generous woman, offering attractive gifts of long life (**3:2, 16**; see 4:10; 9:11; 10:27; Exod. 20:12), riches (**3:16; 8:18, 21**) and honor (**3:16; 8:18**). Riches, honor, and life do not determine the extent of one's happiness but do substantially improve it when received as by-products of wisdom.

A man who displays his knowledge in conversation is scarcer and more to be prized than the abundance of gold and rubies (**20:15**). There are basic reasons for wisdom's superior value (**16:16**). We may use wisdom to acquire wealth, but we cannot acquire wisdom by means of wealth. Wisdom provides not only material riches, but also the wealth of personal satisfaction and happy relationships. Discernment is essential to governmental leaders who need it to develop and administer wise policies that are just, fair, and benevolent (**8:15, 16, 20**).

THE TWO WAYS: WISDOM AND FOLLY

There is power and sound judgment in wisdom (8:14). Sound judgment involves the discerning common sense that leads to continuing practical success.

The prosperity of the wise is pictured by three terms in these texts. First, the Hebrew word, *shālôm*, correctly rendered "prosperity" (3:2) and "peace" (3:17), also means completion, fulfillment, wholeness, and harmony. It includes the qualities of peace, prosperity, health, safety, and happiness in all areas of life.

The second word rendered "prosperity" (8:18) normally means righteousness (see VR) in the sense of conforming to an ethical standard. Some have suggested that it also has a secondary sense of prosperity with which God often blesses the righteous (NIV). Others feel that to understand righteousness as involving success or prosperity is to oversimplify the relationship of rightness to either result.[1] Either "righteousness" or "prosperity" would be an appropriate synonymous parallel to "honor."

For "prospers" in 19:8, see the comment about "prospers" in 16:20 and "good" in VR. Financial prosperity, although included, is not the primary element in any of these terms.

Wisdom is pictured as a tree of life to those who embrace her (3:18; see Gen. 2:9; 3:22; Rev. 2:7; 22:2). In the Book of Proverbs, "tree of life" refers to God's sources of renewal and vitality apart from any cosmic or eschatological significance. In 3:18, the wise are to embrace and lay hold of (see note about 4:4) wisdom, loving her and absorbing her qualities. Wisdom (personified) loves those who love her (8:17; note the similar attitude of the Lord Jesus Christ in John 14:21). Lovers of Wisdom will desire her greatly, vigorously pursue her, and ultimately find her. Happy with her (3:13), they find Wisdom's ways to be pleasant (3:17), delightful, enjoyable.

The person who acquires wisdom shows that he loves his "soul," that is, his life or himself (19:8; see the comment about "zeal" in 19:2). Loving ourselves is a desirable quality that is important for our effectiveness. That is why this attitude is

---

[1] William McKane, *Proverbs: A New Approach* (Philadelphia: Westminster, 1970), 350.

assumed to be commendable. Those who love themselves want what is beneficial and so are attracted to wisdom.

C. Benefits of Wisdom

1. *Life and Health*

4:20–23 "My son, pay attention to what I say; listen closely to my words. Do not let them out of your sight, keep them within your heart; for they are life to those who find them and health to a man's whole body. Above all else, guard your heart, for it is the wellspring of life."

6:20–23 "My son, keep your father's commands and do not forsake your mother's teaching. Bind them upon your heart forever; fasten them around your neck. When you walk, they will guide you; when you sleep, they will watch over you; when you awake, they will speak to you. For these commands are a lamp, this teaching is a light, and the corrections of discipline are the way to life."

11:30 "The fruit of the righteous is a tree of life, and he who wins souls is wise."

13:14 "The teaching of the wise is a fountain of life, turning a man from the snares of death."

15:24 "The path of life leads upward for the wise to keep him from going down to the grave."

For other references to life and health, see 3:1–2, 13–18, 21–26; 4:10–13; 8:32–36. For "life" (**4:22–23; 6:23; 11:30; 13:14; 15:24**), see the comments about 19:23. For the exhortations of **4:20** and **6:20**, see the preceding sections about commands to acquire and to keep wisdom. The exhortations of **4:21a** and **3:21b** are identical.

The important exhortation to guard your heart (**4:23**) includes the thoughts, emotions, and will of the entire person. The modern equivalent to the heart is the mind as the central conditioner and controller for human functioning. For a person to function properly, his mind must function properly. "Mind" is a better rendering than "heart" for this and other texts in which this term focuses on human functioning. Although it can picture the entire person, often "heart" describes specific functions of thinking and feeling; for example, understanding, judgment, desire. Therefore, it is crucial for us to guard diligently (see "protect" in 2:8) our minds as our most precious possession. To protect them, we must filter out sinful, destructive thoughts and attitudes that shatter our confidence and demolish our effectiveness. We must carefully and consistently feed our minds with God-honoring, moral, constructive thoughts and attitudes that build our confidence, enhance our effectiveness, and mold our lives. To protect the supremely important mind, we are urged to guard it "above all else."

The synonymous parallel (see introduction) exhortations of 6:21 use the imagery of binding upon the heart and fastening (e.g., a necklace) around the neck to picture a close and firm attachment (see similar imagery in 3:3). Wisdom so thoroughly saturates our personality that it prompts us both consciously and subconsciously to follow her principles. Such an attachment keeps wisdom constantly within view (4:21), since Wisdom exerts her beneficial influence when we walk, sleep, and awake (6:22)—the gamut of daily life.

In 6:23, Wisdom's commands and teachings are pictured as a lamp and a light, which describe spiritual and moral illumination (see Ps. 119:105). As light removes darkness, Wisdom eliminates foolishness. As light clarifies a person's surroundings, Wisdom enlightens and enables him to function properly and effectively.

Several images picture a major benefit of wisdom—quality life. Corrections by discipline place a person on the way to "the path of life" (15:24) with its upward direction that portrays an improved quality in every dimension of life and avoidance of a premature death. Its fruit or result is a "tree of life" (11:30; see the comment about 3:18). For "fountain of life" and "snares of death" (13:14), see the comments about 14:27, which is identical to 13:14 except that "the fear of the LORD" replaces "the teaching of the wise."

There is an important reason to guard our minds (4:23a): The mind is "the wellspring of life" (4:23b). The word rendered "wellspring" pictures the mind as the source of the thoughts and attitudes that determine a person's perspective toward and direction in life. Two translations of 4:23 capture its thought and urgency especially well. "More than anything else watch your heart, because from it flows your life" (Beck). "Be careful how you think; your life is shaped by your thoughts" (TEV).

The meaning of **11:30b** is unclear. In spite of prevalent evangelical usage, "winning souls" does not refer here to gospel evangelism. For "souls," see "zeal" in 19:2. The word rendered "wins" means "takes"; therefore, literally "he who takes lives is wise." If "taking lives" means "taking life," then it pictures the wise as violently killing people and clashes with the biblical description of their self-control. Thus, some translators and interpreters have followed the pre-Christian Greek translation, which reads "but the souls of the wicked are cut off before their time." It is more plausible to understand "taking lives" as not involving violence and to let the Hebrew text stand as it is. The most likely interpretation is to understand "taking lives" as a wise man's attracting people to himself and taking them to make them wise.

2. Rejoicing Parents

23:15–16 "My son, if your heart is wise, then my heart will be glad; my inmost being will rejoice when your lips speak what is right."

23:24–25 "The father of a righteous man has great joy; he who has a wise son delights in him. May your father and mother be glad; may she who gave you birth rejoice!"

27:11 "Be wise, my son, and bring joy to my heart; then I can answer anyone who treats me with contempt."

These texts all have similar meanings. No parent or teacher can force his child or student to be wise and righteous. There are no guarantees as to the outcomes of their efforts. That is why a son or student who rightly decides to learn, acquire, and use wisdom brings great joy to his parent or teacher. When faced with negative criticism, contempt, and scorn, a parent or teacher can point to a wise son, daughter, or student who has absorbed and is applying the principles of wisdom. For that makes it clear that both teacher and student have done their jobs.

D. Results of Rejecting Wisdom

1:20–33 "Wisdom calls aloud in the street, she raises her voice in the public squares, at the head of the noisy streets she cries out, in the gateways of the city she makes her speech:

THE TWO WAYS: WISDOM AND FOLLY 99

"'How long will you simple ones love your simple ways? How long will mockers delight in mockery and fools hate knowledge? If you had responded to my rebuke, I would have poured out my heart to you and made my thoughts known to you. But since you rejected me when I called and no one gave heed when I stretched out my hand, since you ignored all my advice and would not accept my rebuke, I in turn will laugh at your disaster; I will mock when calamity overtakes you—when calamity overtakes you like a storm, when disaster sweeps over you like a whirlwind, when distress and trouble overwhelm you.

"'Then they will call to me but I will not answer; they will look for me but will not find me. Since they hated knowledge and did not choose to fear the LORD, since they would not accept my advice and spurned my rebuke, they will eat the fruit of their ways and be filled with the fruit of their schemes. For the waywardness of the simple will kill them, and the complacency of fools will destroy them; but whoever listens to me will live in safety and be at ease, without fear of harm.'"

15:10 "Stern discipline awaits him who leaves the path; he who hates correction will die."

19:27 "Stop listening to instruction, my son, and you will stray from the words of knowledge."

21:16 "A man who strays from the path of understanding comes to rest in the company of the dead."

For "rebuke" or "correction" (1:23, 25; 15:10), see VWm. For "mockers" or "mock" (1:22, 26), "simple" (1:22, 32), and "fools" ($k^e s\hat{\imath}l$; 1:22, 32), see VF. For 1:20–21, see Wisdom's Invitation under Exhortations to Obtain Wisdom.

The rhetorical questions of 1:22 picture people's foolish rejection of Wisdom's invitation (1:20–21) and their resulting tragic loss (1:23). Turning a deaf ear to Wisdom's verbal invitation (1:24a) and spurning her beckoning gesture (1:24b), they strayed from knowledge (19:27), that is, lived as if they had never acquired it. These repeated descriptions of rejecting wisdom build up an expectancy of impending doom.

Wisdom's mocking laughter at the plight of those who stupidly mocked and rejected her emphasize their rejection (1:26–27). Calamity comes upon them like the crashing thunder of a devastating storm, which loudly publicizes its unleashing of destruction, or like the furious, destructive, stormy wind ("whirlwind"), which vividly pictures God's judgment (1:27; see Ps. 73:19). These images include both the external calamities and the internal anxieties people face when Wisdom withdraws her invitation and their opportunity for deliverance (1:28). For 1:29–31, see the results of Rejecting Wisdom in chapter three.

Apathy toward wisdom can be fatal. A complacent (1:32) person has no anxieties because he accepts no commitments or responsibilities. Complacency and waywardness, or turning away (1:32), are equally effective ways of departing from wisdom, bringing severe discipline (15:10) that includes death (1:32b). This result is vividly pictured in 21:16. Premature death provides a permanent "rest." The irony is that the person who obtains freedom from the discipline and restraints of wisdom will lose his freedom and his life by his premature death.

In contrast are those who follow wisdom (1:33). They live in safety, are at ease, and do not fear harm.

E. Characteristics of Foolishness

1. The Foolish Repeat Their Foolishness.

26:11 "As a dog returns to its vomit, so a fool repeats his folly."

In the simile of **26:11**, the image of the foolish is gross. No less stupid and repulsive than a dog's eating its indigestible vomit is a foolish person who repeats his foolish and disgusting behavior, even when it has previously harmed him. He is clearly either incapable or unwilling to learn from his mistakes. The first line was later quoted in 2 Peter 2:22 to show that a person's actions indicate what he is like.

2. The Foolish Have Zeal without Knowledge.

19:2 "It is not good to have zeal without knowledge, nor to be hasty and miss the way."

The Hebrew word *nepesh*, rendered "zeal," originally meant "breath." Rendered "soul" in older translations, its modern English equivalent is most often "self," "person," "life." It also pictures a person's thinking, appetites (hunger, thirst), desires (for someone or something), vitality, emotions (love or hate), rejoicing, and enthusiasm. All these human functionings are neutral; what makes them positive or negative, good or bad, right or wrong is *what* we desire or are zealous about. It is not good to have enthusiasm or desires that are unrelated to and unenlightened by knowledge. The key is to use knowledge to direct our desires and enthusiasm in ways that are honorable and constructive.

Equally faulty is for a person to make a decision so quickly that he does not use his wisdom, define his goal, or develop his plan for achieving it. The result is to move rapidly in the wrong direction toward the wrong destination. This is to "miss the way," a central idea in the Hebrew word used here, which also means "to sin" (see VWs).

3. *The Foolish Reject the Knowledge That They Lack.*

14:7 "Stay away from a foolish man, for you will not find knowledge on his lips."

18:2 "A fool finds no pleasure in understanding but delights in airing his own opinions."

23:9 "Do not speak to a fool, for he will scorn the wisdom of your words."

26:4 "Do not answer a fool according to his folly, or you will be like him yourself."

26:5 "Answer a fool according to his folly, or he will be wise in his own eyes."

For "foolish"/"fool" ($k^esîl$; **14:7; 18:2; 23:9; 26:4–5**) and "folly" (*'iwwelet*; **26:4–5**), see VF.

Bored with the wisdom available from others, a fool wants only to convey his opinions (**18:2**), which merely express his stupidity. As a result, he has nothing beneficial to contribute (**14:7**). So it is best to have nothing to do with him (**14:7**). Even the effort to correct him arouses only his contempt (**23:9**).

Both ancient rabbis and recent scholars have observed the apparent contradiction between **26:4** and **26:5**. To consider the two texts contradictory with one as wrong is simplistic. The issue of how to respond to a fool is too complex to be handled adequately by a mere yes or no.

For a wise man to take foolish questions seriously is to fall to a fool's low level (**26:4**) and waste his time. According to an ancient Jewish proverb, "A fool can ask more questions in an hour than ten wise men can answer in a year."[2] To become hopelessly enmeshed in discussing an endless barrage of futile questions is to become like a fool and to lose the value of your own wisdom.

A talkative fool, whom no wise man corrects, may consider himself wise (**26:5**) and present dogmatically his foolish advice, which he believes to be correct and valuable. Such a fool is obnoxious. That is why a perceptive answer may be needed to reject a fool's perspective, to rebuke his folly, and to correct his erroneous views. This is why Paul responded to Corinthian Christian foolishness as he did (2 Cor. 11:16–21; 12:11).

When examined closely, **26:4** and **26:5** are found not to contradict each other. Rather, they complement each other by treating different aspects of the same topic. This means that there are certain occasions when a person should answer a fool and others when he should not. It requires great wisdom to discern which is which. Thus, the most plausible approach is to take both texts together and to combine their contributions toward handling this complex issue. Unfortunately, dealings with fools are so loaded with traps that any response could be wrong, problematic, or ineffective in a specific case. In fact, each of our texts (along with 23:9) states a potentially undesirable result of any response to a fool.

4. The Foolish Detest Turning from the Evil They Plot.

13:19 "A longing fulfilled is sweet to the soul, but fools detest turning from evil."

24:8–9 "He who plots evil will be known as a schemer. The schemes of folly are sin, and men detest a mocker."

In **13:19a**, the word rendered "longing" pictures a burning desire, whether for something good or evil. To make that desire, if good (as here), a reality by achieving it is exquisitely pleasant and immensely satisfying, but this sweet pleasure lasts only if the goal is worthy. For "soul" (person), see "zeal" in 19:2. Similar to **13:19a** is 13:12b. The unrelated statement in **13:19b**

---
[2]Cited by Robert L. Alden, *Proverbs, A Commentary on an Ancient Book of Timeless Advice* (Grand Rapids: Baker, 1983). 186.

indicates the sinful element in foolishness. Fools who love what is morally evil and worthless do not break away from their evil because they do not want to.

In 24:8–9, the words rendered "plots," "schemer," and "schemes" are virtually synonymous and picture carefully planned malevolence. The mocker who is capable of concocting and executing such schemes is despised. For having nothing of value to contribute, his impact is harmful and his presence obnoxious.

5. The Foolish Are Quick-Tempered.

14:17 "A quick-tempered man does foolish things, and a crafty man is hated."

For "quick-tempered," see the comment about 14:29 and 29:8.

The text compares the quick-tempered man's foolish, explosive anger with the crafty man's calm, rational, planned, malicious schemes, which may include violence. It contrasts the stupid with the despicable.

6. The Foolish Are Dangerous, Quarrelsome, Vexing, and Arouse Hostilities.

17:12 "Better to meet a bear robbed of her cubs than a fool in his folly."

22:10 "Drive out the mocker, and out goes strife; quarrels and insults are ended."

27:3 "Stone is heavy and sand a burden, but provocation by a fool is heavier than both."

30:32–33 "'If you have played the fool and exalted yourself, or if you have planned evil, clap your hand over your mouth! For as churning the milk produces butter, and as twisting the nose produces blood, so stirring up anger produces strife.'"

For "fool" ($k^e s\hat{\imath}l$, 17:12), "fool" ($\check{e}w\hat{\imath}l$, 27:3), "play the fool" ($n\bar{a}b\bar{a}l$, 30:32), and "mocker" (22:10), see VF.

An enraged mother bear robbed of her cubs was a classic symbol for ferocity (2 Sam. 17:8; Hos. 13:8). Potentially no less dangerous and destructive is a fool who is irrational, irresponsible, and has an uncontrolled temper (17:12). By constantly annoying people, a foolish man imposes a mental and emotional burden that is more exhausting and annoying than any physical load (**27:3**).

We must remember that the proper response to exalting ourselves foolishly or plotting evil is to close our mouths by clapping our hands over them (**30:32**), just as we would when we realize that we should not have said something we had already said. Quick action will prevent any harm from our foolish schemes, statements, or deeds.

In **30:33**, two similes illustrate the cause-effect relationship between arousing anger and strife. Each of the three lines in **30:33** contains the same two verbs. The verb rendered "churning," "twisting," "stirring up" pictures a vigorous, prolonged pressing or twisting that produces curds from milk or a painful bloody nose with an angry reaction. For the relationship between "nose" and "anger" (same Hebrew word), see the comment about 29:8. Nevertheless, prolonged vigorous arousing of hostile feelings shortens the fuse and fuels an inevitable explosion into bitter strife. The purpose of **30:32–33** is to motivate people to prevent these nasty consequences by avoiding the arrogant attitude and evil schemes that are sure to produce them.

Three similar repetitive words—strife, quarrels, and insults (**22:10**)—emphasize the tensions and conflicts that mockers arouse and intensify. An obvious contribution toward peace is to expel the mocker. Once he is removed, things will calm down.

7. *The Foolish Are Arrogant.*

17:7 "Arrogant lips are unsuited to a fool—how much worse lying lips to a ruler!"

21:24 "The proud and arrogant man—'Mocker' is his name; he behaves with overweening pride."

26:12 "Do you see a man wise in his own eyes? There is more hope for a fool than for him."

In Proverbs 21:24 the mocker is pictured as excessively arrogant and offensive. The cognate words rendered "proud" and "pride" involve an exaggerated sense of self-importance expressed by being presumptuous, defiant, insolent, and rebellious. "Overweening" is excessive.

In **17:7**, "arrogant lips" pictures big talk that exaggerates the speaker's importance. Even more contemptible is a lying ruler or leader who deceives and betrays his constituency.

The greatest obstacle to acquiring wisdom is the deluded impression that a person does not need it (**26:12**). Even a fool has more potential than the arrogant person who does not listen to the wise. There is a slight possibility that a fool may acquire a little wisdom, but there is no such chance for the "wise guy" who wrongly considers himself wise. Identical are **26:12b** and **29:20b**.

8. The Foolish Are Slanderous.

10:18 "He who conceals his hatred has lying lips, and whoever spreads slander is a fool."

Apparently friendly words that conceal hostility are no more reliable than those of a liar. Slander can ruin a person's reputation by describing him as immoral or corrupt. To spread such false information will benefit no one, arouse hostilities, and may bring harm and guilt to the slanderer. That is why such behavior is foolish. Both lines of **10:18** describe conveying a false impression: one by withholding information and the other by conveying false, derogatory information.

9. The Foolish Are Useless to Others.

a. As a Messenger. **26:6** "Like cutting off one's feet or drinking violence is the sending of a message by the hand of a fool."

Only wise, reliable people should be messengers. This text vividly portrays the futility of sending a message by a fool ($k^e s\hat{\imath}l$; see VF). To do so will be as successful as a man without feet who must walk or a violent diplomat.

b. As an Employee. **26:10** "Like an archer who wounds at random is he who hires a fool or any passer-by."

The NIV rendering is a plausible effort to make sense out of the obscure Hebrew text with its unclear meaning. The deliberately ridiculous image pictures an archer who has gone berserk, spraying his arrows indiscriminately toward anyone within range, with destructive, tragic results. It is no less irrational or potentially harmful to hire a fool or any stranger. To have a job done correctly, one should hire a person who is competent and motivated to do it. (See 26:18–19.)

1. *The Foolish Find Certain Items Useless.*
For "fool" (*kᵉsîl*; 17:16; 19:10; 26:1, 7, 8, 9), see VF.

a. Money. 17:16 "Of what use is money in the hand of a fool, since he has no desire to get wisdom?"

Money is useless to a fool who will squander it by his incompetent handling of it. Not wanting to get (see "acquire" in 18:15) wisdom, he has forfeited his only opportunity to learn enough to make his money beneficial.

b. Luxury. 19:10 "It is not fitting for a fool to live in luxury—how much worse for a slave to rule over princes!"

A fool lacks the wisdom to handle luxury. A slave without leadership experience is incompetent to rule, especially over leaders who can govern. The latter situation is worse because it affects more people adversely.

c. Honor. 26:1 "Like snow in summer or rain in harvest, honor is not fitting for a fool."

26:8 "Like tying a stone in a sling is the giving of honor to a fool."

The point of **26:1** is that honoring a fool would be as weird, undesirable, and destructive as these unseasonable and damaging weather phenomena.

The sling (**26:8**) was an ancient lethal weapon used by shepherds to kill wild animals that threatened their flocks and by soldiers to kill their enemies while still at some distance away. To fasten the stone in the sling so that it would not be released would be equivalent to disarming the sling. Disarming one's weapon when threatened is no less ridiculous than honoring a fool.

d. Proverbs. 26:7 "Like a lame man's legs that hang limp is a proverb in the mouth of a fool."

26:9 "Like a thornbush in a drunkard's hand is a proverb in the mouth of a fool."

Lame legs hanging limp (**26:7**) serve no useful function. Nor do Israel's thornbushes that are especially painful to touch or brush against. The details of this image (**26:9**) are unclear. It may picture a drunkard as threatening people by waving a thornbush wildly, or as too far gone to remove a thorn, or as too insensitive to pain to care. Nevertheless, the image is clearly intended to be absurd. A proverb is as useless to a fool as lame legs to a cripple or a thornbush to a drunkard.

F. Results of Foolishness

1. The Foolish Receive Penalties, Beatings, and Death.

19:29 "Penalties are prepared for mockers, and beatings for the backs of fools."

20:30 "Blows and wounds cleanse away evil, and beatings purge the inmost being."

26:3 "A whip for the horse, a halter for the donkey, and a rod for the backs of fools!"

27:22 "Though you grind a fool in a mortar, grinding him like grain with a pestle, you will not remove his folly from him."

For "mockers" (**19:29**), "fools" ($k^e s\hat{\imath}l$; **19:29**; **26:3**), and "fool" ($'\check{e}w\hat{\imath}l$; **10:10**; **27:22**), see VF.

Mockers and fools are so obnoxious that their behavior invites punishment, and they get it (**19:29**). The "penalties" and "beatings" were handed out by a court that found one guilty of violating the law. As whips and halters were necessary to restrain and control horses and donkeys, beatings were necessary to restrain fools (**26:3**). After all, verbal advice is no more persuasive to a fool than to a horse or donkey.

The word rendered "cleanse" (**20:30**), unrelated to atonement, means to "scrape," "scour." These severe beatings were to scrape a person so thoroughly clean as to cleanse his inmost being. By inflicting intense pain, these beatings were the instruments of discipline to stop and change the evildoer's behavior.

In **27:22**, the wise teacher used hyperbole to emphasize how stubbornly a foolish man clings to his foolishness. Two cognate forms of the same Hebrew root are rendered "grind" and "mortar." The mortar and pestle are equipment designed to pound and pulverize grain into fine particles. The picture of a man's undergoing such a vicious, even fatal, beating is a brutal image. However, even if a foolish person should survive such a pulverizing pounding, he would learn nothing from it and change nothing as a result of it. The most drastic means of discipline and punishment are simply ineffective for him.

2. The Foolish Bring Ruin.

10:10 "He who winks maliciously causes grief, and a chattering fool comes to ruin."

The word rendered "winks" describes pinching or narrowing together of eyes, lips, and clay. Here it clearly involves the eyes, although winking is not the normal way to express hostility. The details of the image are unclear. The physical action or expression was, "the ancient Oriental people evidently associated it with perverse behavior such as being deceitful or concocting an evil plot." (6:12–14; 16:30; Ps. 35:19). The resulting grief may be physical, mental, and emotional.

Identical to **10:10b** is 10:8b, although the relationship between the two lines is unclear. A talkative fool whose lips outrun his mind will be thrust away, rejected. Repeated reruns of this pattern bring ruin. See 19:3a.

3. The Foolish Bring Grief to Their Parents.

17:21 "To have a fool for a son brings grief; there is no joy for the father of a fool."

17:25 "A foolish son brings grief to his father and bitterness to the one who bore him."

19:13a "A foolish son is his father's ruin."

These texts picture the negative impact of a foolish son upon his caring parents who experience grief, bitterness, and ruin. See 10:1.

G. Contrasts Between Wise and Foolish

Numerous proverbs exhibit the structure of antithetic parallelism (see introduction). These contrasts use both "wise"/"foolish" and other similar terminology. The following texts are arranged according to what is contrasted.

1. The Wise and the Foolish Do Not Acquire Wisdom with the Same Ease.

14:6 "The mocker seeks wisdom and finds none, but knowledge comes easily to the discerning."

14:33 "Wisdom reposes in the heart of the discerning and even among fools she lets herself be known."

24:7 "Wisdom is too high for a fool; in the assembly at the gate he has nothing to say."

Wisdom rests quietly, settling down within the discerning (**14:33**), since the wise give warm hospitality to her beneficial influence. Although fools have some awareness of wisdom, they neither absorb nor apply it. The contrast is between the wise who are nourished by wisdom and the foolish who derive no benefit from their exposure to wisdom.

Wisdom is difficult for fools to obtain (**24:7**), literally as difficult as obtaining jewels, such as corals. That is why fools contribute nothing significant to public discussions, even when they are talkative!

The discerning acquire wisdom easily (**14:6**), since they have the attitude and discipline to do it. Perhaps attracted by her material benefits of affluence and status, the mocker seeks wisdom. But lacking the fear of the Lord that is the beginning of knowledge, the willingness and discipline to learn, and the openness to a radically different approach to life, the mocker overlooks it.

2. The Wise Enjoy and Keep Wisdom; the Foolish Enjoy Evil and Wander.

10:23 "A fool finds pleasure in evil conduct, but a man of understanding delights in wisdom."

17:24 "A discerning man keeps wisdom in view, but a fool's eyes wander to the ends of the earth."

A fool considers evil conduct to be a sport in which he participates for his own amusement (**10:23**). His evil conduct may result from clever schemes devised to produce immediate pleasure. In contrast, a discerning man enjoys the practice of wisdom as much as his favorite sport.

A discerning man concentrates his energies upon obtaining wisdom—a goal, which he keeps constantly in view (**17:24**). In contrast, a fool is easily distracted. As a result, his progress is paralyzed.

3. The Wise Do Not Trust in Themselves; the Foolish Do.

26:16 "The sluggard is wiser in his own eyes than seven men who answer discreetly."

28:26 "He who trusts in himself is a fool, but he who walks in wisdom is kept safe."

Having an exaggerated impression of his competence, the lazy man (see "Sluggard" under VF) considers himself to have already the wisdom that he is neither motivated nor disciplined enough to acquire (**26:16**). To answer discreetly is to display wisdom in developing an appropriate answer.

It is foolish to trust completely in ourselves (**28:26**; see 3:5) and thus reject the principles of wisdom. Everyone is fallible; however, by following the path of wisdom, a person can improve his capacity to make wise decisions and keep safe, especially from premature death.

4. The Wise Acquire and Follow Knowledge; the Foolish Display Their Foolishness.

12:23 "A prudent man keeps his knowledge to himself, but the heart of fools blurts out folly."

13:16 "Every prudent man acts out of knowledge, but a fool exposes his folly."

14:18 "The simple inherit folly, but the prudent are crowned with knowledge."

15:14 "The discerning heart seeks knowledge, but the mouth of a fool feeds on folly."

15:21 "Folly delights a man who lacks judgment, but a man of understanding keeps a straight course."

Fools inherit folly (**14:18**) and possess it permanently by feeding on it (**15:14**), that is, digesting and absorbing it. Their insatiable appetite for folly stifles any desire for acquiring wisdom. Consequently, they lack judgment; they enjoy folly (**15:21**). They display their stupidity (**13:16**) by acting impulsively. Eager to impress others, fools are often talkative (**12:23**), but their blabbing only makes their foolishness conspicuous.

In contrast, the discerning seek (see the comment about "Look for" in 2:4) the knowledge that characterizes wisdom

(15:14). The prudent are saturated with knowledge (14:18). They do not ostentatiously display their knowledge (12:23), but use good timing to enable what they do share to have maximum impact. They base their actions upon what they know (13:16), acting sensibly and ethically by following a straight (see "Upright" under VR) path that is morally right, straightforward, and honest (15:21).

5. The Wise Are Thoughtful; the Foolish Are Naive and Misguided.

14:8 "The wisdom of the prudent is to give thought to their ways, but the folly of fools is deception."

14:15 "A simple man believes anything, but a prudent man gives thought to his steps."

The equivalent statements of **14:8a** and **14:15b** indicate how the wise develop their conduct (ways or steps). They discern what is wise, morally right, and most probably successful. As a result, their conduct reflects their thoughtful application of the principles of wisdom. In contrast, the simple are gullible (**14:15a**) while fools foolishly deceive both themselves and others (**14:8b**). Both qualities lead to disaster.

6. The Wise Listen to Advice; the Foolish Prefer Their Ways and Quarrel.

12:15 "The way of a fool seems right to him, but a wise man listens to advice."

13:10 "Pride only breeds quarrels, but wisdom is found in those who take advice."

Open to new ideas, wise men welcome perceptive advice from discerning people (**12:15b; 13:10b**). In contrast, fools reject advice, since they consider their own ways the only plausible ones (**12:15a**). The extreme pride in **13:10a** approaches an arrogance capable of arousing sufficiently hostile feelings to produce conflicts and hostilities.

7. The Wise Are Humble; the Proud Are Brought Down.

11:2 "When pride comes, then comes disgrace, but with humility comes wisdom."

16:18 "Pride goes before destruction, a haughty spirit before a fall."

18:12 "Before his downfall a man's heart is proud, but humility comes before honor."

25:6–7 "Do not exalt yourself in the king's presence, and do not claim a place among great men; it is better for him to say to you, 'Come up here,' than for him to humiliate you before a nobleman."

29:23 "A man's pride brings him low, but a man of lowly spirit gains honor."

These texts contrast the humiliating and disastrous results of arrogant pride with the benefits of humility.

These synonymous parallel (see introduction) exhortations (**25:6**) warn against trying to improve our status by seeking more honor, respect, and status than is warranted. "Spirit" (**16:18; 29:23**) and "heart" (**18:12**) refer to our attitude. The virtually synonymous words rendered "pride" (**16:18; 29:23**) and "haughty" (**16:18**) or "proud" (**18:12**) usually picture arrogance and a cynical apathy to human needs. As desirable as positive self-confidence is, it becomes sin when it degenerates into a self-centeredness that arrogantly supplants the God-centeredness generated by the fear of the Lord.

The reason for the command in **25:6** is given in **25:7**. The arrogant person who seeks undeserved honor is brought low (**29:23**) or humiliated (**25:7**); for example, when his distinguished host seats him in a lower place at dinner to reflect his status (**25:7**). Jesus developed a parable when He noticed how guests chose places of honor at a dinner (Luke 4:8–11) to expand the proverb in **25:6–7**. Offensive displays of egotistical arrogance may bring about a person's disgrace (**11:2**) and destruction (**16:18; 18:12**), which could involve the sudden, disastrous decline of his power, influence, financial and social status.

In contrast, humility (**11:2**; see the comments about **15:33**) often pictures the condition of the oppressed and afflicted (**18:12**). Identical are **15:33b** and **18:12b**. The words rendered "bring low" and "lowly" in **29:23** are cognate forms of the same root. This play on words is carefully preserved by the NIV.

To summarize, an arrogant person who seeks honor is

humiliated when snubbed, while a competent, humble person receives honor without pursuing it. As a rabbinic aphorism states, "He who runs after honor, honor flees from him; he who shuns honor, honor pursues him."[3] Since the humble are receptive, they receive wisdom (**11:2**), which produces improved status (**25:7**) and honor (**18:12; 29:23**). For similar themes, see 3:34; 15:33; 16:5, 19; 21:24; and 22:4.

8. The Wise Have Self-Control, Patience, and Good Will; the Foolish Are Quick-Tempered, Express Anger, and Arouse Tensions and Hostilities.

12:16 "A fool shows his annoyance at once, but a prudent man overlooks an insult."

14:9 "Fools mock at making amends for sin, but good will is found among the upright."

14:29 "A patient man has great understanding, but a quick-tempered man displays folly."

14:35 "A king delights in a wise servant, but a shameful servant incurs his wrath."

20:3 "It is to a man's honor to avoid strife, but every fool is quick to quarrel."

29:8 "Mockers stir up a city, but wise men turn away anger."

29:9 "If a wise man goes to court with a fool, the fool rages and scoffs, and there is no peace."

29:11 "A fool gives full vent to his anger, but a wise man keeps himself under control."

The antithetic parallelisms (see introduction) in these texts contrast those who produce harmony with those who arouse conflict, those who possess self-control with those who lack it.

Although the meaning of **14:9a** is debated, it evidently pictures fools as mocking either their guilt or their punishment, which results from their being found guilty. They have no respect for justice through litigation. When taken to court (**29:9**), their hostile bluster—their intense anger and derisive laughter—prevent any settlement and paralyze the course of justice.

A foolish servant's imprudent, unethical, and shameful

---

[3] Cited by A. Cohen, *Proverbs* (New York: Soncino Press, 1952), 198.

actions bring disgrace upon both himself and his king-owner, who is understandably enraged (**14:35**). Mockers are so obnoxious that they can arouse the hostilities of an entire city (**29:8**).

For a fool to give full vent to his anger (**29:11**) is literally to cause all his spirit to go forth. Quick to quarrel (**20:3**), a foolish person expresses his anger (**29:11**) or annoyance (**12:16**) immediately as a psychological reflex action. Unrestrained, the explosive force of his anger lashes out whenever he is irritated. This repetitive pattern of anger surrounds him with tension and hostility.

In **14:29**, the two Hebrew words rendered "quick-tempered" mean literally "short of breath." They picture someone who cannot hold his breath for very long and will soon let it all out. A similar idiom involves a Hebrew word that means "nose," "nostril," "anger" (**29:8**). Also rendered "quick-tempered," this idiom means literally "short-nosed" or "short of nostrils." People express emotions by varied breathing patterns. For example, heavy breathing, dilated nostrils, and a red nose are often signs of anger. To be "short-nosed" or "short of breath" is to have a short fuse, that is, to be short of patience, to be quickly and easily angered. Impulsive, irrational, and often regrettable actions by a quick-tempered man make his foolishness conspicuous so all may see it.

In contrast, the "patient" man (**14:29**) is literally "long-nosed," that is, to have a nose that will take a long time to burn up and release its anger. Similarly, to be long of anger is to take a deep breath and to hold back anger. All these images picture slowness to anger and thus remarkable patience.

A prudent man keeps himself under control. For him to overlook an insult (**12:16**) with its resulting shame is, in effect, to forgive the person who made it. Unlike mockers, the wise turn away anger (**29:8**) by smoothing out differences and by exerting their influence in peaceful ways that avoid hostilities. A wise man keeps himself under control (**29:11**) and soothes his own anger. He maintains his composure, even under infuriating conditions. To avoid strife by promoting harmony is honorable (**20:3**). A king-owner regards favorably his wise slave (**14:35**) who fulfills his responsibilities competently and well. These qualities bring the upright good will, favor, and an honorable reputation (**14:9**).

9. The Wise Build; the Foolish Tear Down.

14:1 "The wise woman builds her house, but with her own hands the foolish one tears hers down."

Using construction imagery, this text figuratively pictures the building up and tearing down of household affairs. A wise woman provides a haven for her husband, builds a strong family unity in an atmosphere of mutual love, and manages her household's business affairs, which contribute to her family's spiritual, social, and financial prosperity. The foolish woman stirs up tension and conflict with her husband and children and dissipates her household's resources, which contributes to her family's spiritual, social, and financial deterioration.

10. The Wise Learn, Grow, Obey, and Avoid Danger; the Foolish Experience Danger, Harm, Ruin, and Death.

10:8 "The wise in heart accept commands, but a chattering fool comes to ruin."

10:14 "Wise men store up knowledge, but the mouth of a fool invites ruin."

10:21 "The lips of the righteous nourish many, but fools die for lack of judgment."

13:20 "He who walks with the wise grows wise, but a companion of fools suffers harm."

22:3 "A prudent man sees danger and takes refuge, but the simple keep going and suffer for it."

27:12 "The prudent see danger and take refuge, but the simple keep going and suffer for it."

The wise store knowledge (**10:14**), which they treasure as well as use by obeying its commands (**10:8**). In contrast, a fool's conversation is destructive, arousing hostilities that produce troubles, which result in their ruin and rejection (**10:14**). Identical are **10:8b** and 10:10b.

Pictured in shepherd's imagery, the righteous "nourish" many (**10:21**) with the spiritual and character-building food of wisdom. But the fool who lacks "judgment" (see "heart" in 4:23) is vulnerable to the dangers that produce premature death.

In **13:20**, both statements describe the effects of a person's associates upon him. Keeping company with the wise enables him to learn from them and to become like them. Companions of fools pick up enough of their qualities to be harmed. The word rendered "suffer harm" means to "shout." In this text it means "to cry out in distress."

The proverbs **22:3** and **27:12** are almost identical. When threatened, the wise man hides himself in a place of shelter. He takes refuge by using appropriate protective measures to avoid danger. In contrast, the simple, oblivious to such dangers, blindly plunge into them and suffer.

11. The Wise Are Rewarded; the Foolish Suffer.

9:12 "If you are wise, your wisdom will reward you; if you are a mocker, you alone will suffer."

10:13 "Wisdom is found on the lips of the discerning, but a rod is for the back of him who lacks judgment."

13:15 "Good understanding wins favor, but the way of the unfaithful is hard."

16:22 "Understanding is a fountain of life to those who have it, but folly brings punishment to fools."

The discerning express wisdom in their conversation (**10:13a**). A benefit of wisdom (**9:12a**) is a good reputation (**13:15a**), for understanding is a fountain of life (**16:22a**; see the comment about **14:27**).

The way of the unfaithful is "hard" (**13:15b**), pictured here as permanently rough. The mocker suffers (**9:12b**) because he carries the heavy burdens of people's rejection and negative responses to his derisive attitudes.

Someone who refuses to learn proper behavior may expect to be beaten with a rod across his back (**10:13b**). With this severe discipline he learns a lesson the hard way. For other references to this theme, see 13:24; 18:6; 19:29; 22:15; 23:13–14; 26:3; 29:15. Although these beatings may seem harsh, they inflict only temporary pain designed to prevent permanent and more serious damage. Even so, they were far more merciful than the vicious physical mutilation practiced by Israel's neighbors for selfish or vindictive motives (e.g., Judg. 1:7; 16:21; 2 Kings 25:7; Amos 1:13).

12. *The Wise Receive and Appreciate Discipline, Correction, and Rebuke; the Foolish Reject and Resent Them and Are Punished and Beaten.*

9:7-9 "Whoever corrects a mocker invites insult; whoever rebukes a wicked man incurs abuse. Do not rebuke a mocker or he will hate you; rebuke a wise man and he will love you. Instruct a wise man and he will be wiser still; teach a righteous man and he will add to his learning."

10:17 "He who heeds discipline shows the way to life, but whoever ignores correction leads others astray."

12:1 "Whoever loves discipline loves knowledge, but he who hates correction is stupid."

13:1 "A wise son heeds his father's instruction, but a mocker does not listen to rebuke."

13:13 "He who scorns instruction will pay for it, but he who respects a command is rewarded."

13:18 "He who ignores discipline comes to poverty and shame, but whoever heeds correction is honored."

15:5 "A fool spurns his father's discipline, but whoever heeds correction shows prudence."

15:12 "A mocker resents correction; he will not consult the wise."

15:32 "He who ignores discipline despises himself, but whoever heeds correction gains understanding."

17:10 "A rebuke impresses a man of discernment more than a hundred lashes a fool."

19:16 "He who obeys instructions guards his life, but he who is contemptuous of his ways will die.

19:25 "Flog a mocker, and the simple will learn prudence; rebuke a discerning man, and he will gain knowledge."

21:11 "When a mocker is punished, the simple gain wisdom; when a wise man is instructed, he gets knowledge."

29:1 "A man who remains stiff-necked after many rebukes will suddenly be destroyed—without remedy."

Appreciative of the need for corrections indicated by perceptive rebukes and instruction, the wise man makes the proper adjustments. He learns and grows, thus increasing his wisdom as a result of accepting teaching (**9:9; 21:11;** see 1:5;

12:15), following discipline (**10:17; 13:1**), respecting (**13:13**) and obeying commands (**19:16**), and being corrected by rebukes (**13:18; 15:5, 32; 19:25**). For "heed" (**10:17; 13:18; 15:5**), "obey," and "guard" (**19:16**), see "protect" in 2:8. For "listen" (**13:1**) and "heed" (**15:32**), see "listen" in 4:1. For "respect" (**13:13**), see "fear" in 1:7. The word rendered "impresses" (**17:10**) pictures the corrective rebuke as penetrating the discerning mind, making a profound impact that generates the needed changes.

Benefits of these responses to instruction, discipline, and corrective rebukes include protection (**19:16**), reward (**13:13**; see "prosperity" in 3:2), honor (**13:18**), and a happy, productive, satisfying life (**10:17**; see the comments about "life" in 19:23 and 15:24). That is why the wise man loves discipline and knowledge (**12:1**) and those who rebuke him (**9:8b**), since he is enthusiastic enough to give them top priority.

Fools and mockers stubbornly ignore discipline and corrective rebukes (**10:17; 13:1, 18; 15:32; 29:1**). They ignore (**10:17**) or abandon the guidelines prescribed by correction and prompt others to do likewise. They do not even listen to correction (**13:1**), but ignore (**13:18; 15:32**) or reject it. Equivalent are the "stiff-necked" (**29:1**), that is, stubborn, insensitive, adamant in rejecting or ignoring rebukes.

Fools and mockers hate those who rebuke them (**9:8; 12:1**), are contemptuous of Wisdom's commands (**19:16**), scorn instruction (**13:13**), resent correction (**15:12**), and spurn discipline (**15:5**). The "contemptuous" (**19:16**) and scornful (**13:13**) are mocking, cynical, and sarcastic toward whoever and whatever is contrary to their desires.

Mockers insult and abuse those who rebuke them (**9:7**). The mocker's vicious verbal assault is designed to bring shame to the one who dares to correct him.

Whoever ignores discipline shows that he despises himself (**15:32**). He has such a low self-esteem that he is willing to casually throw away himself, his potential for productive achieving, and even his life. Such rejection is acting stupidly (**12:1**), that is, reflecting an animal's inability to think, analyze, and evaluate.

Harm and even disaster come to those who reject corrective rebukes. They pay for rejecting wisdom (**13:13**) by experiencing destruction (29:1), poverty and shame (13:18), by beatings (17:10), and by death (19:16). The word rendered "pay" (13:13) uses either the imagery of debt to picture the necessity of suffering the consequences of scorning instruction or, more likely, of the sudden ruin or destruction involved (29:1). There will be no remedy (29:1) and thus no possibility of being restored. Identical are 29:1b and 6:15b; see also 1:20–33. Poverty (13:18) pictures destitution, the desperate condition of those whose finances are severely lacking and whose future prospects are gloomy. Ignoring discipline (13:18) produces financial and social ruin. Death (19:16) could result either from a court's decision finding someone guilty of a capital crime or from a violent reaction to someone's offensive behavior.

Since verbal rebukes were ineffective, beating a fool with a whip (17:10) was necessary just to get his attention. Normally forty lashes were considered the maximum for such punishment. One hundred lashes may be an hyperbole, exaggerating the duration of the beatings (much as we mention "millions" without being mathematically precise). Nevertheless, even an excessively long and severe beating would have less impact upon a stubborn, unresponsive fool than a verbal rebuke upon a person with the discernment to take it seriously.

It is futile to attempt to reform mockers (9:7–9; 13:1; 15:12). Yet even ineffective efforts to do so may have an impact upon the simple (19:25; 21:11) who are open enough to learn by example. Whether enduring a painful flogging (19:25) from a whip or paying a fine (21:11; see the comment about 22:3), a mocker was punished as the result of a court's verdict that found him guilty of a criminal offense. By hearing about or perhaps observing these judicial procedures and their results, the simple find the punishments repugnant and decide to reform. In this process they begin to learn prudence.

13. *The Wise Are Praised; Warped (Foolish) Minds Are Despised.*

12:8 "A man is praised according to his wisdom, but men with warped minds are despised."

In contrast with the wise who attract praise are those who have warped minds (see "heart" in 4:23). The word rendered "warped" pictures people whose twisted, distorted thinking makes them incapable of sound judgment and thus produces erroneous attitudes and decisions. Such people will be regarded with contempt.

14. The Wise Become Wealthy; the Foolish Experience Folly and Poverty.

14:24 "The wealth of the wise is their crown, but the folly of fools yields folly."

21:5 "The plans of the diligent lead to profit as surely as haste leads to poverty."

21:20 "In the house of the wise are stores of choice food and oil, but a foolish man devours all he has."

By applying the principles of wisdom in the financial realm, the wise obtain wealth that adorns them like a crown (**14:24**). Innovative plans combined with hard work by the diligent are likely to succeed and be profitable (**21:5**). Wealth brought such benefits as "choice food" and "oil" (**21:20**). The Hebrew terms rendered "choice food" (NIV) picture desirable, luxurious treasures that brought pleasure and delight to the rich. Olive oil, used in ancient Hebrew homes for cooking, cosmetics, medicine, ointment, and lamps, was a natural symbol of prosperity (Deut. 33:24; Job 29:6). Through careful planning and astute management of their financial affairs, the wise rich can afford the signs of affluence in their homes.

Folly is foolish (**14:24**). Hasty decisions may be a shortcut to nowhere (**21:5**; see 19:2; 28:20). Get-rich-quick schemes often waste time, energy, and resources without producing the desired prosperity, or even leading to losses and poverty. The rich fool is wasteful (**21:20**), extravagantly squandering his wealth without replenishing it.

15. The Wise Bring Joy; the Foolish Bring Grief to Their Parents.

10:1 "A wise son brings joy to his father, but a foolish son brings grief to his mother."

15:20 "A wise son brings joy to his father, but a foolish man despises his mother."

28:7 "He who keeps the law is a discerning son, but a companion of gluttons disgraces his father."

29:3 "A man who loves wisdom brings joy to his father, but a companion of prostitutes squanders his wealth."

Similar statements occur in 17:21, 25; 23:15–16, 24–25; 27:11. Identical are 10:1a and 15:20a. A man who loves, grows, and lives by wisdom is a joy to his parents (10:1; 15:20; 29:3). Being discerning, he carefully obeys the law (28:7), that is, wise teaching.

In contrast, a foolish son despises (15:20) and grieves (10:1) his parents. "Companion" (28:7; 29:3) includes friends, neighbors, and associates, both close and casual. "Gluttons" (28:7), who eat unnecessarily large amounts of food, are considered worthless people who squander their resources (see 23:20–21). Their expensive tastes and greedy excess combine with their limited work output to bring them to unnecessary poverty, poor health, and disgrace. This tragic condition, displaying the lack of significant parental influence, disgraces a father by publicly humiliating him.

II. For Further Study

1. Use a concordance to trace biblical references to wise and fool, wisdom and folly or foolishness throughout the Bible. What do these terms include? How are they contrasted?

2. Why is it so important to absorb, digest, and internalize the principles of wisdom? How do you do this? How do you motivate others to do it?

3. Why is self-control so important? What are its benefits? How do you obtain it? In what situations do you find self-control helpful, if not essential? In what situations have you lost control?

4. How valuable is wisdom? What are its benefits? How should your awareness of its value affect your attitude toward it and your desire for it? Does your awareness of wisdom really affect these areas?

5. What is involved in guarding your heart or mind (4:23)? Why is this essential? How do you do it? With what positive elements should you deliberately and regularly feed your mind? What negative elements should you deliberately and consist-

ently avoid? Think of specific examples from your experience that you should cultivate, that you should avoid.

6. Why is discipline and correction so important and so highly valued by the wise? What do they contribute? Why are they needed? What experiences of discipline and correction have you had? In what ways should discipline and correction be incorporated in your church?

7. What is the relationship between wisdom and wealth? Does wisdom necessarily produce wealth? Does wealth necessarily produce wisdom? What other factors are involved?

Chapter 6

The Two Ways: Righteousness and Wickedness

Many proverbs present the ethical elements in both wisdom and foolishness by describing the qualities and results of righteousness and wickedness. They include antithetic parallelisms (see introduction) that contrast righteousness with wickedness.

We have structured the material to develop an orderly discussion of righteousness. To treat each verse with an antithetic parallelism as a unit, we have included its contrasting statement about wickedness in our discussion of righteousness. We have discussed verses that mention only wickedness in connection with contrasting statements to which they fit.

A. Qualities of the Righteous and the Wicked

1. The Righteous Walk Straight Paths of Integrity and Uprightness.

a. The Path of the Upright. 11:3 "The integrity of the upright guides them, but the unfaithful are destroyed by their duplicity."

15:19 "The way of the sluggard is blocked with thorns, but the path of the upright is a highway."

21:8 "The way of the guilty is devious, but the conduct of the innocent is upright."

25:19 "Like a bad tooth or a lame foot is reliance on the unfaithful in times of trouble."

For "integrity" (**11:3**) and "upright" (**11:3; 15:19; 21:8**), see

VR. For "devious" (21:8), see "perverse" in VWs. For "sluggard" (15:19), see VF.

Thorns block the sluggard (15:19) who does not prevent their taking over his yard, which was a familiar scene in Israel. In contrast, the construction of a "highway" included the hard work of building it higher than its immediate surroundings and of making it smooth by removing obstacles. So the "highway" pictures the straight, smooth, uplifted path that the upright follow.

Antithetic parallelisms (see introduction) contrast the perverse qualities of the guilty with the straightforward ways of the innocent (21:8), the integrity of the upright with the duplicity of the unfaithful (11:3). Treachery by the unfaithful will backfire to ruin them and thus reduce them to nothing. In contrast, the "innocent" who are pure and sincere have a clean conscience with no sense of guilt.

The vivid similes of **25:19** portray the futility of relying upon an unfaithful person whose response is erratic and unpredictable. For a disloyal, unreliable person may hinder us as much as a lame leg that cannot handle body weight or as the searing pain of a badly decayed tooth that puts us out of action.

b. The Path of Integrity. 4:25–27 "Let your eyes look straight ahead, fix your gaze directly before you. Make level paths for your feet and take only ways that are firm. Do not swerve to the right or the left; keep your foot from evil."

11:5 "The righteousness of the blameless makes a straight way for them, but the wicked are brought down by their own wickedness."

13:6 "Righteousness guards the man of integrity, but wickedness overthrows the sinner."

16:17 "The highway of the upright avoids evil; he who guards his way guards his life."

20:7 "The righteous man leads a blameless life; blessed are his children after him."

For "fix (your gaze) directly" (before you) "make straight" or "upright" (**4:25; 11:5; 16:17**), and "integrity" or "blameless" (**11:5; 13:6; 20:7**), see "upright" and "integrity" under VR.

The antithetic parallelism (see introduction) of **11:5** contrasts the smooth, straight path of the righteous who have integrity with the obstacles that trip up the wicked (see 11:3). To be "brought down" or to "fall" may involve either a physical accident or, more likely, a sinister damaging event that produces permanent ruin or even death. For wickedness overthrows the sinner (**13:6**) by twisting, perverting, and ruining him.

Several synonymous exhortations emphasize the urgency of following the straight path (**4:25-27**). A wise person concentrates upon moving directly toward his goal without permitting any distractions (**4:25**). He removes obstacles that hinder his progress (**4:26**). He avoids evil, not swerving from the desired path (**4:27**; **16:17**; see the comment about "persuasive" in 7:21). His straight path preserves his way on "the highway of the upright" (**16:17**). For "highway," "life," and "guards" (also in 13:6), see the comments about "highway" in 15:19, *"zeal" in 19:2*, "protect" and "guard" in 2:8. Benefiting greatly are the children of those who develop integrity by carefully following these principles (**20:7**).

c. **The Path of the Wicked.** 4:14–17 "Do not set foot on the path of the wicked or walk in the way of evil men. Avoid it; do not travel on it; turn from it and go on your way. For they cannot sleep till they do evil; they are robbed of slumber till they make someone fall. They eat the bread of wickedness and drink the wine of violence."

17:11 "An evil man is bent only on rebellion; a merciless official will be sent against him."

21:10 "The wicked man craves evil; his neighbor gets no mercy from him."

For "wicked" (**4:14, 17**; **21:10**), "evil" (**4:14, 16**; **17:11**; **21:10**), see VWs.

The repetitious piling up of synonymous statements of the same prohibition emphasize the urgency of avoiding evil ways (**4:14-15**). A man with a ravenous appetite for evil expresses no mercy or favorable treatment to his neighbors (**21:10**), who may become the victims of his vicious schemes. Such an evil man who hungers (see comment on "look for" in 2:4) for rebellion (**17:11**) will encounter a merciless, cruel official, who will give him the punishment he deserves.

The wicked's craving for evil and compulsion to lure others into evil are so intense and addictive that they actually force sleep from him, rob him of it (**4:16**) if his desire is frustrated. To "make someone fall" (**4:16**) usually describes a physical falling; however, here it pictures a spiritual and moral falling. The NT concept of a stumbling block (Rom. 14:13) may have been derived from this and similar texts (e.g., 4:19).

The imagery of eating and drinking pictures the wicked as continually absorbing evil and violence (**4:17**). With a steady diet of wickedness and violence infiltrating and saturating their minds, it should be no surprise to see their mental digestive systems excrete repulsive, sickening, violent, sinful deeds.

d. The Brightly Shining Path of the Righteous. 4:18–19 "The path of the righteous is like the first gleam of dawn, shining ever brighter till the full light of day. But the way of the wicked is like deep darkness; they do not know what makes them stumble."

13:9 "The light of the righteous shines brightly, but the lamp of the wicked is snuffed out."

The imagery of light and darkness is used to contrast the path of the righteous with that of the wicked (**4:18–19; 13:9**). The well-lit path (**4:18**) and the brightly shining lamp (**13:9**) enable the righteous to see clearly where to go. Figuratively light pictures the Lord's presence, wisdom, life, blessing, happiness, and prosperity—reasons for rejoicing.

In contrast, darkness pictures a lack of the Lord's presence, ignorance, death, disaster, misery, and poverty. The wicked cannot see where to go safely in the deep darkness (**4:19**; see Exod. 10:21–23), either of his unlit path or of his home, when his lamp has been extinguished (see the comments about 20:20 and 24:20). So he stumbles (see the comment about "make fall" in 4:16) and does not know why. For without the light of wisdom, he cannot perceive what is tripping him.

2. *The Righteous Devise Just Plans.*

12:5 "The plans of the righteous are just, but the advice of the wicked is deceitful."

The antithetic parallelism (see introduction) of **12:5** contrasts the ethical thinking and planning of the righteous with the deceptive advice of the wicked.

3. The Wicked Plot Violent Plans.

1:10-19 "My son, if sinners entice you, do not give in to them. If they say, 'Come along with us; let's lie in wait for someone's blood, let's waylay some harmless soul; let's swallow them alive, like the grave, and whole, like those who go down to the pit; we will get all sorts of valuable things and fill our houses with plunder; throw in your lot with us, and we will share a common purse'—my son, do not go along with them, do not set foot on their paths; for their feet rush into sin, they are swift to shed blood. How useless to spread a net in full view of all the birds! These men lie in wait for their own blood; they waylay only themselves! Such is the end of all who go after ill-gotten gain; it takes away the lives of those who get it."

16:27 "A scoundrel plots evil, and his speech is like a scorching fire."

16:29 "A violent man entices his neighbor and leads him down a path that is not good."

16:30 "He who winks with his eye is plotting perversity; he who purses his lips is bent on evil."

21:7 "The violence of the wicked will drag them away, for they refuse to do what is right."

30:11-14 "'There are those who curse their fathers and do not bless their mothers; those who are pure in their own eyes and yet are not cleansed of their filth; those whose eyes are ever so haughty, whose glances are so disdainful; those whose teeth are swords and whose jaws are set with knives to devour the poor from the earth, the needy from among mankind.'"

Examples of evil behavior are recorded in **30:11-14** without further comment. A curse (**30:11**) is the absence of blessing and especially involves slighting a person by giving less than what the relationship calls for, e.g., ignoring or not taking care of one's parents when needed. It includes wishing or bringing harm to another. Any form of cursing one's parents violates the fifth commandment to honor parents (Exod. 20:12; see also Prov. 20:20).

"Filth" (**30:12**) refers physically to human excrement (Isa. 36:12). The text pictures morally filthy people who, although contaminated by their spiritual excrement, nevertheless consider themselves pure with no need for cleansing (see 20:9). The eyes and glances of some people express their arrogant, presumptuous self-exaltation (**30:13**). For "haughty," see the comment about 6:17.

People whose teeth and jaws are pictured as weapons (**30:14**) are psyched to kill. The words rendered "devour" and "knife" are cognates. The devouring may involve their slicing the poor into pieces (see "oppressed" in 15:15). This vicious metaphor pictures the unscrupulous use of power by the wicked against the helpless to satisfy their excessive greed.

In **16:27**, the Hebrew word ($b^e l\hat{i}ya\cdot al$), rendered "scoundrel," pictures a person or action as morally worthless, wicked, corrupt, unscrupulous. As Belial, it referred to Satan in the intertestamental pseudepigraphical literature and in the NT (2 Cor. 6:15). The "plot" involves trapping someone by an evil scheme; the "scorching fire" vividly portrays the destructive fury and extensive damage inflicted on those who hear a scoundrel talk (see James 3:5–6).

Winking eyes and pursed (or compressed) lips were perceived as "body language" that suggests the brewing of a perverse plot (**16:30**; see the discussion in 6:13–14 and 10:10). Those "bent on evil" are determined to carry out their destructive plots to completion. A violent man exploits his relationship with his neighbor by persuading him (**16:29**) to join in using violence to achieve destructive goals, which is vividly portrayed in 1:10–19.

The sinners' plan was to lurk in a dark area, to ambush, mug, and murder innocent victims (**1:11–12**). These victims were attacked for no good reason or "for the fun of it" (TEV, an idea conveyed by a Hebrew word untranslated by NIV in 1:11b). Their purpose was to acquire wealth (**1:13**) in the form of plunder from armed robbery. Their invitation was to participate in this ancient "get-rich-quick" scheme and to have one purse shared by all (**1:14**). The idea of communal sharing did not remain effective for long, even among honorable Christians in the early church in Jerusalem (Acts 4:32–34; 5:1–11; 6:1). How could it be expected to work among thieves who had obtained their wealth by violence? The shares were larger with fewer people to receive them. Consequently, the only remaining questions were who would be liquidated and when would the liquidations be stopped.

The wise are to reject such schemes (1:10, 15), no matter how profitable they may seem. For the participants are quick to commit violent sins, such as murder (1:16; see 6:18; Isa. 59:7; Rom. 3:15). Both senseless violence for money and permitting victims to observe the setting of a trap intended for them are exercises in futility (1:17). Perhaps the text also suggests that the youth who perceives the dangerous nature of the trap carefully described in 1:10–19 should have the good sense to avoid it.[1]

The repetition of the verbs "lie in wait" and "waylay" in 1:11 and 1:18 emphasize the irony that the violent schemes of the violent (1:11) will backfire (1:18). Thus, they are lurking to ambush and destroy themselves. For the violence perpetrated by the wicked has the boomerang effect of coming back upon them and dragging them away (21:7). The word rendered "violence" also includes any forms of injustice or social evils. The word rendered "drag away" is a fishing term, which describes dragging a net through water to catch fish, and is also used to picture capturing men by force (Hab. 1:14–15).

In 1:19, the conclusion of 1:18 is restated as a general principle. Greedy, covetous people who use violent, dishonest, and other unethical means to achieve their financial goals will become the victims when their schemes boomerang.

4. The Righteous Care about Justice.

29:7 "The righteous care about justice for the poor, but the wicked have no such concern."

For "righteous" and "wicked," see VR and VWs.

The quality of justice for the poor, oppressed, and helpless is the barometer to measure the quality of a nation's justice, since that is where injustice most easily occurs. Justice that is not equally applicable to all is hardly just.

The righteous who fear God love their neighbors and are thus concerned about having an equally high quality of justice for all. The words rendered "care" and "concern" mean "know"

---

[1] Robert L. Alden, *Proverbs* (Grand Rapids: Baker, 1983), 25.

and "knowledge" (see VWm). Here they refer to the sympathetic knowledge involved in caring.

5. Justice Requires Both Sides to Be Heard.

18:17 "The first to present his case seems right, till another comes forward and questions him."

By hearing the arguments and counter-arguments of both litigants, a judge places himself in a better position to evaluate the evidence and to render a just verdict.

6. The Wicked Pervert Justice; the Righteous Impart Justice.

17:23 "A wicked man accepts a bribe in secret to pervert the course of justice."

17:26 "It is not good to punish an innocent man, or to flog officials for their integrity."

18:5 "It is not good to be partial to the wicked or to deprive the innocent of justice."

19:28 "A corrupt witness mocks at justice, and the mouth of the wicked gulps down evil."

24:23–25 "These also are sayings of the wise: To show partiality in judging is not good: Whoever says to the guilty, 'You are innocent'—peoples will curse him and nations denounce him. But it will go well with those who convict the guilty, and rich blessing will come upon them."

24:26 "An honest answer is like a kiss on the lips."

28:21 "To show partiality is not good—yet a man will do wrong for a piece of bread."

For "innocent" (**17:26; 18:5; 24:24**), see "righteous" under VR.

The wicked find a money-making opportunity in the processes of justice (**17:23**). A corrupt judge is secretly bribed to render a favorable verdict to the undeserving or guilty person who paid him. Or a witness is bribed to commit perjury to alter the judge's verdict. This perverts the course of justice and turns it into injustice.

For "corrupt" (**19:28a**), see the comment about "scoundrel" in 16:27. A corrupt witness scorns justice by saying whatever the one paying him wants, which may involve a false accusation and deliberately distorted testimony for destructive purposes. The wicked have a ravenous appetite for evil that involves frequent exposure and participation (**19:28b**).

To a desperately hungry man, the value of even ordinary food greatly exceeds its worth in money. Such a man may transgress to get it (**28:21b**). Even though a judge may be sympathetic in such a case, he should nevertheless uphold the law (Exod. 23:3; Lev. 19:15).

Punishing (fining) the innocent and beating honest officials (**17:26**) with a whip are repugnant perversions of justice. So is preferential treatment in court (**24:23b; 28:21a**), especially to the wicked (**18:5**). Such favoritism by a judge is prohibited (Deut. 1:17; 16:18–19), since it may motivate a judge to convict the innocent and to acquit the guilty (**24:24**). Either way the innocent are deprived or turned away from justice (**18:5**), which produces vehement verbal reactions of cursing and denouncing those who perpetrate such injustice (**24:24**).

To "convict" (**24:25**; see "rebuke" in VWm) is also a standard juridical term that pictures a judge's verdict of "guilty." It will be pleasant for those who handle this important responsibility with integrity and equity. Integrity, impartiality, and equity are essential ingredients of justice.

An honest, just verdict is as refreshing and delightful as a kiss on the lips (**24:26**) that expresses genuine love. An intriguing alternative to the interpretation of the word rendered "kiss" has been recently suggested.[2] J. M. Cohen observed an uncommon connotation of that word: "press the lips together," a meaning attested outside of the OT. When pressed together, lips remain still or silent. The idea of **24:26** is this: "A just verdict silences hostile lips." Although there is no word for "hostile" in the Hebrew text, its presence is implied by the context (**24:24**). Cohen suggested this flow of thought: the importance of impartial judgment (**24:23**), the curses and denunciations faced by the corrupt judge (**24:24**), the blessings received by the honest and just judge (**24:25**), the silence that neutralizes the curses and denunciations of **24:24** (**24:26**). Although involving a

---

[2] Jeffrey M. Cohen, "An Unrecognized Connotation of *NSQ PEH* with Special Reference to Three Biblical Occurrences," *Vetus Testamentum* 32, 4 (New York: E. J. Brill, Inc., 1982), 416–24.

less frequent meaning than "kiss," this interpretation is plausible, fits the context well, and merits serious consideration.

7. The Righteous Are Generous; Man Is Never Satisfied.

12:10 "A righteous man cares for the needs of his animal, but the kindest acts of the wicked are cruel."

21:25–26 "The sluggard's craving will be the death of him, because his hands refuse to work. All day long he craves for more, but the righteous give without sparing."

27:20 "Death and Destruction are never satisfied, and neither are the eyes of man."

30:15–16 " 'The leech has two daughters. "Give! Give!" they cry. There are three things that are never satisfied, four that never say,"Enough!": the grave, the barren womb, land, which is never satisfied with water, and fire, which never says, "Enough!" ' "

The righteous man is generous (**21:26b**) and wisely provides for his animal (**12:10**). For "cares," see the note about 29:7. In contrast are the wicked man's cruelty (**12:10**) and the lazy man's ravenous appetite, which is frustrated by his refusal to work to fulfill it (**21:25–26a**).

No matter how many creatures die, Death is pictured as constantly looking for more to pour into its bottomless pit (**27:20**). This grisly image pictures man's insatiable desire for more. As long as man strives to satisfy his desires by means of material things, he will be frustrated by their incapability to provide a lasting satisfaction.

Common in Israel, especially in stagnant water, the "leech" (**30:15**) is a blood-sucking worm with a sucker at each end of its body and with an insatiable appetite. It hangs on so tightly that the term "leech" has been used figuratively for a greedy person who continually requests favors and becomes annoying. The "daughters" may be the two sucking ends of the ravenous leech that constantly wants more.[3] The three lines in **30:15** form a triple synonymous parallelism with a consecutive numerical sequence of 2, 3, and 4 (see Synonymous Parallelism and

---

[3] F.S. North, "The Four Insatiables," *Vetus Testamentum* 15 (New York: E. J. Brill, Inc., 1965), 281–82.

Numerical Sayings in the introduction). Each line describes a desire for more than what is possessed.

The four examples of dissatisfied entities with their incessant desires for more (**30:16**) include (1) Death for corpses, (2) a barren womb for an embryo, (3) parched land for water, and (4) fire for fuel. The wise teacher may have mentioned these natural phenomena to picture sarcastically the greedy whose insatiable desires are never satisfied.

8. *The Righteous Are Careful.*

12:26 "A righteous man is cautious in friendship, but the way of the wicked leads them astray."

21:29 "A wicked man puts up a bold front, but an upright man gives thought to his ways."

To "put up a bold front" (**21:29**) literally is to "harden his face," that is, to "look tough." This may express a wicked man's defiant, insolent attitude. In contrast, the upright establishes in his life the righteous ways that will define his behavior. This includes carefully examining his close friend (**12:26**) to be certain that neither his relationship nor his friend's ways will cause him to compromise his own righteous principles. For the wrong friend may lure him away from the righteous path.

9. *The Wicked Are Arrogant.*

21:4 "Haughty eyes and a proud heart, the lamp of the wicked, are sin!"

For "haughty" and "heart," see the comments about "haughty" in 6:17 and "heart" in 4:23. A "proud heart" pictures a broad or "big head." An attitude that is conceited, arrogant, excessively self-conscious, and apathetic to others is sinful.

10. *The Righteous Keep the Law.*

29:18 "Where there is no revelation, the people cast off restraint; but blessed is he who keeps the law."

For "law" and "keeps," see the comments about "teaching" in VWm, and "protect" in 2:8. To "cast off" is to "let loose," to abandon all inhibitions in effect by the influence of the Law or the principles of wisdom. The word rendered "revelation" means "vision," specifically a prophetic revelatory vision that reflects the Lord's guidance and will. It has nothing to do with what people may visualize in achieving their goals. The KJV, "where there is no vision, the people perish" has been misinterpreted at this point. The point of the text is to contrast the moral anarchy that results from ignoring God's Word with the blessed happiness experienced by those who follow the wise principles that He has revealed.

11. The Righteous Hate What Is False and Dishonest.

13:5 "The righteous hate what is false, but the wicked bring shame and disgrace."

29:27 "The righteous detest the dishonest; the wicked detest the upright."

In **13:5**, the word rendered "shame" means "abhor," "stink" (as the nauseating odor of dead flies in perfume in Eccl. 10:1). It pictures evil deeds as having a rotten stench to God and to the people affected. "Shame" and "disgrace" are similar in meaning and are often virtually synonymous when paralleled.

The righteous and wicked despise each other (**29:27**). The righteous disapprove of wicked behavior; the wicked, of righteous condemnation. See 3:32; 8:7; 15:9; 24:9.

12. The Wicked Bring Shame, Disgrace, and Hostility.

18:3 "When wickedness comes, so does contempt, and with shame comes disgrace."

19:26 "He who robs his father and drives out his mother is a son who brings shame and disgrace."

29:10 "Bloodthirsty men hate a man of integrity and seek to kill the upright."

Contempt, shame, and disgrace often accompany wickedness (**18:3**), especially in such forms as a man's seizing control of his (perhaps senile) father's property and evicting both parents (**19:26**).

The hostility of the wicked against the righteous may be expressed in violence (**29:10**). Bloodthirsty (literally, "men of blood") men are quick to kill to obtain what they want or to liquidate those whom they hate.

The meaning of **29:10b** is unclear. A literal rendering (similar to the KJV) is "The upright seek his life." In the OT, this statement often indicates intent to kill, a puzzling description of the upright. A more likely alternative is to consider the text as an incomplete synonymous parallelism with "bloodthirsty" men as the subject of "seek," who energetically strive to kill the upright (RSV and NIV).

13. The Righteous Are Bold and Resist the Wicked.

28:1 "The wicked man flees though no one pursues, but the righteous are as bold as a lion."

28:4 "Those who forsake the law praise the wicked, but those who keep the law resist them."

For "wicked," "righteous," and "law" (teaching), see VWs, VR, and VWm.

The wicked, perhaps overly sensitive to their guilt, run away even when there is no danger of pursuit (**28:1**). In contrast, the righteous, who trust God and perceive their security in Him, have the confidence to act with courage.

The only possible basis for praising the wicked is to reject the Law and wisdom (**28:4**) as a means to guide and evaluate behavior. Those who prize and guard the Law and wisdom vigorously oppose the wicked.

14. The Righteous Bounce Back from Adversity.

24:15-16 "Do not lie in wait like an outlaw against a righteous man's house, do not raid his dwelling place; for though a righteous man falls seven times, he rises again, but the wicked are brought down by calamity."

For "calamity" ("evil"), see VWs.

The words rendered "house" and "dwelling" picture home as a secure, peaceful, restful place where a person may be refreshed. A righteous man's home is not to be attacked and destroyed (**24:15**) because the righteous display remarkable resilience in rebounding from adversity (**24:16**; see Mic. 7:8). However, disaster pulls down the wicked.

B. Evaluation of the Righteous and Wicked

1. Conduct Indicates Character.

20:11 "Even a child is known by his actions, by whether his conduct is pure and right."

One can discern what a youth is like by observing what he does. See Matthew 7:20.

2. The Righteous Are Polluted by Giving Way to the Wicked.

25:26 "Like a muddied spring or a polluted well is a righteous man who gives way to the wicked."

For "righteous" and "wicked," see VR and VWs. When animals wade in spring water, they stir up the dirt, making the water muddy and undrinkable (Ezek. 32:2; 34:18–19). Long-lasting pollution may ruin a spring or well as a source of decent drinking water. These depressing images vividly portray the ruinous moral pollution of righteous people who slip and succumb to the pressures and attractions of the wicked. The sins of the wicked are not nearly as conspicuous or noticeable as the fall of a righteous person. The loss of his reputation may be permanent.

3. Better to Be Righteous and Poor Than to Be Unjust, Arrogant, or Perverse.

16:8 "Better a little with righteousness than much gain with injustice."

16:19 "Better to be lowly in spirit and among the oppressed than to share plunder with the proud."

19:1 "Better a poor man whose walk is blameless than a fool whose lips are perverse."

28:6 "Better a poor man whose walk is blameless than a rich man whose ways are perverse."

For "blameless" ("Integrity"), see VR.

Poverty, however unpleasant, is by no means the worst condition to experience. Being poor and righteous is better than becoming affluent by unethical means (**16:8**; see 15:16). For such wealth breeds the misery of a guilty conscience and fear of exposure with its resulting shame. Having lowly status and oppressed associates is superior to associating and sharing (perhaps by entertaining) with the arrogant the wealth they may have obtained so unethically and illegally as to be called "plunder" (**16:19**). Poverty with integrity is less undesirable than perversity, whether in the form of a rich man with twisted ways (**28:6**) or a fool's talk (**19:1**). Identical are **19:1a** and **28:6a**. Thus, a person's character is far more important than his financial or social status.

4. People Rejoice When the Righteous Prosper, but Hide from the Powerful Wicked.

11:10 "When the righteous prosper, the city rejoices; when the wicked perish, there are shouts of joy."

28:12 "When the righteous triumph, there is great elation; but when the wicked rise to power, men go into hiding."

28:28 "When the wicked rise to power, people go into hiding; but when the wicked perish, the righteous thrive."

29:2 "When the righteous thrive, the people rejoice; when the wicked rule, the people groan."

For "righteous" and "wicked" in each of these texts, see VR and VWs.

Most people want honest and just government leaders and fear the capricious manipulations and unscrupulous policies developed by wicked rulers. Thus, they rejoice when the wicked are destroyed (**11:10**) and when the righteous triumph (**28:12**), prosper (**11:10**; see "good" under VR), and thrive (**28:28**; **29:2**). The word rendered "thrive" means "be great," "be many," "be much" in various, mostly quantitative, senses. It includes financial prosperity and, as here, substantial political influence and power. The word rendered "rejoice" (**11:10**) and "triumph" (**28:12**) pictures the joy experienced in victory, success, or blessing.

In contrast, when the wicked acquire political power and influence, people hide and groan (**28:12, 28; 29:2**). Their groaning reflects their misery under the oppressive rule by the wicked (**29:2**) That is why they go into hiding (or perhaps "underground") to such an extent that only an extremely thorough search may find them (**28:12, 28**). Almost identical are **28:12b** and **28:28a**.

5. The Wicked's Religious Practices Are Detestable.

21:27 "The sacrifice of the wicked is detestable—how much more so when brought with evil intent."

28:9 "If anyone turns a deaf ear to the law, even his prayers are detestable."

For "law," see "teaching" under VWm.

There is no intent to repudiate sacrifices (21:27) or prayer (28:9), which were sanctioned by the law of Moses. But unethical behavior contrary to that law makes even these basic religious practices detestable. The wicked person's unspecified evil intent, perhaps his putting on a deceptive religious veneer to carry out his evil schemes more effectively, make his sacrifices and prayers even more despicable. Almost identical in the Hebrew text, except for the explicit reference to Yahweh in 15:8, are **21:27a** and 15:8a.

C. Results of Being Righteous or Wicked

1. The Righteous Are Delivered; There Is Trouble for the Wicked.

a. The Righteous Go Free; the Wicked Are Punished. 11:21 "Be sure of this: The wicked will not go unpunished, but those who are righteous will go free."

For "Be sure of this," see the comment about 16:5 to understand the imagery in this guarantee. The guarantee is that, in spite of appearances to the contrary, the evil man will not get away with his sins. He will be found guilty and appropriately punished. The righteous will be delivered from a wrongly unfavorable verdict in court. Since human courts are not always accurate, this principle points to God's justice.

b. The Righteous Are Delivered From Trouble; the Wicked Encounter Trouble. 11:8 "The righteous man is rescued from trouble, and it comes on the wicked instead."

12:21 "No harm befalls the righteous, but the wicked have their fill of trouble."

13:17 "A wicked messenger falls into trouble, but a trustworthy envoy brings healing."

22:5 "In the paths of the wicked lie thorns and snares, but he who guards his soul stays far from them."

These texts present the general principle that the lives of the wicked are saturated with the problems and troubles that they deserve. The "thorns and snares" (**22:5**) picture these

THE TWO WAYS: RIGHTEOUSNESS AND WICKEDNESS   139

difficulties as formidable obstacles and dangerous plots. Israel's thorns are nasty and thick, capable of ripping one's clothes and cutting anybody that tries to go through them (see 15:19). Another general principle in these texts pictures the righteous who avoid evil ways as delivered from such troubles (see 16:17). For "guards" and "soul" (**22:5**), see the comments about "protect" in 2:8 and "zeal" in 19:2. These general principles are applied specifically to the envoy (**13:17**).

    c. The Wicked Have Trouble. 22:8 "He who sows wickedness reaps trouble, and the rod of his fury will be destroyed."

    24:1–2 "Do not envy wicked men, do not desire their company; for their hearts plot violence, and their lips talk about making trouble."

    Do not envy the wicked (**24:1**) who convey the impression of success. The similar words rendered "envy" (see the comment about 3:31) and "desire" (see "longing" in 13:19) both picture an intense urge, perhaps to indulge in sinful fun or to obtain material wealth. The latter term occurs in the tenth commandment, which prohibits coveting another's possessions (Deut. 5:21). The wicked express such desires in their conniving talk to devise unethical schemes to produce fast profits. Consequently, their envy and lust are translated into sinful deeds (**24:2**).

    The agricultural metaphors of sowing and reaping in **22:8a** picture a person's actions as having consequences, here undesirable (see Gal. 6:7). The "rod" (**22:8b**) pictures figuratively the power of the wicked to inflict far more terrifying trouble than even a severe physical beating. "Fury" pictures an intense, boiling anger that cannot be suppressed. Evidently in **22:8b**, the intense hostility of the wicked will be thwarted either by defeat, by death, or by dissipation upon the wicked themselves. For the latter, "He who sows injustice reaps disaster, and the rod of his anger falls on himself" (JB).

    d. Righteousness Delivers the Righteous; Evil Desires Trap the Unfaithful. 11:6 "The righteousness of the upright delivers them, but the unfaithful are trapped by evil desires."

    Being righteous saves us (**11:6a**) from many problems encountered by those who break God's rules and con the people around them. In contrast, the unfaithful fall into a trap set by their own cravings—the boomerang effect. Variants of 11:6b are 11:3b and 11:5b.

e. Righteousness Delivers from Death; Ill-Gotten Wealth Is Worthless. 10:2 "Ill-gotten treasures are of no value, but righteousness delivers from death."

11:4 "Wealth is worthless in the day of wrath, but righteousness delivers from death."

These two texts, variants of each other, have the same theme: wealth, highly regarded in the Book of Proverbs, is inferior to righteousness and worthless without it. "Ill-gotten treasures" (10:2) are unethically and perhaps illegally obtained. They provide no protection against calamity or death. Identical are 10:2b and 11:4b, which picture the saving benefit of righteousness. Deliverance from death by righteousness in these texts involves rescue from premature death and thus a long life. The issue of eternal life is not in view.

2. The Righteous Are Secure; the Wicked Fall.

6:12–15 "A scoundrel and villain, who goes about with a corrupt mouth, who winks with his eye, signals with his feet and motions with his fingers, who plots evil with deceit in his heart—he always stirs up dissension. Therefore disaster will overtake him in an instant; he will suddenly be destroyed—without remedy."

10:9 "The man of integrity walks securely, but he who takes crooked paths will be found out."

10:25 "When the storm has swept by, the wicked are gone, but the righteous stand firm forever."

10:30 "The righteous will never be uprooted, but the wicked will not remain in the land."

12:3 "A man cannot be established through wickedness, but the righteous cannot be uprooted."

12:7 "Wicked men are overthrown and are no more, but the house of the righteous stands firm."

14:11 "The house of the wicked will be destroyed, but the tent of the upright will flourish."

14:32 "When calamity comes, the wicked are brought down, but even in death the righteous have a refuge."

28:18 "He whose walk is blameless is kept safe, but he whose ways are perverse will suddenly fall."

For "integrity"/"blameless" (**10:9; 28:18**), see VR.

The antithetic parallelisms (see introduction) in most of these texts contrast the security of the righteous with the impending destruction of the wicked.

In **6:12–14**, the wicked are described by several parts of the human body: mouth, eye, feet, fingers, heart—each of which pictures metaphorically the evil character of the entire person. The physical movements mentioned in **6:13** picture "body language" associated then with concocting evil schemes. For "winks," see the comments about 10:10 and 16:30. With his perverse talk (**6:12**) and deceptive schemes, the scoundrel (**6:12**; see the comments about 16:27) constantly arouses and fuels tensions and hostilities (**6:14**).

The consequences of wickedness are disastrous. A perverse man is found out (**10:9**), literally "known" for what he is, since his wickedness cannot establish him (**12:3**). That he will not remain to live in the land (**10:30**) anticipates either his premature death or his moving away, perhaps into exile or slavery. Several of the texts picture a permanent destruction of the wicked, probably involving ruin or premature death from a sudden unexpected catastrophe (**6:15; 12:7; 14:11, 32; 28:18**) by human vengeance or the punishment resulting from God's judgment. Identical are **6:15b** and 29:1b. The imagery of the violent storm (**10:25**) dramatizes the sudden devastation of God's judgment and punishment. Their overthrow or destruction will be complete and permanent; the wicked will be no more (**10:25; 12:7**).

In contrast, the righteous are kept safe (**28:18**). The word rendered "kept safe" means to "save," "deliver," "give victory." They are delivered from threats in this life that damage or destroy the wicked, so they are secure (**10:9**; see the comment about 14:26). They stand firm (**10:25; 12:7**), so solidly established that they will not be moved by violent storms or the punishments that destroy the wicked. Jesus' parable of the two houses—one built on sand; the other, on rock—also teaches this (Matt. 7:24–27). The word rendered "forever" (**10:25**) and "never" (**10:30**) indicates here a distant but not eternal future (see the note about 8:23). In botanical imagery, the righteous will never (see "eternity" in 8:23) be uprooted (**10:30; 12:3**), that is, they are very firmly rooted. This metaphor pictures great security, stability, and prosperity, especially when its basis is God's deliverance and protection.

Not only do the righteous flourish (**14:11**) and prosper in life, they even have a refuge in death (**14:32**), remarkably a future life after death. For "refuge," see the comment about "refuge" in 14:26. Although providing no further details about future life and not mentioning heaven (a NT doctrine), the text is evidently an exception to the nearly constant concentration upon this life in the Book of Proverbs.

3. *The Righteous Attain Life; the Wicked, Punishment and Death.*

a. The Wicked Have No Future Hope. 11:7 "When a wicked man dies, his hope perishes; all he expected from his power comes to nothing."

24:19–20 "Do not fret because of evil men or be envious of the wicked, for the evil man has no future hope, and the lamp of the wicked will be snuffed out."

The word rendered "do not fret" (**24:19**) pictures heated or burning anger. For "be envious," see "envy" in 3:31. The apparent prosperity and success of the wicked should never prompt a response either of envy or of burning anger from the righteous. In spite of appearances, they are not better off. See 3:31–32; 23:17–18; 24:1; Ps. 37:1 (which is almost identical).

In **24:20**, for "future," see the comments about 23:18. The Hebrew text contains no word here for "hope." It merely states that the wicked man has no future. This and having one's lamp suddenly extinguished both picture a wicked man's life as prematurely terminated (see 13:9 and 20:20 with comments). Virtually identical are **24:20b** and 13:9b.

The wicked man's confidence in his own ideology, ingenuity, strength, and achievements is futile. For his hopes and expectations will be liquidated by his death (**11:7**). For what he builds through financial investments and political power will not affect him when he dies. Even his influence loses its momentum when he is no longer around.

b. Mistreatment of Parents Is Wrong and Often Fatal. 20:20 "If a man curses his father or mother, his lamp will be snuffed out in pitch darkness."

28:24 "He who robs his father or mother and says, 'It's not wrong'—he is partner to him who destroys."

30:17 "The eye that mocks a father, that scorns obedience to a mother, will be pecked out by the ravens of the valley, will be eaten by the vultures."

In **28:24**, to "rob" may picture an unwarranted attempt by adult children to take illegal control of their aging parents' property. To claim that such a vicious violation of their parents' rights is not a transgression is to display either moral blindness or ingenious rationalization. Either way, it is violently destructive behavior.

A scornful attitude toward parents (**30:17**) is arrogant, cynical, and contrary to the fifth commandment, which tells us to honor our parents (Exod. 20:12). The unusually severe and violent consequences of this offensive attitude indicate physical death. For ravens and vultures do not gouge out and devour human eyeballs unless the eyeballs are motionless, in the unresponsive face of a corpse. This ghastly image was not merely theoretical (2 Sam. 21:8–10; Jer. 16:3–4).

In **20:20**, for "curses" and "snuffed out," see the comments about 30:11 and 24:20. The extinguished lamp and "pitch darkness" picture the complete absence of light in the endless darkness of the grave (see Ps. 88:10–12). This sombre picture is consistent with the law of Moses, which classifies cursing parents as a capital offense (Exod. 21:17; Lev. 20:9).

c. The Apparently Right Way Leads to Death. 14:12 "There is a way that seems right to a man, but in the end it leads to death."

16:25 "There is a way that seems right to a man, but in the end it leads to death."

These identical texts focus on this life, not the life beyond. What seems right may be wrong, since wrong moral decisions may reflect a defective moral standard. They may produce a low quality of life or even premature physical death. Unethical behavior is deceptive, promising more than it can deliver, conveying an impression of success and prosperity that is inaccurate and unrealistic. It is, thus, crucial for a person to base his ethical standards and behavior upon the teachings of God's Word that records His wisdom.

d. The Righteous Live Long. 16:31 "Gray hair is a crown of spendor; it is attained by a righteous life."

28:15–16 "Like a roaring lion or a charging bear is a wicked man ruling over a helpless people. A tyrannical ruler lacks judgment, but he who hates ill-gotten gain will enjoy a long life."

Cruel, cantankerous, and extremely dangerous when hungry or enraged, the lion and the bear (**28:15**) form a vivid, sinister picture of helpless people in the clutches of a wicked ruler with no spiritual awareness, social sensitivity, or ethical inhibitions. The tyrannical ruler (**28:16**) abuses his authority by oppressing, crushing, and impoverishing his people/victims. He violates God's standard (14:31; Zech. 7:8–10) and displays his lack of discernment to govern competently and responsibly. A ruler's refusal to get rich at the expense of his people avoids such burdensome policies that alienate them, which stabilizes his administration and extends his life.

Gray hair (**16:31**) is a sign of old age, which is attained by following a righteous path, which avoids the pitfalls that lead to premature death. The text envisions the honor and prestige of old age rather than its weaknesses and failings. The apocryphal Wisdom of Sirach (25:3–8) perceptively develops this theme: "If you have gathered nothing in your youth, how can you find anything in your old age? How fine a thing: sound judgment with gray hairs, and for graybeards to know how to advise! How fine a thing: wisdom in the aged, and considered advice coming from men of distinction! The crown of old men is ripe experience, their true glory, the fear of the Lord" (JB).

e. The Righteous Attain Life; the Wicked Are Punished and Die. 10:11 "The mouth of the righteous is a fountain of life, but violence overwhelms the mouth of the wicked."

10:16 "The wages of the righteous bring them life, but the income of the wicked brings them punishment."

11:19 "The truly righteous man attains life, but he who pursues evil goes to his death."

12:28 "In the way of righteousness there is life; along that path is immortality."

21:21 "He who pursues righteousness and love finds life, prosperity and honor."

Violence, perhaps including violent schemes, malicious talk, deliberately concealed aggressive hostility, and curses, saturates the conversation of the wicked (**10:11**). Identical are **10:11b** and **10:6b**. The "income" (**10:16**) or result of wickedness is "punishment," or more precisely, "sin" (see VWs). Wickedness breeds a deeper and broader involvement in sin with its natural undesirable results (see Rom. 1:18–32). Those who aggressively work to experience and become evil will die (**11:19**), probably prematurely.

All of these texts associate closely the qualities of righteousness and life (see the comment about 19:23). The righteous find (**11:19; 21:21**), receive (**10:16**), follow (**12:28**), and produce (**10:11**) life. Those who aggressively work to develop righteousness and love experience life, prosperity (see comment on "prosperity" in **8:18**), and honor (**21:21**). For "love" (21:21) and "fountain" (**10:11**), see the comments about 16:6 and 14:27.

The words rendered "immortality" mean literally "no death" (**12:28**). This glimpse beyond the dominant OT focus on this present life perceives the truth of the immortality of the righteous.[4] The text provides no details as to what is involved in it. See 14:32 and comment.

f. You Get What You Seek. **11:27** "He who seeks good finds good will, but evil comes to him who searches for it."

14:22 "Do not those who plot evil go astray? But those who plan what is good find love and faithfulness."

17:13 "If a man pays back evil for good, evil will never leave his house."

Evil comes to those who search for it (**11:27**), plot it (**14:22**), and bestow it (**17:13**). Concocting evil schemes leads people astray (**14:22**) from God's moral standard into more evil. To do evil or bring harm to a person who has done good to you (**17:13**) is the most reprehensible reversal of the Golden Rule (Luke

---

[4] M. Dahood, "Immortality in Proverbs 12:28," *Biblica* 41 (Rome, Italy: Biblical Institute Press, 1960): 176–81.

6:31, but see Luke 6:27–30), so it is no wonder that evil will cling to him permanently.

Vigorous searching (**11:27**) and careful planning (**14:22**) will naturally produce good will (**11:27**), love (**14:22**), and faithfulness. What we seek is what we get is a general principle equally applicable to both good and evil.

4. The Righteous Get What They Want; the Wicked, What They Dread.

10:24 "What the wicked dreads will overtake him; what the righteous desire will be granted."

11:23 "The desire of the righteous ends only in good, but the hope of the wicked only in wrath."

These texts teach the general principle that the righteous get the good for which they have a burning desire. Since this implies a God-centered perspective, it may suggest the need for the righteous to be careful in determining what they want.

Another general principle is that what the wicked man dreads is what will happen to him (**10:24**). The fears in his mind are actualized—inhibiting him, frustrating his hopes and efforts, and terminating in wrath (**11:23**). It is unclear whether the wrath is expressed by the frustrated wicked or toward them. When this happens to a righteous man (Job 3:25), it is an exception to the general pattern pictured here.

5. The Righteous Are Blessed; the Wicked Are Punished.

10:6 "Blessings crown the head of the righteous, but violence overwhelms the mouth of the wicked."

10:7 "The memory of the righteous will be a blessing, but the name of the wicked will rot."

28:20 "A faithful man will be richly blessed, but one eager to get rich will not go unpunished."

Faithful (**28:20**) and righteous people (**10:6–7**) experience blessing as a way of life and are favorably remembered. The word rendered "eager" (**28:20**) means "haste" and pictures someone who is in a hurry. Such a person is vulnerable to unethical get-rich-quick schemes that expose his dishonesty and bring about deserved punishment, perhaps in court. Violence

THE TWO WAYS: RIGHTEOUSNESS AND WICKEDNESS   147

dominates both word and deed of the wicked (**10:6**). Identical are **10:6b** and 10:11b. See the comments about 10:11b. The word rendered "name" (**10:7**) also includes the ideas of "existence," "character," "reputation." A rotten reputation is repulsive. Its decaying elements deteriorate until there is nothing left.

6. The Righteous Are Rewarded; the Wicked Get What They Deserve.

11:18 "The wicked man earns deceptive wages, but he who sows righteousness reaps a sure reward."

11:31 "If the righteous receive their due on earth, how much more the ungodly and the sinner!"

14:14 "The faithless will be fully repaid for their ways, and the good man rewarded for his."

Both righteous and wicked (**11:18, 31**) or faithless (**14:14**) "receive their due" (**11:31**), that is, get what they deserve—reward or punishment. The deceptive wages of the wicked (**11:18**) are disappointing, falling far short of what they have been led to expect. The righteous can count on receiving their reward or wage (**11:18**), that is, all they have earned. The Hebrew text for **11:18** contains a pun based upon the similar sounding, but contrasting words *shāqar* (deceptive) and *seker* (reward). Since the righteous pay the consequences for their moral failures, the wicked will surely experience what they deserve as a result of their sins (**11:31**). This is a general principle in this present life. A variant form of **11:31** is quoted in 1 Peter 4:18.

7. The Righteous Prosper; the Wicked Fail and Fall.

11:28 "Whoever trusts in his riches will fall, but the righteous will thrive like a green leaf."

12:12 "The wicked desire the plunder of evil men, but the root of the righteous flourishes."

13:21 "Misfortune pursues the sinner, but prosperity is the reward of the righteous."

13:22 "A good man leaves an inheritance for his children's children, but a sinner's wealth is stored up for the righteous."

13:25 "The righteous eat to their hearts' content, but the stomach of the wicked goes hungry."

15:6 "The house of the righteous contains great treasure, but the income of the wicked brings them trouble."

28:10 "He who leads the upright along an evil path will fall into his own trap, but the blameless will receive a good inheritance."

For "blameless" (28:10), see "integrity" in VR.

These texts present the general principle that the righteous prosper, while the wicked encounter trouble and fall.

The wicked, in spite of their burning desire for the plunder of evil men (12:12), fail to acquire what they covet. They go hungry (13:25), lacking enough food to satisfy them. Chased by misfortune (13:21), their evil ways produce trouble (15:6), that is, fury and wrath (see the comment about "fury" in 22:8). Victimized by their own scheme to captivate the upright and lure them into doing evil (28:10), they fall (11:28; see the comment about "brought down" in 11:5). For even great material wealth and large incomes can evaporate as a result of a collapsing economy or reduced market. It cannot deliver a man from the consequences of his sins. Whatever wealth a sinner may accumulate, he will eventually lose it (13:22), either by having no children to inherit it or by handling it incompetently.

The righteous thrive (11:28), flourish (12:12), and prosper (13:21; see "good" in VR), accumulating much wealth (15:6). They eat well and feel full and contented (13:25). They receive a good inheritance (28:10), which is sufficiently substantial to pass through at least two generations (13:22).

8. The Wicked Are Victimized by Their Evil Schemes and Deeds.

5:22–23 "The evil deeds of a wicked man ensnare him; the cords of his sin hold him fast. He will die for lack of discipline, led astray by his own great folly."

26:27 "If a man digs a pit, he will fall into it; if a man rolls a stone, it will roll back on him."

The synonymous parallel (see introduction) images of a trap in the form of a pit or rolled stone (26:27) picture the sinister plots of the wicked backfiring, thus giving them what they deserve. The boomerang effect makes them the victims of their own or some similar malicious schemes. See 28:10; Ps. 7:15–16; 9:15–16; 57:6; Sirach 27:25–27). Caught in his own trap by his evil deeds, he is held fast by the cords of his sin (**5:22**). Referring to a sturdy rope (Josh. 2:15; Isa. 33:23; Jer. 38:6), the word rendered "cords" pictures figuratively the binding (habit forming?) effects of his sin that has trapped him. His lack of discipline to control the sinful desires that have captivated him has led him astray, even to death (**5:23**; see 1:30–32).

9. *The Righteous Experience Joy; the Wicked Encounter Deceit, Traps, Terror, and Futility.*

10:28 "The prospect of the righteous is joy, but the hopes of the wicked come to nothing."

12:20 "There is deceit in the hearts of those who plot evil, but joy for those who promote peace."

21:15 "When justice is done, it brings joy to the righteous but terror to evildoers."

29:6 "An evil man is snared by his own sin, but a righteous one can sing and be glad."

Evil schemes utilize deceit (**12:20**; see 6:14a). Nevertheless, the boomerang effect springs the trap to ensnare the schemer in his own trap (**29:6**). As a result, his hopes are demolished (**10:28**). He is dismayed by the ruin that justice brings to him (**21:15**). Identical are **21:15b** and **10:29b**. In contrast, the application of justice and beneficial effects of their good deeds prompt the righteous, who advocate peace, to rejoice enthusiastically (**10:28; 12:20; 21:15; 29:6**). These proverbs also picture people as getting what they deserve (see 26:27 and 28:10). Using proper ethical means to achieve worthy goals helps to develop a positive attitude and, therefore, a healthy approach to life.

10. *The Wicked Are Hampered and Tormented by Their Guilt.*

28:17 "A man tormented by the guilt of murder will be a fugitive till death; let no one support him."

29:24 "The accomplice of a thief is his own enemy; he is put under oath and dare not testify."

A thief's accomplice is his own enemy (**29:24**), that is, he literally hates himself. The problem for the thief's accomplice is whether to confess his guilt in court or to commit perjury in an attempted cover-up. Either perjury or withholding evidence was considered sin that could bring a person under a curse (Lev. 5:1). No matter what he does, he is in trouble.

A murderer tormented by guilt feels pursued (**28:17**), threatened, and insecure for the rest of his life, especially in an ancient Oriental culture where vengeance by the victim's kin was legal. Any kind of support to a fleeing murderer was prohibited. As a result, his guilt-ridden feelings would never abate.

11. Righteousness Exalts and Establishes a Nation; Wickedness Is Detested and Disgraceful

14:34 "Righteousness exalts a nation, but sin is a disgrace to any people."

16:12 "Kings detest wrongdoing, for a throne is established through righteousness."

20:28 "Love and faithfulness keep a king safe; through love his throne is made secure."

25:4–5 "Remove the dross from the silver, and out comes material for the silversmith; remove the wicked from the king's presence, and his throne will be established through righteousness."

29:4 "By justice a king gives a country stability, but one who is greedy for bribes tears it down."

29:14 "If a king judges the poor with fairness, his throne will always be secure."

A sinful nation experiences disgrace (**14:34**), that is, the shame and reproach resulting from contemptible behavior. A wise king abhors evil (**16:12**), which undermines any government that it infects. Bribes that enrich greedy government officials (**29:4**) are destructive and rip apart that administration when its angry victims rebel.

The removal of impurities or "dross" (**25:4**) in the refining process produces a silver of high quality. Similarly, with the removal of wicked officials, the resulting righteous government will be firmly established (**16:12; 25:5**). Moral purification is much more important than metallic purification. Close variants are **16:12b** and **25:5b**.

The treatment of the poor (**29:14**) by the judicial process is an accurate indicator of the quality of justice administered. For the poor are the most likely to suffer from judicial inequities. Justice of the highest quality treats rich and poor alike, favoring neither. Genuine justice with fairness, equity (**29:4**), and love (**20:28**; see the comment about 16:6) builds the loyalty and respect needed to protect and secure a government. A nation with these qualities will be honored with an excellent reputation (**14:34**). Isaiah prophesied that the Messiah would follow these principles by establishing His kingdom with justice and righteousness (Isa. 9:6–7).

12. The Righteous Benefit at the Expense of the Wicked.

14:19 "Evil men will bow down in the presence of the good, and the wicked at the gates of the righteous."

21:18 "The wicked become a ransom for the righteous, and the unfaithful for the upright."

29:16 "When the wicked thrive, so does sin, but the righteous will see their downfall."

Transgression increases as the wicked prosper and thus gain more power and influence (**29:16**). With no hint as to when it will occur, the righteous will observe the collapse and ruin of the wicked. The wicked will "bow down" (**14:19**) before the righteous; not as an act of worship, but as an expression of respect and submission while conceding defeat.

In **21:18**, for "ransom," see the comment about "atoned for" in 16:6. The wicked are not to be sacrificed (like Christ) to obtain atonement for the righteous, for human sacrifice was prohibited by the Law (Lev. 18:21). This text displays an innovative use of atonement terminology to picture the prosperity of the righteous at the expense of the wicked. See Isaiah 43:3–4 for similar use of this terminology. See 11:8 for a more direct statement of the principle.

13. Sins Are Universal, but Are to Be Confessed and Renounced.

20:9 "Who can say, 'I have kept my heart pure; I am clean and without sin'?"

28:13 "He who conceals his sins does not prosper, but whoever confesses and renounces them finds mercy."

The rhetorical question in **20:9** emphasizes that the claim to be pure or clean morally is valid for no one. This is equivalent to the doctrine of universal human sinfulness (1 Kings 8:46; Eccl. 7:20; Rom. 3:10–12, 23).

To "prosper" (**28:13**) is to achieve successfully what we have set out to do. For a man to hypocritically hide the reality of his sinfulness is to prevent his complete success by hampering his effectiveness. To confess our sins is to acknowledge their reality and presence. To renounce them is to depart from them, to forsake them, to abandon them. To acknowledge and to abandon our sins brings God's pardon and peace (see Ps. 32:1–5; 1 John 1:8–10).

D. For Further Study

1. Read the references in Proverbs discussed in this chapter and list the ones that state general principles rather than absolute truths. Observe that not all of them were specifically mentioned as such in this commentary. What is the value of having general principles in Scripture?

2. Why is integrity desirable? Why is it so rare? How do you develop it?

3. Use a concordance to trace the use of justice, judge, judgment throughout Scripture. What are the differences between God's judgment and human judgment?

4. Why is justice important? What are the qualities of true justice? To whom does it apply? How can it be developed in our judicial system? How can corrupt courts be avoided?

5. What is wrong with greed? Why are the greedy never satisfied? How often do you encounter greed in your circles? How can you avoid being greedy?

6. Why is it better to be poor and righteous than to be rich and perverse? How do you develop an appreciation for right-

eousness that values it more than the obvious benefits and attractions of wealth? How do you learn to feel the way you should feel?

7. What do you think of this principle: You get what you seek (11:27)? What illustrations of it can you cite from your experience? What impact should this principle have upon defining personal goals? Does it?

Chapter 7

Human Relationships

The Book of Proverbs presents general principles for developing harmonious, happy, and mutually satisfying relationships with one's spouse, children, servants, friends, and neighbors. Its realistic treatment of marriage includes both its beneficial and irritating aspects. It pictures the benefits of constructive conversation and the damages of destructive talk.

A. The Adulterous Woman

Several passages vividly picture the adulterous woman as alluring and seductive, while they warn that no pleasure is worth the disastrous consequences of becoming involved with her. Those who succumb to the immoral woman are no less sinful than she is, since the sins of adultery and fornication occur only when *two* people participate. The frequency, length, and intensity of these passages suggest that adultery and fornication were major problems in ancient Israel, just as they are today.

1. Descriptions of the Adulteress and Her Deadly Path

2:16–19 "It [Wisdom] will save you also from the adulteress, from the wayward wife with her seductive words, who has left the partner of her youth and ignored the covenant she made before God. For her house leads down to death and her paths to the spirits of the dead. None who go to her return or attain the paths of life."

The wise teacher described several benefits of wisdom

(2:1–11). One benefit is that a man may be saved from the devious ways of perverse men (2:12–15) and seductive women (2:16) by listening to wisdom and moving away from their clutches. "Adulteress" and "wayward wife" (2:16) are the connecting synonymous terms in a step parallelism construction (see introduction). Throughout the Book of Proverbs these synonymous terms picture women, both foreign and Hebrew, who were strangers to God's Law and thus uninhibited by its moral standard. Both words were standard designations for the immoral woman. Her seductive (literally, "smooth") words were flattering, enticing, and manipulative (7:14–20). By leaving her husband (2:17) and committing adultery, she has ignored (rejected) both the covenant (pact) between God and Israel (Exod. 20:14) and her marriage covenant—both prohibit adultery.

The synonymous parallel lines in 2:18 convey the same idea. Her "house" and "paths" indicate the context and direction of her sinful activities that bring the participants down to her low level of death (see the comment about 14:27) from which there is no return (2:19). The path of life (see the comment about 19:23) is beyond the reach of her clientele.

5:3–6 "For the lips of an adulteress drip honey, and her speech is smoother than oil; but in the end she is bitter as gall, sharp as a double-edged sword. Her feet go down to death; her steps lead straight to the grave. She gives no thought to the way of life; her paths are crooked, but she knows it not."

Lips that drip honey and speech (literally, "mouth") that is smoother than oil (5:3) are both metaphors that picture seductive talk. The adulteress makes her invitation seem so exciting and delightful that a man would need much wisdom to discern its deadly nature. For "adulteress" and "smoother," see the comments about 2:16.

In 5:4–6, the wise teacher penetrates the attractive veneer of the adulteress and exposes her for what she really is—a woman who leaves a bitter taste. The word rendered "bitter" (5:4) pictures realistically a bitter taste that makes water undrinkable (Exod. 15:23) and figuratively the anguish felt in a distressing situation. The word rendered "gall" refers to "wormwood," a bitter herb that came to symbolize anything especially bitter or distressing. The aftermath of the adultery that promised pleasure leaves the sinner with a bitter, disgusting, nauseating taste. The parallel image "sharp as a double-edged sword" pictures the painful aspect that may include danger, damage, ruin, and even death. For "death" and "grave" (**5:5**), see the comments about 14:27 and 15:11. The immoral woman is determined to continue her sinful ways in spite of their disastrous consequences.

The word rendered "crooked" (**5:6**) means "shaking," "staggering," "wandering." It pictures her sinful rebellion (see Jer. 14:10) and moral instability. She is unaware of the deadly character and implications of her evil ways because she does not stop long enough to evaluate them.

6:23-29 "For these commands are a lamp, this teaching is a light, and the corrections of discipline are the way to life, keeping you from the immoral woman, from the smooth tongue of the wayward wife. Do not lust in your heart after her beauty or let her captivate you with her eyes, for the prostitute reduces you to a loaf of bread, and the adulteress preys upon your very life. Can a man scoop fire into his lap without his clothes being burned? Can a man walk on hot coals without his feet being scorched? So is he who sleeps with another man's wife; no one who touches her will go unpunished."

See the previous discussion about 6:23. Proper application of Wisdom's teachings will prevent a man from being ensnared by an adulteress, whether an immoral wife or a prostitute (**6:24**; see also 2:16). For "keeping," "immoral woman," "smooth" and "wayward wife," see the comments about "protect" in 2:8, "evil" in VWs, "seductive" and "wayward wife" in 2:16.

In **6:25**, the wise teacher warns against lust, an uncontrolled selfish desire, for an immoral woman. Lust, a violation of the tenth commandment, which prohibits coveting (same word in Hebrew text of Exod. 20:17), may also motivate him to violate the seventh commandment, which prohibits adultery (Exod. 20:14). See also our Lord's warning (Matt. 5:27-28), which this exhortation anticipates! A beautiful, immoral woman "captivates" (see the comment about "wins" in 11:30) a man by arousing his sexual desire for her. She seduces him with her eyes.

Morally equivalent to the prostitute is the adulteress (literally, "a man's wife," that is, an immoral wife looking elsewhere). To "prey" (**6:26**) is to hunt, whether for animals to eat or another person to destroy. This pictures her determined, planned, vigorous search and strategy to capture her victim. When she has him, she wants more than he can provide and constantly presses him for more. Her insatiable appetite consumes his financial resources, as does the prostitute. The adulterer retains only the bare essentials of life (bread). His affair destroys his honor and threatens his life, whether by physical violence or legal process. In ancient Israel adultery was a capital offense.

The rhetorical questions in **6:27–28** indicate that certain acts inevitably produce severe results. Fire in your lap will burn your clothes and probably you also (**6:27**). Does the fire picture insatiable sexual lust? Walking on hot coals will burn your feet (**6:28**). No less foolish and disastrous is the act of adultery (**6:29**), which also has its inevitable undesirable results. The word rendered "sleeps with" means literally "goes into," an explicit OT expression for sexual intercourse. For a man to "touch a woman" is an OT euphemism for sexual intercourse (Gen. 20:6).

6:30–35 "Men do not despise a thief if he steals to satisfy his hunger when he is starving. Yet if he is caught, he must pay sevenfold, though it costs him all the wealth of his house. But a man who commits adultery lacks judgment; whoever does so destroys himself. Blows and disgrace are his lot, and his shame will never be wiped away; for jealousy arouses a husband's fury, and he will show no mercy when he takes revenge. He will not accept any compensation; he will refuse the bribe, however great it is."

Although some people may even sympathize with a desperately hungry man who steals to survive (**6:30**), stealing was a violation of the eighth commandment (Exod. 20:15) and vigorously condemned. When caught, a thief is required by the Law to pay up to fivefold (Exod. 22:1–9). The "sevenfold" in **6:31** exceeds what the Law required, so it may be a hyperbole, that is, it emphasizes the necessity of his punishment by exaggerating the penalty prescribed by the Law. The thief is liable for the full penalty, even if compelled to forfeit all of his possessions, including his home and land, and be forced into slavery.

The adulterer lacks common sense (6:32). No momentary sinful pleasure is worth the physical beatings, disgrace, shame (6:33), ruin, and perhaps the premature termination of life. The punishment for adultery is inevitable and permanent, since he will never outlive the shame for his sin. Where high moral standards prevail, adultery is considered intolerable and results in social suicide. In 6:33, "blows and disgrace" are his lot, and his shame will never be wiped away; for jealousy arouses a husband's fury" (6:34. See "wrath" in 15:1, "envy" in 3:31, and "jealousy" in 27:4). In his intense rage the husband will mercilessly exact the full measure of revenge allowed by the procedures of justice, even death. No compensation or bribe, no matter how large, will ever be enough (6:35).

7:4–27 "Say to wisdom, 'You are my sister,' and call understanding your kinsman; they will keep you from the adulteress, from the wayward wife with her seductive words. At the window of my house I looked out through the lattice. I saw among the simple, I noticed among the young men, a youth who lacked judgment. He was going down the street near her corner, walking along in the direction of her house at twilight, as the day was fading, as the dark of night set in. Then out came a woman to meet him, dressed like a prostitute and with crafty intent. (She is loud and defiant, her feet never stay at home; now in the street, now in the squares, at every corner she lurks.) She took hold of him and kissed him and with a brazen face she said: 'I have fellowship offerings at home; today I fulfilled my vows. So I came out to meet you; I looked for you and have found you! I have covered my bed with colored linens from Egypt. I have perfumed my bed with myrrh, aloes and cinnamon. Come, let's drink deep of love till morning; let's enjoy ourselves with love! My husband is not at home; he has gone on a long journey. He took his purse filled with money and will not be home till full moon.' With persuasive words she led him astray; she seduced him with her smooth talk. All at once he followed her like an ox going to the slaughter, like a deer stepping into a noose till an arrow pierces his liver, like a bird darting into a snare, little knowing it will cost him his life. Now then, my sons, listen to me; pay attention to what I say. Do not let your heart turn to her ways or stray into her paths. Many are the victims she has brought down; her slain are a mighty throng. Her house is a highway to the grave, leading down to the chambers of death."

See the previous discussion about 7:4. A wise man, with his priorities in perspective, avoids adultery (7:5). For "adulteress," "wayward wife," and "seductive," see the comments about 2:16.

In 7:6–23, the wise teacher vividly portrays a typical approach by an immoral woman. Observing from his home (7:6), he notices a naive (see "Simple" in VF) young man who lacked common sense (7:7). Either oblivious or apathetic to the danger threatening him, he wandered into an area where temptations lurked (7:8). Five words in 7:9 that collectively describe the interval from dusk to the darkness of night indicate that his wandering was prolonged.

With her clothes doubtless designed to emphasize her sex appeal, the meeting (7:10) reflected the immoral woman's intent to encounter a man. Her loud defiance (7:11) openly expressed her rebelliousness. Rarely staying at home, she circulated in various public places, lurking for customers (7:12). Interestingly, the word rendered "lurks" also pictures lying in wait to ambush someone.

The immoral woman's impudent facial expression and passionate embrace and kiss (7:13) won his attention and interest. Claiming to have fulfilled her religious vows by making a fellowship or peace offering (Lev. 7:11–36), she had an excess of meat (7:14) that provided an opportunity for feasting and partying. Her claim to look for him to meet him (7:15) was insincere flattery, since she was looking for any man.

She intimately described the preparations of her bed with elegant colorful coverings (7:16) and exotic erotic fragrances (7:17). Her sensuous appearance, actions, and talk led up to her frank statement of her purpose (7:18)—to spend the night together, wildly indulging themselves in the pleasures and delights of sexual love. The two Hebrew words rendered "love," evidently synonymous, cover the entire broad range of meaning as "love," including God's love, and human love for God, spouse, family, neighbor, things, and illicit sexual lust.

With her husband out of town on a long trip (7:19–20), she assured him that they would not be caught.

Using "smooth" (see "seductive" in 2:16) words, she persuaded him (7:21) and overcame his resistance and influenced him to move in her direction. Here the word rendered "seduced" pictures her as forcing him to go with her by appealing to his senses, while ignoring his common sense. He *saw* her attractiveness. He *heard* her flattering invitation. He *touched* and *tasted* her lips during their embrace. He *smelled* her perfume and (in his imagination) the fragrances in her bed. When she succeeded in getting him to visualize what she was offering, to emotionalize his involvement with her, and to arouse his desire for her, there was no stopping him. By these highly effective techniques she virtually forced his seduction. Such is the irresistable power and extreme danger of being sexually aroused by an immoral woman and dwelling upon its possibilities. This passage dramatizes our Lord's perceptive wisdom in His warning against the sin of lust (Matt. 5:27–28).

Suddenly the young man followed her (7:22). The stupidity and ignorance behind his decision was illustrated by three situations involving animals that were maneuvered or lured into grave danger while unaware of any threat (7:22–23). Similarly the adulterer is unaware that he has foolishly stepped into a trap, which will ruin his reputation and could easily cost him his life.

Even after his narrative with its obvious point, the wise teacher is motivated to warn his readers not to slip into the ways of sexual immorality (7:24–25). Throughout history adultery has been an immensely destructive force. Many people have suffered broken marriages, severed relationships, social and financial ruin, and death as a result of this sin (7:26). Since the same sins and their tragic aftermath reoccur in each generation, these warnings are repeated urgently and often in the Book of Proverbs. For the path of sexual immorality leads to the "chambers of death" (7:27), probably the interiors of tombs, a grisly picture of death. For "grave" and "death," see the comments about "death" in 14:27 and 15:11.

9:13–18"The woman Folly is loud; she is undisciplined and without knowledge. She sits at the door of her house, on a seat at the highest point of the city, calling out to those who pass by, who go straight on their way. 'Let all who are simple come in here!' she says to those who lack judgment. 'Stolen water is sweet; food eaten in secret is delicious!' But little do they know that the dead are there, that her guests are in the depths of the grave."

As wisdom was previously personified, Folly (see "fool," *kᵉsîl* in VF) is personified here as an aggressive adulteress (**9:13–18**). Loud (see the note about 7:11), ignorant (**9:13**), and shameless, she makes herself conspicuous in public places (**9:14**). Attracting their attention (**9:15**), she invites men to join her (**9:16**). It is striking that the invitations of both Wisdom (**9:4**) and Folly (**9:16**), are both addressed to the simple (see VF) who do not know any better and use the same words, just as the vocabulary of love and that of seduction may be identical. She uses the attractive qualities of "sweet" and "delicious" (**9:17**) to embellish her enticing invitation. "Stolen water" and "food eaten in secret" are both metaphors for illicit sex (**9:17**; see 5:15, 20; Song of Songs 4:11–5:1 for similar sexual imagery). Her seductive imagery is designed to emphasize the ecstatic delight of forbidden sexual pleasures. What she neglects to inform the simple who will become her victims is that her invitation involves the grisly prospect of joining the ranks of the dead (**9:18**).

Throughout this entire series of passages the wise teacher vividly contrasts the exciting, exquisite delights of forbidden sexual sin as pictured by the adulteress' seductive talk to its stark realities of unrelieved pain and guilt, irretrievably shattered relationships, broken families, financial ruin, social disgrace, and even premature physical death. The consequences of adultery are horrendous, even before we consider modern data about sexual diseases.

2. Warnings to Avoid the Adulteress

5:7–20 "Now then, my sons, listen to me; do not turn aside from what I say. Keep to a path far from her, do not go near the door of her house, lest you give your best strength to others and your years to one who is cruel, lest strangers feast on your wealth and your toil enrich another man's house. At the end of your life you will groan, when your flesh and body are spent. You will say, 'How I hated discipline! How my heart spurned correction! I would not obey my teachers or listen to my instructors. I have come to the brink of utter ruin in the midst of the whole assembly.' Drink water from your own cistern, running water from your own well. Should your springs overflow in the streets, your streams of water in the public squares? Let them be yours alone, never to be shared with strangers. May your fountain be blessed, and may you rejoice in the wife of your youth. A loving doe, a graceful deer—may her breasts satisfy you always, may you ever be captivated by her love. Why be captivated, my son, by an adulteress? Why embrace the bosom of another man's wife?"

The severe danger of sexual temptation prompted the wise teacher to urge his readers to listen carefully and follow diligently his instructions (**5:7**). The most effective way to prevent sexual temptation is to avoid any person with seductive intentions (**5:8**; see 2 Tim. 2:22), even to the point of avoiding visual contact. A promiscuous man dissipates his energy and makes himself vulnerable to decline and ruin (**5:9**). Whether manipulating him into pampering her with expensive gifts or blackmailing him, the cruel adulteress keeps digging into him until his ruin is complete. She brings him misery and poverty. Whatever income and property he has will benefit someone else, whether the adulteress or strangers who capitalize on his vulnerability (**5:10**).

In **5:11–14**, the wise teacher describes the foolish adulterer's regret at experiencing the miserable consequences of his sin. Perhaps reduced to exhaustion and poverty, his groans (**5:11**) express his anguish and despair. His "spent" body pictures the ruinous depletion of his strength, which results from excessive sexual indulgence and perhaps some form of venereal disease. Profoundly regretting his rejection of discipline and correction (**5:12–13**; see in VWm), he experienced the wages of sin as public shame, disgrace, ruin (**5:14**), and death, perhaps soon to come.

In **5:15–20**, the wise teacher contrasts marital bliss with the wasteful dissipation of promiscuity. Wells and cisterns (**5:15**) were important sources of water in ancient Israel because of limited rainfall, dry seasons, and droughts. Therefore, it was important for each man to have his own cistern or well, which he and his household would use exclusively. "Drinking water" (5:15) is a metaphor for sexual intercourse (see similar imagery in 23:27 and Song of Songs 4:12, 15). For a man to drink water from his own well or cistern is for him to enjoy sexual pleasure and satisfaction from his own wife, which pictures marital faithfulness. To allow his springs to overflow into the streets (5:16) pictures his sexual activities with prostitutes or other loose women. The one is as stupidly wasteful as the other. A man's sexual prowess and its result, children, are to be limited to his wife, not to be shared with other women (5:17).

In 5:18–19, the wise teacher visualizes the sexual joys of marriage by using erotic metaphors also found in the Song of Songs. "Fountain" (5:18; see note about 14:27) is another sexual metaphor that pictures a man's wife as the proper source of his children. The exhortation is for him to enjoy his ecstatic sexual pleasures only with the woman he married as a young man, to find joy and delight exclusively with her.

The affectionate comparison of a man's beloved wife with animals that move easily and gracefully among the high, sometimes steep, slopes of the mountains, occurred often in ancient Oriental poetry (5:19; see Song of Songs 2:9, 17; 4:5; 7:3). Her satisfying breasts are more explicit sexual imagery that picture an abundance of sexual pleasure that completely fulfills his desires. It is most desirable and delightful for a man to be captivated by his wife's love. The word rendered "captivated" pictures being led astray by strong drink (20:1) and by an adulteress (5:20). It describes a man's being so intoxicated or captivated by the adulteress that he cannot control himself. What a beautiful and striking thought in 5:19—a man can be captivated by his beloved wife through the immense power of her sexual attraction for him. Here the word conveys the associated figurative idea of "captivated" entirely apart from its root idea of "go astray." The captivating power and delights of a man's wife are no less than those of the most alluring adulteress and even more satisfying as exquisite expressions of genuine, mutual love.

This treatment of the legitimate sexual pleasures of marriage (**5:15, 18–19**) is an important supplement to the classic picture of the prudent wife (31:10–31), which does not mention her sexual role. Together the two passages beautifully portray a wife's role in marriage.

The answers to the rhetorical questions involving adultery (**5:20**) are obvious. Such a sinful act is a senseless betrayal of a man's wife, who has so much more to give him.

31:1–3 "The sayings of King Lemuel—an oracle his mother taught him: 'O my son, O son of my womb, O son of my vows, do not spend your strength on women, your vigor on those who ruin kings.' "

For "King Lemuel" (**31:1**) and "oracle" (probably here a burden or corrective rebuke), see "authorship" in introduction. Repeatedly emphasizing her concern (**31:2**) for his lifestyle, King Lemuel's mother urged him not to dissipate his strength by sexual overindulgence (**31:3**). She warned that his sexual overindulgence might so reduce his capability that he would lose his credibility as a leader, which would result in the destruction of his authority. Was she reflecting the impact of the earlier treatments of illicit sex in Proverbs (discussed above)?

3. Negative Qualities of an Adulteress

11:22 "Like a gold ring in a pig's snout is a beautiful woman who shows no discretion."

22:14 "The mouth of an adulteress is a deep pit; he who is under the LORD's wrath will fall into it."

23:26–28 "My son, give me your heart and let your eyes keep to my ways, for a prostitute is a deep pit and a wayward wife is a narrow well. Like a bandit she lies in wait, and multiplies the unfaithful among men."

29:3 "A man who loves wisdom brings joy to his father, but a companion of prostitutes squanders his wealth."

30:20 " 'This is the way of an adulteress: She eats and wipes her mouth and says, "I've done nothing wrong." ' "

In **11:22**, the emblematic parallelism (see introduction) uses humor to stress the obvious inappropriateness of sexual immorality. Gold rings in her nose or ears were luxurious ornaments designed to beautify affluent Oriental women in ancient times. A beautiful woman "shows no discretion" when she turns away and deliberately rejects what is right, appropriate, and involves good taste. The exquisite physical beauty of a woman whose uninhibited promiscuity makes her morally hideous is as wasted and useless as a beautiful gold ring decorating a filthy stinking pig.

Apathetic and casual about her sin, an adulterous woman displays her lack of discretion by her astonishing moral insensitivity to feel no sense of wrongdoing or shame (**30:20**). Her eating and wiping her mouth was probably a euphemism for sexual intercourse (see 5:15–16; 9:17 for similar euphemisms).

The "deep pit" (**22:14; 23:27**) was a metaphor for corruption, destruction, irretrievable ruin, and the place of the dead. The three images of the deep pit, narrow well (**23:27**), and bandit (**23:28**) all picture the adulteress or prostitute as lurking to ambush her victim by springing her seductive trap upon him. The adulteress' "mouth" or seductive words (see 2:16; 5:3; 7:5, 14–20) bait a trap, which will ensnare, ruin, and destroy anyone who succumbs to her wiles (**22:14**). Her successes substantially increase the number of men who betray their wives by violating their vows of marital loyalty (**23:28**). Those under the Lord's wrath will be vulnerable to her enticement and to the bitter and disastrous consequences of being caught in her trap (**22:14**). For "adulteress" (**22:14**) and "wayward wife" (**23:27**), see the comments about 2:16.

Constant association with and use of prostitutes is addictive and expensive enough to destroy a man's wealth by dissipating it (**29:3b**). The only return for his "investment" is the fleeting pleasures of sin followed by the permanent, bitter, disastrous consequences of adultery. The dissipation of his wealth reduces him to poverty so that he can no longer afford the prostitutes he doubtless still craves.

B. The Wife

In contrast to the prostitute and adulteress is the moral wife who remains faithful to her husband; however, the wise teacher recognizes that not all marriages are happy and mutually satisfying. Thus, his references to the wife are mixed. The contrast between the quarrelsome and prudent wife make clear the urgency of a man's using great care and discernment to decide whom to marry. Analogous principles also apply to women. The combined characteristics of husband and wife interrelating with each other in a dynamic relationship determine the quality of their marriage.

1. Unbearable Situations

30:21–23 "Under three things the earth trembles, under four it cannot bear up: a servant who becomes king, a fool who is full of food, an unloved woman who is married, and a maidservant who displaces her mistress.'"

For "three" and "four," see "Numerical Sayings" in the introduction. The "earth" (**30:21**) is personified to picture human reactions. The "trembling" may be a hyperbole, to emphasize its point by exaggerating the intensity of the reaction. "Cannot bear up" is to find a situation intolerable. Four unbearable examples include (1) a servant who becomes king and abuses his authority; (2) a stuffed fool (*nābāl*, see VF) who is arrogant and offensive; (3) an unloved wife who is frustrated and miserable; (4) a female slave who replaces her mistress and abuses her authority.

2. A Quarrelsome Wife

19:13 "A foolish son is his father's ruin, and a quarrelsome wife is like a constant dripping."

21:9 "Better to live on a corner of the roof than share a house with a quarrelsome wife."

21:19 "Better to live in a desert than with a quarrelsome and ill-tempered wife."

25:24 "Better to live on a corner of the roof than share a house with a quarrelsome wife."

27:15–16 "A quarrelsome wife is like a constant dripping on a rainy day; restraining her is like restraining the wind or grasping oil with the hand."

All five texts use the same words to refer to the "quarrelsome wife." The word rendered "quarrelsome" also means "dissension," "conflict," and probably includes the perpetual nagging, which makes a marriage miserable. In their commentaries, Toy and Kidner mention an old Arab proverb: "Three things make a house intolerable: *tak* (the leaking through of rain), *nak* (a wife's nagging), and *bak* (bugs)."¹

These texts picture an incessantly nagging and argumentative wife as worse than several irritating situations. One such situation is a constant dripping of water, perhaps leaking through the roof on a rainy day or night (19:13b; 27:15). Restraining her is like quieting a howling wind or grasping vegetable oil in your hand (27:16). No matter what you do. the wind blows and the oil slips out, just like her unceasing torrent of nagging words.

In 21:9 and in the virtually identical 25:24, the comparative image is "a corner on the roof." Whether that means the flat roof with its exposure to hot sun and rain, a cramped attic, or a compact guest room nestled against the roof, it is an intolerable situation for a man to endure in his own house. Yet even that degree of isolation and discomfort is preferable to incessant nagging. The next step is to move away to the desert (21:19). To live in the desert is to experience hardship, discomfort, and loneliness in a desolate, uninhabited area. Each of these difficult situations offers two things that he will not experience while living with a quarrelsome and nagging wife—peace and quiet. That makes it worthwhile.

3. Noble Character; Disgraceful Character

12:4 "A wife of noble character is her husband's crown, but a disgraceful wife is like decay in his bones."

The word rendered "noble character" pictures a person with strength, courage, integrity, ability, and competence. Such a wife strengthens her husband's social status, helps and motivates him to achieve his goals, and is delighted for him to be respected, honored, and loved. The man who finds and marries a woman like this has been immensely favored and blessed by the Lord who brought her to him (18:22; 19:14).

In the Book of Proverbs, the word rendered "disgraceful" pictures the public shame brought upon an individual's spouse

---

[1] C. H. Toy, *A Critical and Exegetical Commentary of the Book of Proverbs* (Philadelphia: T & T Clark, 1899), 373; Derek Kidner, *The Proverbs* (Wheaton: Tyndale, 1964), 133. See also Franz Delitzsch, *Biblical Commentary on the Proverbs of Solomon* (Grand Rapids: Eerdmans, reprint of 1872 ed.), 2:27.

or parents as a result of his or her imprudent or immoral behavior. Actions by a wife that produce such disgrace include her nagging, quarreling, and marital unfaithfulness. Such a woman is like rot or decay in his bones (see the comment about 14:30). She is an annoying irritant that keeps gnawing away at a man's strength, marital happiness, morale, and even the quality of his life until all these are gone.

4. Beautiful Qualities of a Prudent Wife

31:10–31 "A wife of noble character who can find? She is worth far more than rubies. Her husband has full confidence in her and lacks nothing of value. She brings him good, not harm, all the days of her life. She selects wool and flax and works with eager hands. She is like the merchant ships, bringing her food from afar. She gets up while it is still dark; she provides food for her family and portions for her servant girls. She considers a field and buys it; out of her earnings she plants a vineyard. She sets about her work vigorously; her arms are strong for her tasks. She sees that her trading is profitable, and her lamp does not go out at night. In her hand she holds the distaff and grasps the spindle with her fingers. She opens her arms to the poor and extends her hands to the needy. When it snows, she has no fear for her household; for all of them are clothed in scarlet. She makes coverings for her bed; she is clothed in fine linen and purple. Her husband is respected at the city gate, where he takes his seat among the elders of the land. She makes linen garments and sells them, and supplies the merchants with sashes. She is clothed with strength and dignity; she can laugh at the days to come. She speaks with wisdom, and faithful instruction is on her tongue. She watches over the affairs of her household and does not eat the bread of idleness. Her children arise and call her blessed; her husband also, and he praises her: 'Many women do noble things, but you surpass them all.' Charm is deceptive, and beauty is fleeting; but a woman who fears the LORD is to be praised. Give her the reward she has earned, and let her works bring her praise at the city gate."

This classic poem about the wealthy prudent wife is an acrostic (see introduction). To maintain the acrostic structure, the poem moves at random from one topic to another with some repetition. This positive, appreciative picture more than offsets the negative two-liners about the quarrelsome wife.

For "noble character" in **31:10**, see the note about **12:4**. A woman with such exceptional wisdom, prudence, competence, endurance, strength, motivation, leadership, and loyalty is an extremely rare individual. Her value is immeasurable, greater than rubies. Her husband's confidence in her competence and reliability to handle what he delegates to her frees him to take on other responsibilities (**31:11**). Her business skills and prudent management generate enough income that he acquires what he wants. Her lifelong pattern is to bring good (see in VR) in all of its many connotations to her husband (**31:12**). She avoids harming (see "evil" under VWs) him. She carefully selects materials of high quality and enthusiastically works to make clothes for her family (**31:13**).

Like the merchant ships (**31:14**), she learns where to do her selling, trading, and buying for maximum profitability, quality, and economy. Then she carefully organizes her business and marketing trips. Lacking modern refrigeration and canning techniques, the responsibility for obtaining, preparing, and cooking food is an ongoing, daily task. Both a hard worker and an efficient administrator, the prudent wife gets up before sunrise to prepare food for her household and perhaps to organize and assign work to her servant girls (**31:15**).

Astute in real estate, she invests some of her earnings to buy a field and plants a vineyard on it (**31:16**). Grapes and wine were staples in ancient Israel, especially with water erratic in both quantity and quality. She works vigorously (**31:17**), possessing sufficient strength, energy, and endurance to handle her rigorous work. Astute in both buying and selling, her business transactions (**31:18**) are regularly profitable (see "good" in VR).

The reference to her lamp's not going out (**31:18**) has often been interpreted to picture her continuous hard work, even into the late night hours. Being wise, however, she is unlikely to cause premature burnout by starting her day's work well before sunrise and continuing it late at night. More likely it referred to her tending to her lamp at night. The ordinary lamp used in homes in OT times was a small bowl containing oil and a wick to be lit. It held enough oil to burn all night, but the wick had to be adjusted periodically. The prudent wife will get up once or twice during the night to take care of the wick to keep it going.[2] By doing this she has a flame to start her fire in the morning. For the lamp to go out was considered a sign of tragedy or extreme poverty.[3]

Although the words rendered "distaff" and "spindle" (**31:19**) are obscure, they evidently refer to equipment used by the prudent wife to make clothes for her family and perhaps also for the poor (**31:20**). She made scarlet clothes that protected her family from freezing weather (**31:21**). Her "coverings" (**31:22**) were probably spreads or quilts. The scarlet, fine linen (from Egypt), and purple (probably colored by a dye from Canaan or Phoenicia) were expensive materials of top quality (**31:21-22**). Clothing made from them was thus a sign of affluence. These products displayed her skill as a designer and weaver.

Her husband is respected (literally, "known") by the community leaders who assembled near the city gate (**31:23**). The prudent wife's competence, wisdom, and productivity frees her husband to become a community leader, even part of the city council.

The prudent wife's making and selling (**31:24**) attractive and fashionable clothing geared for the affluent market doubtless produces a healthy income supplement. The "linen garments" may have been some sort of outer garment or nightgown for women. The "sash" was an expensive ornamental belt or sash. The clothes-making prudent wife is herself "clothed with strength and dignity" (**31:25**). With several ways to produce income and substantial financial reserves, she has no worries about her temporal future. The principles of wisdom (see the note in VWm) saturate her conversations (**31:26**). As a capable administrator, she alertly observes and efficiently supervises the activities of her household (**31:27**).

Naturally the prudent wife's family appreciates and praises her (**31:28**). Her husband considers her an achiever superior to even those women who do noble (see the note about 12:4) deeds

---

[2] J. Rea, "Lamp," *The Zondervan Pictorial Encyclopedia of the Bible*, edited by M. C. Tenney, et al., (Grand Rapids: Zondervan, 1975), 3:866.

[3] A Cohen, *Proverbs* (New York: Bloch Publishing Company, Soncino Press, 1952), 213.

(31:29). For most men, their first impression of a woman is her "charm and beauty" (31:30) or physical attractiveness. Yet this is deceptive, providing no reliable information as to what she is like. Physical beauty is "fleeting" because it is only transitory. It has little connection with capability or happiness. Of far greater value and significance is a woman's "fear of the LORD" (see the comment about 1:7), which expresses her spiritual commitment. A spiritual woman has an inner beauty that does not fade as her age increases. For her many achievements and remarkable character, the prudent wife clearly deserves her reward and praise (31:31).

5. Amazing Romantic Love

30:18–19 "'There are three things that are too amazing for me, four that I do not understand: the way of an eagle in the sky, the way of a snake on a rock, the way of a ship on the high seas, and the way of a man with a maiden.'"

For "three" and "four" (30:18), see "Numerical Sayings" in the introduction. The word rendered "amazing" means "wonderful," "incomprehensible"—an apt description of God's providential care. The examples cited (30:19) are (1) the ability of a large eagle to fly high; (2) the maneuverability of a slithering snake; (3) the qualities of water that enable a ship to move through it; and (4) the beautiful maneuvers of a young couple in love. The word rendered "maiden" pictures a young woman of marriageable age and includes the gamit from courtship to sexual intimacy, presumably in marriage.

C. Family Relationships and Practices

1. General Observations

a. A Man Who Strays from Home Is Lost. 27:8 "Like a bird that strays from its nest is a man who strays from his home."

Straying or aimlessly wandering away from home, abandoning helpless dependents, is tragic, whether by a mother bird or human father. By rejecting his family, a man both fails to fulfill his responsibility to them and deprives himself of his strongest source of social and emotional support.

b. A Man Who Troubles His Family Forfeits His Future.

11:29 "He who brings trouble on his family will inherit only wind, and the fool will be servant to the wise."

15:27 "A greedy man brings trouble to his family, but he who hates bribes will live."

17:2 "A wise servant will rule over a disgraceful son, and will share the inheritance as one of the brothers."

In **15:27a**, the word rendered "greedy" pictures one who "cuts off what is not one's own" or "rips off" someone else. The trouble brought by a greedy man upon his family (**11:29; 15:27**) involves many forms, such as his misappropriating family resources to fulfill his selfish desires by dishonest "get-rich-quick" schemes, bribes, and unscrupulous business deals. It includes his depriving them of food, clothes, love, and recreation together. By troubling his family, a man deprives himself of the loving family relationships that make life rich, happy, and satisfying. Through his efforts to satisfy his greed, he will inherit wind (**11:29**), that is, come up empty and have nothing. The foolish man who destroys his relationships and dissipates his resources will eventually serve the wise man who develops friendly relationships and builds up his resources (**11:29**).

A wise servant might be valuable enough to deserve authority over a son involved in scandal (for "disgraceful," see the comment about 12:4), or even to share the family inheritance (**17:2**). Yet there is no provision in the law of Moses for such developments (see Num. 27:8–11 and Deut. 21:15–17 for the usual procedures). There is limited evidence that a slave could or did obtain his master's estate or part of it under special circumstances (e.g., Gen. 15:2–3; 2 Sam. 16:1–4; 1 Chron. 2:34–35). The OT data are too limited to provide a complete picture of inheritance procedures with regard to slaves.

c. There Is Misery in Family Hostilities.

15:17 "Better a meal of vegetables where there is love than a fattened calf with hatred."

17:1 "Better a dry crust with peace and quiet than a house full of feasting with strife."

Both proverbs are saying that who you eat with is more important than how delicious your food is. An atmosphere of love, friendship, and harmony can make a portion of greens (more accurate than NIV "vegetables" in **15:17**) or a piece of dry, stale bread (**17:1**) enjoyable and satisfying. In contrast to this minimal meal for the poor is the juicy, tender sirloin steaks from the fattened calf (**15:17**) or from the substantial remains of a peace offering that was followed by feasting (**17:1**), since the ancients had no way to preserve the meat. Yet even such sumptuous eating, regularly affordable only by the rich, can be ruined by an atmosphere of hostility and conflict.

d. There Is Glory in Youth, Respect in Age. 20:29 "The glory of young men is their strength, gray hair the splendor of the old."

Young men are often proud of their physical strength. Gray hair, usually a sign of old age, indicates survival. It is also a sign of honor if a man has acquired maturity and wisdom that make him a valued citizen, if not a leader. Even when retired, wise old men are still excellent advisers.

2. *Children*

The Value of Training Children. 22:6 "Train a child in the way he should go, and when he is old he will not turn from it."

The word rendered "train" means "inaugurate," "begin," "start." (Its cognate noun is *Ḥanukkah*, the name of a Jewish feast.) Starting a child in the right direction as perceived by mature parental judgment involves parental teaching and guidance. No methods or content of the beginning training are specified; rather, it is implied to teach whatever he needs to know to function effectively in life. The training may include first steps in fearing the Lord, in developing wisdom, in learning what is right and what is wrong, in acquiring good manners and learning to relate to people, in building confidence, and in developing a good positive attitude. The training should begin right after birth, even before a baby learns to talk. Learning patterns may be developed very early and more advanced levels of this training added as the baby grows from infancy through childhood and adolescence into adulthood.

The idea is that if you mold a child rightly, he will not deviate from that way for the rest of his life. Like many proverbs, this is a general principle that is true in the vast bulk of cases, but it should not be pressed as an absolute truth with no exceptions. Generally children do reflect their upbringing.

b. The Importance of Disciplining Children. 13:24 "He who spares the rod hates his son, but he who loves him is careful to discipline him."

19:18 "Discipline your son, for in that there is hope; do not be a willing party to his death."

22:15 "Folly is bound up in the heart of a child, but the rod of discipline will drive it far from him."

23:13–14 "Do not withhold discipline from a child; if you punish him with the rod, he will not die. Punish him with the rod and save his soul from death."

29:15 "The rod of correction imparts wisdom, but a child left to himself disgraces his mother."

29:17 "Discipline your son, and he will give you peace; he will bring delight to your soul."

Children have a natural attraction to foolishness. For their folly has been tightly bound to them and is becoming part of them (**22:15**). They are not wise enough to avoid their sinful and foolish inclinations. Training and the drastic means of physical punishment are needed to drive their folly from them (**22:15**) and to impart the wisdom (see 20:30) needed to enable them to avoid the traps and unnecessary troubles that they will otherwise encounter (**29:15**). Proper disciplinary physical punishment will not kill a child (**23:13**). Rather, its unpleasantness and pain will teach him a lesson that will prevent future beatings and save his life (**23:14**; for "soul," see the comment about "zeal" in 19:2). This text does not convey the idea of a later evangelistic expression, but describes the deliverance of the child from a premature death. Physical discipline provides a confident hope for the child to avoid a foolish premature death (**19:18**).

Discipline expresses parents' love for their child by showing that they care enough to take an unpleasant action (**13:24**). They are following the Lord's example (3:12; see Heb. 12:5–11). A properly disciplined son will give his parents peace and delight (**29:17**) because they will have no anxieties concerning him.

A child "left to himself" ("let loose") is unrestrained

because of his lack of discipline (**29:15**). He will become increasingly sinful and foolish to the point of bringing public shame upon his parents and making probable his premature death (**19:18**). A parent's apathetic inaction with regard to physical punishment expresses his hatred (**13:24**) by his willingness for his child to die prematurely (**19:18**).

c. **Relationships Between Generations.** 17:6 "Children's children are a crown to the aged, and parents are the pride of their children."

Implicit behind this beautiful closing of the "generation gap" is the development of wisdom by parents who, in turn, impart it to their children who, likewise, continue the process. Through deliberate cultivation of family relationships, these children honor their parents, whom they find beautiful, and delight their grandparents.

3. **The Importance of Disciplining Servants.** 29:19 "A servant cannot be corrected by mere words; though he understands, he will not respond."

29:21 "If a man pampers his servant from youth, he will bring grief in the end."

Ineffective ways of handling slaves were pampering (indulging) a slave who was growing up in his household (**29:21**) and using only verbal rebukes to correct (see "discipline" in VWm) the unresponsive slaves (**29:19**). Undisciplined slaves caused grief (**29:21**), probably resulting from their incompetence and lack of discipline. Implicit was the need for disciplinary physical punishment to teach a slave his place and his responsibility to do his work. Yet the Law required that the punishment not inflict permanent physical damage (Exod. 21:20, 26–27). These principles helped people to function effectively within an already existing system of slavery, which the wise teacher did not question.

D. **Friends**

1. **Unfriendliness Is Selfish and Unsound.** 18:1 "An unfriendly man pursues selfish ends; he defies all sound judgment." The word rendered "unfriendly" means "separated." It pictures someone who is unsociable, who does not get along with others and prefers to go his own way because he is

interested primarily in his selfish interests and desires. Apathetic toward the interests of others and even toward those of his community, he does not hesitate to disregard their interests, ignore their standards, and argue about both. This attitude lacks "sound judgment" (common sense).

2. A Friend Is Faithful.

17:17 "A friend loves at all times, and a brother is born for adversity."

18:24 "A man of many companions may come to ruin, but there is a friend who sticks closer than a brother."

20:6 "Many a man claims to have unfailing love, but a faithful man who can find?"

27:6 "Wounds from a friend can be trusted, but an enemy multiplies kisses."

In **20:6**, there is a contrast between the frequency of talk about loyalty and love (see the comment about 16:6) and the scarcity of faithfulness expressed when needed.

In **27:6**, the words rendered "enemy" and "friend" mean "one who hates" and "one who loves" respectively. Numerous expressions of affection and friendship by an enemy are insincere, worthless, and perhaps treacherous (e.g., those of Judas Iscariot). In contrast, a friend's corrective rebuke, however painful, expresses his loyalty, concern, and desire for our welfare.

To have many unreliable companions (**18:24**) may bring about our ruin. Genuine friendship is a stable relationship that is not altered by changing circumstances (**17:17**). A true friend, like a brother who is unquestionably loyal and reliable, is there to help you or encourage you when you need him (**18:24**), especially during adversity (**17:17**).

3. Do Not Forsake Your Friend.

27:10 "Do not forsake your friend and the friend of your father, and do not go to your brother's house when disaster strikes you—better a neighbor nearby than a brother far away."

We should never abandon genuine friends, especially family friends in long, durable relationships. When struck by disaster, we should go to a neighbor-friend's house. For a neighbor is in a far better position to be helpful than the most cordial and beneficent brother who lives several hours away and is virtually inaccessible. This is consistent with 17:17, which advocates a brother's help. For neither text covers all variables, such as timing and the nature of the relationship. There are some brothers to go to and others to avoid, some times to approach a brother and other times to leave him alone. The same is true for our neighbors.

4. Love Covers Wrongs.

10:12 "Hatred stirs up dissension, but love covers over all wrongs."

17:9 "He who covers over an offense promotes love, but whoever repeats the matter separates close friends."

27:5 "Better is open rebuke than hidden love."

An atmosphere of hatred incites quarreling (**10:12a**). In contrast is the love that overlooks, ignores, and forgives the wrongs done to people (**10:12b**). Peter quoted **10:12b** (1 Peter 4:8), and Paul may have alluded to it (1 Cor. 13:5) in his teachings about love. The statements in **10:12b** and **17:9a** picture interrelated qualities of love and the covering or forgiving of sins as expressing and promoting each other.

By constantly dwelling upon and repeating (**17:9b**) such negative matters as points of contention, unpleasant disagreements, and hostile confrontations, even close friends may be sufficiently alienated to damage permanently their relationship. This kind of behavior can ruin a good marriage as easily as a close friendship.

The idea in **27:5** balances the other two texts. It is sometimes necessary to rebuke a loved one. To speak frankly and tactfully about a matter is a beneficial expression of love in spite of temporary pain (see 28:23). To say nothing when we should because we are afraid of hurting another's feelings or arousing his anger is to hide our love by not expressing it. It is to let another's wrongs cover our love rather than having our love cover their wrongs.

E. Neighbor

1. Do Not Visit Your Neighbor Too Often.

25:17 "Seldom set foot in your neighbor's house—too much of you, and he will hate you."

Occasional visits with a neighbor are valuable and pleasant. Overdoing it decreases the value and pleasure of each visit. Eventually they become tiresome, and even a nuisance. Without some relief, a man's neighbor may not want to see him at all. When his attitude has deteriorated to hate, there is no more friendship or neighborliness between them.

2. Do Not Put Off Your Neighbor.

3:27-28 "Do not withhold good from those who deserve it, when it is in your power to act. Do not say to your neighbor, 'Come back later; I'll give it tomorrow'—when you now have it with you."

Being ready and eager to provide prompt help whenever needed is part of what is involved in being a good neighbor or friend (3:27). Available aid is not to be postponed (3:28). Procrastination is the first step in avoiding your responsibility. A little help given when urgently needed is far more valuable and appreciated than much help given later.

3. Sharpen One Another.

27:17 "As iron sharpens iron, so one man sharpens another."

This text presents an analogy between metallic and human sharpening. Metal is usually the means of sharpening the cutting edges of tools and weapons. Similarly, people sharpen each other and rise to new levels of competence and performance by means of friendly competition, mutual encouragement, and sharing ideas and methods.

F. Kindness or Ruthlessness

1. Kindness Brings Respect; Ruthlessness, Only Wealth.

11:16 "A kindhearted woman gains respect, but ruthless men gain only wealth."

The word rendered "kindhearted" pictures a woman's

charming, gracious personality that causes her to be highly regarded. A man who exerts his power to produce terror is likely to inflict cruel oppression. Although he may succeed in becoming financially rich, he lacks the richness of respect, honor, and love.

2. Kindness Is Beneficial; Cruelty, Harmful.

11:17 "A kind man benefits himself, but a cruel man brings trouble on himself."

A kind man who treats others graciously generates good will that will be benefical to him (see Isa. 58:10–11; Luke 6:38). In contrast, a harsh man who harms and troubles others generates ill will that will bring harm and trouble to him.

3. Kindness to the Needy Is Blessed; Hatred Is Sinful.

14:21 "He who despises his neighbor sins, but blessed is he who is kind to the needy."

Hostility against neighbor or friend is sinful, especially if that person has needs (see 14:31; 17:5). Refusal to help a needy neighbor is equivalent to a hostile act.

To be "kind" to the needy is to "be gracious," "act favorably" toward them. The parallelism of the text suggests that "neighbor" and "needy" are similar, if not equivalent terms here. This suggests the broad interpretation of neighbor as anyone in need, as Jesus developed it in His parable of the Good Samaritan (Luke 10:25–37; see also also Prov. 19:17; Lev. 19:18).

G. Encouragement; Discouragement

1. Joy; Bitterness

14:10 "Each heart knows its own bitterness, and no one else can share its joy."

No one completely understands how another feels, either positively or negatively. Both bitterness and joy are very private experiences. No one else perceives fully either the impact of what produces these emotions or the intensity and depth of the feelings produced.

2. Deceptive Appearances

14:13 "Even in laughter the heart may ache, and joy may end in grief."

These synonymous parallel lines both state that outward appearances do not necessarily indicate accurately our inner realities. Laughter may cover up an inner ache that may never be expressed. With life's uncertainties happiness may be followed by grievous tragedy. The words rendered "ache" (see "crushes" in 15:13 and 17:22) and "grief" usually picture mental and emotional anguish and sorrow that may not be separable from physical pain.

3. Expressive Appearances

15:13 "A happy heart makes the face cheerful, but heartache crushes the spirit."

27:19 "As water reflects a face, so a man's heart reflects the man."

As water reflects a man's face, his facial expressions and outward bearing reflect his attitude, whether joyful or sad (**15:13; 27:19**). A happy attitude gives extra bounce and vitality. Heartache (**15:13**) "crushes the spirit." It destroys morale, and shatters self-confidence and motivation, making energetic, successful action impossible (see the comment about 17:22). Therefore, to an extent, we can "read" each other.

These texts with 14:13 state valid general principles that convey different aspects of people's understanding each other. However, inner attitudes may be expressed (**15:13; 27:19**) or concealed (**14:13**). Thus, these texts are not contradictory since each covers only part of the total picture.

4. Good Attitude; Poor Attitude

14:30 "A heart at peace gives life to the body, but envy rots the bones."

17:22 "A cheerful heart is good medicine, but a crushed spirit dries up the bones."

18:14 "A man's spirit sustains him in sickness, but a crushed spirit who can bear?"

In these texts "heart," "body," "bones," and "spirit" all

designate the entire person. These psychosomatic texts picture the effects of attitudes upon mental, emotional, and physical health.

A peaceful, healthy person is full of vitality and energy (**14:30**). His cheerful, happy attitude improves and strengthens his mental, emotional, and physical health (**17:22**). Good morale helps to overcome physical disease (**18:14**), even to the point of living and working productively in spite of it. A spirited man has the will and determination to live, be healthy, and be successful.

The rotting (14:30) effect of envy (see the comments about 3:31) pictures an inevitable, ongoing decay, like a cancer. It produces miserable physical health and decaying emotional health. If prolonged, it can be so destructive as to render a person ineffective. A person with a crushed or broken spirit (**17:22; 18:14;** see the comment about 15:13) is depressed, despondent, demoralized, functionally paralyzed, stripped of positive desires, and burdensome to be around. Shattered morale "dries up the bones" (**17:22**), not "making them fat" or prospering (**28:25; 15:30**). It produces deteriorating mental, emotional, and physical health.

5. Fulfilled Desires; Deferred Desires

13:12 "Hope deferred makes the heart sick, but a longing fulfilled is a tree of life."

To put off something indefinitely that has been eagerly anticipated is discouraging, frustrating, depressing, and even sickening. To experience the fulfillment of a strong desire is delightfully satisfying, invigorating, and exhilarating. For "longing" and "tree of life," see the comments about 13:19 and 3:18.

6. Kind Words; Anxious Hearts

12:25 "An anxious heart weighs a man down, but a kind word cheers him up."

Anxiety is an emotional condition that distracts from our concentration and hinders our effectiveness. Like a heavy burden, it weighs a man down, slows his pace, exhausts his strength, and destroys the quality of his life. A friendly, encouraging word, especially during a difficult time, brings joy that helps to relieve the burden.

7. Cheerfulness; Oppression

15:15 "All the days of the oppressed are wretched, but the cheerful heart has a continual feast."

15:30 "A cheerful look brings joy to the heart, and good news gives health to the bones."

25:13 "Like the coolness of snow at harvest time is a trustworthy messenger to those who send him; he refreshes the spirit of his masters."

25:25 "Like cold water to a weary soul is good news from a distant land."

The word rendered "oppressed" (**15:15**) often refers to the poor who are financially pressed, socially defenseless, vulnerable to oppression, and often in distress. Throughout their wretched lives, they suffer in misery under the endless grind of struggling desperately just to survive.

A cheerful (see "good" in VR) person continually enjoys his life as much as he does a special banquet (**15:15**) in virtually all circumstances. His cheerful disposition and positive attitude determine the quality of his experience. He is happy because he has decided to be happy, no matter what happens. A "cheerful look" (**15:30a**) is the meaning of the words rendered literally, "the light of the eyes," which picture the sparkling eyes and radiant expression that convey good will. It quickly warms the social atmosphere.

Snow (**25:13**) during a June harvest in Israel was virtually impossible. More likely, the "snow" was the cold water from the melting snows in the mountains of Lebanon. Just as refreshing as cold water on a hot day to an exhausted thirsty man is a reliable messenger to his masters (**25:13**) or the hearing of good news, especially from a distant place from which news is not often heard (**25:25**). The psychological impact of good news is also described in physical imagery (**15:30b**). It strengthens our mental, emotional, and physical health. For "health" (literally "fat"), see the comment about "prosper" in 28:25 and its opposite image in 17:22.

H. Conversation

1. Human Words Are Deep Waters.

18:4 "The words of a man's mouth are deep waters, but the fountain of wisdom is a bubbling brook."

20:5 "The purposes of a man's heart are deep waters, but a man of understanding draws them out."

For "wisdom" and "understanding," see VWm.

The key to understanding these difficult texts is to explain the enigmatic metaphor "deep waters." The word rendered "deep" pictures profound thoughts (Ps. 92:5), cunning plots (Ps. 64:6), the obscure speech of a foreign language (Ezek. 3:5–6), the depths of sin (Hos. 9:9), and the grave (Job 11:8).

Biblical metaphors involving water are amazingly varied. They picture the Lord as a spring of living water (Jer. 17:13) and as the wells of salvation (Isa. 12:2–3). Constantly flowing streams provide nourishment and growth (Ezek. 31:1–5). Drinking poisoned water (Jer. 9:15) portrays the suffering involved in the waters of affliction (Isa. 30:20). Water that wears away stones (Job 14:19), a driving rain (Isa. 28:2), and the roar of rushing waters (Ezek. 43:2) display great power. The flooding of mighty waters pictures trouble, destruction, and death. The overwhelmed victims who "passed through the waters" (Isa. 43:2), engulfed by them, experienced terror (Job 22:10–11) and despair (Ps. 88:15–18) that made them feel "poured out like water" (Ps 22:14–16). Loss of confidence and morale make people as weak as water (Ezek. 7:17). Elsewhere "deep waters" picture danger (2 Sam. 22:17–18; Ps. 18:16–17) and severe distress from discouragement and even depression (Ps. 69:1–3, 14–15).

In **18:4** and **20:5**, "deep waters" may describe profound thought or what is too deep to grasp, but is not limited to either. "Deep waters" pictures the total range of thoughts, attitudes, feelings, plans, and decisions that combine in many complex ways to characterize the ordinary human mind. Old Testament references to "deep" and "water" suggest that these include profundity, encouragement, happiness, sex, obscurity, cunning, sin, weakness, restlessness, anger, terror, loss of confidence and morale, suffering, affliction, distress, discouragement, and depression. "Deep waters" is a voluminous and flexible enough metaphor to cover these elements and more.

A person expresses the "deep waters" within himself (see the comment about "heart" in 4:23) by his speech (**18:4**). Nevertheless, it requires discernment to draw out these "deep waters" (**20:5**), to ascertain the information needed, perhaps for counseling.

For "fountain" (**18:4**), see the comments about 14:27. The "bubbling brook" (**18:4**) pictures a steadily flowing stream that provides clear and abundant water. Here it is a metaphor for the steady and rich flow of wisdom from its source, which is in contrast to the "deep waters" of the human mind.

2. *The Wise Limit What They Say; the Foolish Talk Too Much.*

10:19 "When words are many, sin is not absent, but he who holds his tongue is wise."

11:12 "A man who lacks judgment derides his neighbor, but a man of understanding holds his tongue."

17:27 "A man of knowledge uses words with restraint, and a man of understanding is even-tempered."

17:28 "Even a fool is thought wise if he keeps silent, and discerning if he holds his tongue."

These texts commend controlling our talk and condemn excessive talk. Talking too much involves sin (**10:19**; see "transgression" under VWs), perhaps the implicit self-exaltation of the speaker. It may also include the lack of judgment (or mind; see the comment about "heart" in 4:23) involved in deriding our neighbors (**11:12**). Such a foolish practice presumptuously involves a judgmental role that belongs only to God, ultimately disrupts harmonious relationships, and may provoke hostilities that benefit no one.

The wise man "holds his tongue" (**10:19**), thereby restraining (**17:27**) and controlling his talk. He is "even-tempered" (**17:27**), literally "cool of spirit," that is, keeping calm, maintaining composure under pressure, having self-control. This enables him to listen, learn, evaluate, and ascertain the best time for him to speak with maximum impact, since people are often more receptive on some occasions than others. Another word rendered "holds his tongue" (**11:12**) means to "keep silent" (**17:28**), to "say nothing." If you cannot say something that is positive, helpful, constructive, encouraging, then it is better to say nothing. A third word rendered "holds his tongue" (**17:28**) means literally to "shut up." Then, even a fool may conceal his stupidity and convey the impression of having some discernment (**17:28**).

3. *A Wise Man's Conversation Increases Knowledge; a Foolish Man's Talk Gushes Folly and Evil.*

10:31 "The mouth of the righteous brings forth wisdom, but a perverse tongue will be cut out."

15:2 "The tongue of the wise commends knowledge, but the mouth of the fool gushes folly."

15:7 "The lips of the wise spread knowledge; not so the hearts of fools."

15:28 "The heart of the righteous weighs its answers, but the mouth of the wicked gushes evil."

16:23 "A wise man's heart guides his mouth, and his lips promote instruction."

18:13 "He who answers before listening—that is his folly and his shame."

29:20 "Do you see a man who speaks in haste? There is more hope for a fool than for him."

Four texts (**10:31; 15: 2, 7, 28**) use antithetic parallelisms (see introduction) to contrast wise and foolish, righteous and wicked.

It is foolish and shameful to answer without listening (**18:13**). Your irrelevant reply will make clear your inattention, which displays your apathetic, impolite, and insulting manner.

A man who rushes to speak (**29:20**), without wisely thinking through his response, is worse off than one who lacks wisdom. Even a fool may learn enough to begin to control what he says, but hasty, thoughtless talk nullifies wisdom by neglecting it. The result is rash talk, which may be malicious, offensive, harmful, foolish, and boring. Identical are **29:20b** and 26:12b.

There is no way for fools to convey knowledge that they lack (**15:7**), since fools gush folly (**15:2**) as the wicked gush evil (**15:28**). The word rendered "gush" pictures an uncontrolled pouring or flooding, here a torrent of words either from a fool who lacks the sense to remain silent when he has nothing to contribute, or from a wicked person who refuses to shut up even when his comments are vicious and offensive. The perverse tongue will be cut off (**10:31**), either by physical removal or death.

The moral quality of wisdom is clear when the righteous are described as acting wisely (**10:31; 15:28**). Several parts of the body (tongue, lips, mouth, heart) picture the functioning of the entire person (**10:31; 15:2, 7, 28; 16:23**).

Positive input into the mind produces positive output (**16:23**). By constantly absorbing wisdom, the wise man's conversations reflect its insights. He thereby promotes (literally, "increases") instruction by helping others to learn.

The righteous man "weighs" his answers (**15:28**), that is, he carefully thinks through what he is going to say before he speaks to make his comments intelligent, perceptive, and constructive. The wise and righteous share their wisdom. To "bring forth" (**10:31**) is to bear fruit. Like a plant, the righteous man grows and produces the fruit of wisdom in his conversation. To "commend" (**15:2**) is to do well in using and sharing knowledge skillfully and attractively. The wise "spread" knowledge (**15:7**; see 10:13a); they disperse what they know by what they say.

4. The Wise Speak What Is Fitting; the Foolish, What Is Perverse.

4:24 "Put away perversity from your mouth; keep corrupt talk far from your lips."

10:32 "The lips of the righteous know what is fitting, but the mouth of the wicked only what is perverse."

By means of their wisdom, the righteous know what is fitting (**10:32**), that is, acceptable, regarded favorably. They develop their conversation accordingly and exclude the wicked's perverse talk, which is to be eliminated (**4:24**). For "perversity" and "perverse," see VWs. For "corrupt," see "devious" in 14:2. When they permanently remove perverted conversation from their presence, the righteous prevent its infiltration into their lives again. This means that we should not only eliminate our own perverse talk, but also remove ourselves from the presence of any people engaged in such degrading talk. Conversation reveals what we are like.

HUMAN RELATIONSHIPS

5. Wise Conversation Is Valuable; Wicked Talk Is Not.

10:20 "The tongue of the righteous is choice silver, but the heart of the wicked is of little value."

"Choice silver" has been refined, carefully examined, and found to be pure. Righteous speech, like choice silver, has exquisite value because it is beautiful, beneficial, and extremely rare. In contrast, the wicked mentality is so undesirable, harmful, common, and easily available that it has no value at all.

6. Apt Words Are Delightful.

15:23 "A man finds joy in giving an apt reply—and how good is a timely word!"

25:11 "A word aptly spoken is like apples of gold in settings of silver."

The "word aptly spoken" (**25:11**), "apt reply," and "timely word" (**15:23**) describe what is said as well-conceived, appropriate, perceptive, apt, and timed well. To give such an answer or statement is most satisfying. The simile in **25:11** pictures an exquisite, beautiful, delightful object; however, it is not clear whether it uses imagery of precious metals to picture the beauty of colorful fruit or the imagery of fruit to picture an exquisite gold and silver ornament.

7. Gracious, Gentle Speech Is Powerful and Influential.

15:1 "A gentle answer turns away wrath, but a harsh word stirs up anger."

22:11 "He who loves a pure heart and whose speech is gracious will have the king for his friend."

25:15 "Through patience a ruler can be persuaded, and a gentle tongue can break a bone."

A "pure heart" (**22:11**; see the comment about 4:23) pictures someone whose mind is spiritually and morally clean. His gracious speech is tactful, sensitive, and likely to evoke a favorable response. For "patience" in **25:15**, see the comment about 14:29. Patient persistence accomplishes wonders, even with rulers.

The word rendered "wrath" (**15:1**) pictures rage, hot anger, intense fury. In contrast, a harsh, cutting retort that inflicts emotional pain is likely to be inflamatory, which intensifies heated, hostile feelings. The soothing, conciliatory impact of a soft or gentle answer (**15:1**; **25:15**) can either powerfully avert even severe anger (**15:1**) or break a bone (**25:15**). For "break" (**25:15**), see the comment about "crush" in 15:4, where it pictures the crushing of a person's spirit. Breaking a bone (**25:15**) evidently means damaging the entire person. The violence perpetrated by the tongue in destroying self-esteem and honor is far more destructive than the physical damage done by a rigorous beating. Similarly, gentle, persistent, persuasive talk can eventually break down even the most stubborn will either for righteous or wicked purposes. Is this not an element in television advertising?

8. *Speech Is Powerful in Affecting Life Quality.*

18:21 "The tongue has the power of life and death, and those who love it will eat its fruit."

To love the tongue is to use it often, to talk incessantly. In view of the tongue's immense power, we should use it carefully and wisely. The level of a person's success reflects how he talks, both to others and (silently) to himself. A statement in the apocryphal wisdom of Sirach 37:17–18, perhaps derived from our text, is an excellent mini-commentary: "Thoughts are rooted in the heart, and this sends out four branches; good and evil, life and death, and always mistress of them all is the tongue" (JB). For "life" and "death," see the comments about 19:23 and 14:27.

9. *Beneficial Talk Brings Good.*

12:14 "From the fruit of his lips a man is filled with good things as surely as the work of his hands rewards him."

13:2 "From the fruit of his lips a man enjoys good things, but the unfaithful have a craving for violence."

18:20 "From the fruit of his mouth a man's stomach is filled; with the harvest from his lips he is satisfied."

All three texts teach that what you receive reflects what you speak. They imply that wise, righteous, positive, encouraging conversation will be beneficial. The first lines of these texts are virtually equivalent to each other. For "fruit," see the comment about 11:30. The second lines are related to their preceding lines by repetition (**18:20**), analogy (**12:14**), and contrast (**13:2**; see the discussion about 4:23).

10. Righteous Talk Benefits; Wicked Talk Brings Conflict and Destruction.

11:9 "With his mouth the godless destroys his neighbor, but through knowledge the righteous escape."

11:11 "Through the blessing of the upright a city is exalted, but by the mouth of the wicked it is destroyed."

Destructive talk by the godless (**11:9**) produces a neighbor's ruin that may be physical, social, or financial. It may ruin a neighbor's reputation by slander or destroy a city by disrupting its unity and weakening its stability (**11:11**).

In contrast, the righteous use their knowledge to escape (**11:9**), being delivered from threatened destruction. The beneficial influence of the upright honors a city by giving it a good reputation (**11:11**).

11. The Righteous Escape Trouble; the Wicked Talk Themselves into Trouble.

12:6 "The words of the wicked lie in wait for blood, but the speech of the upright rescues them."

12:13 "An evil man is trapped by his sinful talk, but a righteous man escapes trouble."

13:3 "He who guards his lips guards his life, but he who speaks rashly will come to ruin."

14:3 "A fool's talk brings a rod to his back. but the lips of the wise protect them."

18:6 "A fool's lips bring him strife, and his mouth invites a beating."

18:7 "A fool's mouth is his undoing, and his lips are a snare to his soul."

21:23 "He who guards his mouth and his tongue keeps himself from calamity."

To "lie in wait for blood" (**12:6**) is to plot an ambush. The "words of the wicked" (**12:6**), pictured by the imagery of violent robbery, attack their victims as viciously as do gossip, slander, false accusations, and false testimony in court.

An evil man's sinful talk backfires and harms him. For "trapped" (**12:13**) and "snare" (**18:7**), see the comment about "snare" in 14:27. If not so tragic, it would be almost comical to watch the villain be victimized by his own schemes when the trap he sets catches him. His malicious talk leaves him open to shameful exposure, retaliation, legal penalties, and even destruction. Speaking rashly, which includes tactless and offensive talk, arouses hostile reactions that bring him ruin (**13:3b**) as well as conflicts and beatings (**14:3a; 18:6**), some as a result of court action. For "beating," see the comment about 19:29.

The righteous escape trouble by moving away from it (**12:13b**). By carefully controlling his conversation, a wise man protects himself and avoids calamity (**13:3a; 14:3b; 21:23**) that can result from rash and arrogant talk. The speech of the upright also rescues (**12:6**), pulling people away from danger. Perhaps they do this by encouragement and verbal defense.

12. A Man Is Trapped by Rash Vows.

20:25 "It is a trap for a man to dedicate something rashly and only later to consider his vows."

We should carefully consider what we dedicate or vow to God before doing it, for God expects vows to be fulfilled (Lev. 27; Deut. 23:21–22). Impetuous vows that are painful, difficult, or impossible to fulfill are disrespectful to God and will probably cause trouble.

13. An Undeserved Curse Is Futile.

26:2 "Like a fluttering sparrow or a darting swallow, an undeserved curse does not come to rest."

For "curse," see the comments about 30:11. A curse is undeserved if there has been no offensive act or sin to prompt someone to utter it. As a bird flits from one place to another, an undeserved curse floats around without coming to its destination to inflict its ugly damage. For a curse not to come to rest is for it not to be fulfilled or brought to reality (e.g., Deut. 23:4–5; 1 Sam. 17:43; Jer. 15:10). In some cases the curse may boomerang to inflict the one who uttered it with what he wished for another.

14. Wise Conversation Heals; Reckless, Deceptive Words Hurt and Demoralize.

12:18 "Reckless words pierce like a sword, but the tongue of the wise brings healing."

15:4 "The tongue that brings healing is a tree of life, but a deceitful tongue crushes the spirit."

16:24 "Pleasant words are a honeycomb, sweet to the soul and healing to the bones."

"Reckless words" (**12:18a**) describe thoughtless, tactless, insensitive statements that may be painful and harmful. Cutting words pierce like a sword and may be no less destructive of a healthy self-esteem (see Ps. 57:4, which pictures tongues as sharp swords).

The word rendered "deceitful" (**15:4b**) means "twisted," "distorted," "perverted." A perverted tongue speaks with twisted, evil intent that may include treachery (11:3) and bring ruin (19:3). To "crush" (break, smash) a person's spirit is to destroy his morale and to shatter his self-confidence to the point of rendering him ineffective. The childish verse "Sticks and stones may break my bones, but words can never hurt me" is clearly false in the light of these texts.

In contrast is the healing brought by the tongue of the wise. For "tree of life" (**15:4**), see the comment about 3:18. These texts picture the therapeutic impact of perceptive, constructive, comforting, and encouraging words (see 4:22; 13:17; 16:24). Such words soothe hostile feelings, cement growing relationships, and promote a benevolent atmosphere. Like the "honeycomb" (**16:24**), which supplies sweet and nutritious raw honey that has medicinal value, these words have a delightful, beneficial, morale-boosting impact that develops the positive attitudes conducive to health and vitality in all areas. The parallel terms, "soul" and "bones," refer to the entire person. These texts suggest the exciting prospect of a healing ministry through comforting, constructive, and encouraging talk, not only for an individual but also for an entire church. For such people, using wisdom and love to control their talk, will make immense contributions toward improving the spiritual, mental, emotional, and physical vitality of those around them.

15. Wicked Talk Is Deceptive, Malevolent, and Produces Anger.

25:23 "As a north wind brings rain, so a sly tongue brings angry looks."

26:23-26 "Like a coating of glaze over earthenware are fervent lips with an evil heart. A malicious man disguises himself with his lips, but in his heart he harbors deceit. Though his speech is charming, do not believe him, for seven abominations fill his heart. His malice may be concealed by deception, but his wickedness will be exposed in the assembly."

The "north wind" (**25:23**) usually brought rain to Egypt, but clear, dry, cold weather to Israel (Job 37:21-22). This proverb may have originated in Egypt and been imported by Israel (Eccl. 12:9).[4] The word rendered "sly" pictures the secretive method of spreading vicious slander. Such malicious conversations arouse intense anger that is observable in facial expressions.

People who convey the impression that they are good by concealing their malicious intentions are described metaphorically (**26:23**), directly (**26:24-26a**), and as publicly exposed (**26:26b**). The NIV rendering "coating of glaze over earthenware" (**26:23**) reflects recent insights that have clarified what used to be considered an obscure image.[5] Pottery vessels were dipped in glaze to make them smooth, shiny, and more attractive. The point of the image was to picture an attractive covering that was designed to conceal the less attractive reality under it.

This is an appropriate metaphor to picture a person who conceals his malicious intentions with a veneer of "fervent lips" (**26:23**), "disguises" (**26:24**), and "charming" (**26:25**) talk. He uses his intense expressions of concern, deception in concealing his real intentions, and gracious conversation to deftly con people into thinking him friendly, caring, and honest. But lurking behind this attractive facade is malicious (**26:24, 26**)

---

[4] Derek Kidner, *The Proverbs* (Wheaton: Tyndale, 1964), 160; William F. McKane, *Proverbs, A New Approach* (Philadelphia: Westminster, 1970), 582-83.

[5] Robert L. Alden, *Proverbs* (Grand Rapids: Baker, 1983), 189; William F. McKane, *Proverbs, A New Approach* (Philadelphia: Westminster, 1970), 603-04.

intent and an evil (**26:23**), deceitful (**26:24**) mind filled with seven abominations (**26:25**). The "abominations" involve what is morally repulsive and detestable.

People who conceal their malevolent intentions behind the favorable impressions conveyed by personal charm are especially dangerous and not to be trusted. Such people should be avoided or, at least, watched closely. For by conveying a false impression, they hope to achieve their sinister objectives. No matter how brilliantly his verbal disguise covers up his malevolent intentions, he will eventually be publicly exposed as a hypocrite (**26:26**).

16. A Blessing Can Be a Curse.

25:20 "Like one who takes away a garment on a cold day, or like vinegar poured on soda, is one who sings songs to a heavy heart."

27:14 "If a man loudly blesses his neighbor early in the morning, it will be taken as a curse."

On a cold day it is cruel to take away a garment (**25:20**) needed for warmth. Vinegar and "soda" (material obtained from alkaline lakes in Egypt) are incompatible and inappropriate for mixing. The "heavy heart" may picture sorrow, distress, or a foul mood. It is inappropriate and cruel to sing songs to a troubled person who does not want to hear them and may resent them (see Rom. 12:15).

To bestow a blessing loudly (**27:14**) is offensive to those whom it awakens before they are ready. To bestow a blessing in an offensive way is hypocritical and equivalent to a curse. For it would be better if it had not been uttered. How, when, and why a blessing is bestowed is even more important than whether it is bestowed or what it involves.

17. Boasting Is Futile.

25:14 "Like clouds and wind without rain is a man who boasts of gifts he does not give."

27:1 "Do not boast about tomorrow, for you do not know what a day may bring forth."

27:2 "Let another praise you, and not your own mouth; someone else, and not your own lips."

In Israel's dry climate, the signs of an approaching storm that brought no rain (**25:14**) provided only frustration. No less galling is the man who brags about his plans for large gifts that never materialize.

We should not be cocky (**27:1**), especially about future developments that no man can control (see Luke 12:16–21; James 4:13–16). For by its very nature man's existence is precarious and the continuation of his prosperity and temporal life uncertain. That is why he must depend upon God for both his temporal and eternal future (**16:1; 19:21**).

Let someone else praise you (**27:2**). A favorable reaction from others without a vested interest in the impact of their statements will accurately indicate your status and help your reputation. But to praise yourself is to indulge in arrogant boasting that is boring, trite, and foolish (**30:32a**). It does not improve your reputation. In fact, listeners will be much quicker to conclude that your self-praise has been overdone than you will.

18. Flattery Is Harmful, Threatening, and Brings No Favor.

26:28 "A lying tongue hates those it hurts, and a flattering mouth works ruin."

28:23 "He who rebukes a man will in the end gain more favor than he who has a flattering tongue."

29:5 "Whoever flatters his neighbor is spreading a net for his feet."

Those "hurt" (**26:28a**) by hostile lies, such as slander, are physically and emotionally crushed by the damage experienced.

In all three texts, "flattery" pictures smooth talk that hypocritically praises, perhaps to manipulate with malevolent intent. Flattery's spreading a net (**29:5**) metaphorically pictures traps set for people. Someone who allows flattery to lower his defenses is likely to be tripped up and made vulnerable to harm and even ruin (**26:28b**). Sometimes the trapping effort backfires, catching the trapper in his own trap, much to his embarrassment and consternation.

Far more beneficial is a perceptive, appropriate rebuke (**28:23**) spoken in truth and love. Even if it produces a temporary alienation, it will eventually bring appreciation for its beneficent intent and result.

19. The Sins of Lying and Perjury

a. Liars Listen to Malice. 17:4 "A wicked man listens to evil lips; a liar pays attention to a malicious tongue."

What people say and attentively hear shows what they are like. The listeners are no better than the talkers! For only evil people tolerate malicious talk and plotting.

b. Riches Gained by Lies Are Brief. 21:6 "A fortune made by a lying tongue is a fleeting vapor and a deadly snare."

"And a deadly snare" (NIV) renders an ancient Greek translation (Septuagint) and some Hebrew manuscripts. Most Hebrew manuscripts read "for those who seek death," an obscure expression. Perhaps this verse says that a man who uses unethical means to acquire material wealth will not experience the honor, harmony, happiness, and fulfillment that enrich life. Experiencing a life devoid of its enriching ingredients, he not only endures a deathly existence but is also headed toward death. Even his material wealth is an easily dispersed "fleeting vapor," empty and futile (13:11a). The most that he can claim is to be miserable in style until his ill-gotten wealth is dispersed by the wind.

c. Poverty Is Better Than Lying. 19:22 "What a man desires is unfailing love; better to be poor than a liar."

There is no clear connection between the two lines of this verse, which express unrelated ideas. "Unfailing love" is obviously a most desirable quality both to give and to receive. No amount of material wealth is worth the price of integrity. That is why it is better to be poor and honest than a rich liar.

d. Liars Get into Trouble. 17:20 "A man of perverse heart does not prosper; he whose tongue is deceitful falls into trouble."

Twisted thinking and motivation with deceptive talk provoke unforeseen hostility and opposition that prevent a perverse person from achieving his goals.

e. Lying Lasts Briefly. 12:19 "Truthful lips endure forever, but a lying tongue lasts only a moment."

The text observes the enduring quality of truth that holds

firm even after a thorough scrutiny. The word rendered "forever" indicates continuation for as long as is relevant, such as the remainder of a person's life. In contrast, the benefits of lies are transitory, for lies will eventually be exposed, thereby ruining the credibility of the liar.

f. A Deceptive Joker Is Dangerously Reckless. 26:18–19 "Like a madman shooting firebrands or deadly arrows is a man who deceives his neighbor and says, 'I was only joking!'"

Insanely shooting arrows at anyone within range for no reason is terrifying and dangerous. This simile pictures the irrational and irresponsible qualities of the deceptive joker that make him as dangerous as a crazy man's handling deadly weapons. Both can do irreparable harm. See 26:10.

g. False Testimony Is Malicious and Dangerous. 25:18 "Like a club or a sword or a sharp arrow is the man who gives false testimony against his neighbor."

No weapon is dangerous by itself, but in the hands of a violent man, any of these weapons is lethal enough to harm or destroy people. Similarly, the harm done by perjury with its resulting distortion of justice may be just as great as that inflicted by lethal weapons wielded by violent men.

h. False Accusation and Betraying a Confidence Are Prohibited. 3:29–30 "Do not plot harm against your neighbor, who lives trustfully near you. Do not accuse a man for no reason—when he has done you no harm."

24:28–29 "Do not testify against your neighbor without cause, or use your lips to deceive. Do not say, 'I'll do to him as he has done to me; I'll pay that man back for what he did.'"

25:8–10 "What you have seen with your eyes do not bring hastily to court, for what will you do in the end if your neighbor puts you to shame? If you argue your case with a neighbor, do not betray another man's confidence, or he who hears it may shame you and you will never lose your bad reputation."

These texts prohibit actions that antagonize a neighbor. They forbid plotting harm, especially against someone who trusts you (**3:29**). They also forbid any unjustified quarreling, fighting, or litigation (**3:30**).

They prohibit unwarranted testimony in court and deceptive talk (**24:28**). In ancient Israel some people apparently gave incriminating evidence (even perjury) against their neighbor in court to gain revenge for some previous gripe.

Their prohibition of revenge (**24:29**; see 20:22; 24:17–18; 25:21–22; Luke 6:27–31; Rom. 12:17, 19) corresponds to the law of Moses. Its "eye-for-an-eye" principle was designed to remove vengeance from the angry avenger and to give the court the responsibility to determine guilt and to hand out punishment appropriate for the crime (Exod. 21:22–25; Lev. 24:19–20; Deut. 19:15–21). These texts emphasize the natural tendency of ancient Hebrews to seek their own revenge. The widespread misunderstanding and abuse of the "eye-for-an-eye" principle to justify personal revenge and the frequent ignoring of verse 29 make it clear that the desire for personal revenge has continued unabated since then.

There is evidently an error in verse division in chapter 25. The verse division wrongly placed what should be the first line of **25:8** as the last line of 25:7. This text prohibits rushing into court without a strong case (**25:8**), since direct observations may be incomplete, inaccurate, or wrongly interpreted. To invalidate an eyewitness testimony brings public disgrace.

These verses prohibit using privileged information in court against a neighbor (**25:9**). To do so demonstrates disloyalty and untrustworthiness. Such a lack of integrity will produce a legitimate defamation of character that will never be erased (**25:10**).

i. A False Witness Lies. 12:17 "A truthful witness gives honest testimony, but a false witness tells lies."

14:5 "A truthful witness does not deceive, but a false witness pours out lies."

14:25 "A truthful witness saves lives, but a false witness is deceitful."

These antithetic parallelisms (see introduction) contrast true witnesses with false ones. False witnesses are liars (perjurers in court) who present false or misleading information that perverts the course of justice (**12:17**; **14:5**). Truthful witnesses present accurate information that delivers (**14:25**) people from wrongful penalties by avoiding the distortions of perjury.

j. A False Witness Will Be Punished. 19:5 "A false witness will not go unpunished, and he who pours out lies will not go free." **19:9** "A false witness will not go unpunished, and he who pours out lies will perish."

21:28 "A false witness will perish, and whoever listens to him will be destroyed forever."

These texts state that perjurers, guilty of illegal conduct (Deut. 19:16–19), will die with no chance of being declared free of guilt or of being rescued from death. Almost identical are **19:5** and **19:9**.

The Hebrew text for **21:28b** is difficult to understand. The NIV footnote, which reads, "but the words of an obedient man will live on," is better than the rendering of the NIV text. It pictures the obedient as continuing to speak, and thus to live, in contrast to the perjurer whose words are cut off by his death.

20. The Sins of Gossip and Slander

a. Gossip Penetrates Deeply. 18:8 "The words of a gossip are like choice morsels; they go down to a man's inmost parts."

26:22 "The words of a gossip are like choice morsels; they go down to a man's inmost parts."

In these identical texts the image of eating delicious food pictures man's voracious appetite for and enjoyment of malicious talk, in spite of its being prohibited by the Law (Lev. 19:16). His "inmost parts," referring to his lower abdomen, is digestive imagery to picture his thorough mental digesting and absorbing of the malicious gossip into the deepest recesses of his mind. Penetrating even his subconscious, it will remain permanently as part of him.

b. Gossip Betrays Confidence. 11:13 "A gossip betrays a confidence, but a trustworthy man keeps a secret."

20:19 "A gossip betrays a confidence; so avoid a man who talks too much."

These texts emphasize that to publicize information received confidentially is to betray that confidence. To spread malicious information and misrepresentations that will discredit a person is to be disloyal. That is why gossip and slander may be acts of treachery. A person who betrays another by sharing his secrets with you is likely to betray you in a similar way behind your back, so you should avoid a person who talks incessantly **(20:19b)** and cannot keep a secret. In contrast, a trustworthy person (11:13b) shows his loyalty to his friends and neighbors by withholding (concealing) from the public any information that is confidential or would damage their reputation.

c. Gossip Separates Close Friends. 16:28 "A perverse man stirs up dissension, and a gossip separates close friends."

Twisted, perverted attitudes and malicious gossip are also divisive. They arouse hostilities powerful enough to alienate close friends, even when both are viciously victimized by the gossip.

d. Gossip Fuels Quarrels. 26:20 "Without wood a fire goes out; without gossip a quarrel dies down."

As wood fuels a fire, gossip fuels a quarrel by arousing hostilities. Removal of the fuel terminates both.

e. Slander Provokes Curses and Punishment. 30:10 " 'Do not slander a servant to his master, or he will curse you, and you will pay for it.' "

One who slanders another will not go unpunished. Either the master or the slandered servant may resent the unwanted publicity and curse the slanderer. His guilt is established; his punishment, inevitable.

21. Quarrels

a. Quarrelsome Men Stir Up Conflicts. 15:18 "A hot-tempered man stirs up dissension, but a patient man calms a quarrel."

26:21 "As charcoal to embers and as wood to fire, so is a quarrelsome man for kindling strife."

29:22 "An angry man stirs up dissension, and a hottempered one commits many sins."

For "hot-tempered" (**15:18; 29:22**), "sins" (**29:22**), and "patient" (**15:18**), see the comments about "wrath" in 15:1, "transgression" in VWs, and "patient" in 14:29.

The imagery in **26:21** is similar to that in 26:20. As charcoal and wood fuel a fire, a quarrelsome man has an inflammatory effect upon conflicts. A man who is easily irritated and quick to express hostility arouses and intensifies tensions (**15:18; 29:22;** see 15:1b), since his quarrelsome attitude is contagious. Sustained anger involves us in many transgressions by overriding our normal moral commitment. A variant of **15:18a** is **29:22a**. In contrast, a patient man (**15:18b**), who is slow to anger, has a soothing effect upon an angry confrontation (see 15:1a).

    b. Quarreling Involves Sin. 17:19 "He who loves a quarrel loves sin; he who builds a high gate invites destruction."

As in 29:22, quarreling may involve transgression. Aggressively argumentative people seem to enjoy offending others.

The image in **17:19b** is not altogether clear. The word rendered "gate" means "opening." It may picture either an entrance or the opening of the mouth to talk. The use of a high, inaccessible gate in ancient Israel is undocumented. More likely, a person's raising high his mouth pictures big talk with an arrogant attitude. The idea evidently is that a man who arrogantly engages in big talk with big promises is actively pursuing his humiliation and destruction. Or, could it be that "building a high gate" was an ancient idiom similar to our "raising the roof"?

    c. It Is Dangerous to Meddle in Another's Quarrel. 26:17 "Like one who seizes a dog by the ears is a passer-by who meddles in a quarrel not his own."

For "seizes" and "quarrel," see the comments about "hold on to" in 4:13 and "strife" in 30:33.

To grab a strange wild dog by the ears would be extremely hazardous; it would virtually assure the dog's reaction of attacking and biting. It is no less foolish and dangerous for a stranger to jump into an argument that is none of his business. For he may infuriate both parties, who might turn their combined anger, and perhaps violence, against him.

    d. Quarrels Are Difficult to End. 17:14 "Starting a quarrel is like breaching a dam; so drop the matter before a dispute breaks out."

The danger of breaching a dam is that more water may be let loose than can be predicted, controlled, or stored. Similarly a quarrel may easily explode, thereby becoming bitter, vicious, and even violent. It can disrupt relationships and destroy friendships permanently. It is preferable, therefore, to drop the matter and refuse to participate in the argument.

    e. Quarrelers Do Not Back Down. 18:19 "An offended brother is more unyielding than a fortified city, and disputes are like the barred gates of a citadel."

Although the meaning of the Hebrew text is obscure, evidently it means that it is more difficult to deal with an offended brother victimized by your transgression than to attack and conquer a strongly fortified city. Gates strengthened by sturdy beams were extremely difficult to break down. Hostilities aroused and barriers erected by vigorous and extended quarreling are even more difficult to overcome.

f. Avoid Quarrelsome People. 19:19 "A hot-tempered man must pay the penalty; if you rescue him, you will have to do it again."

22:24–25 "Do not make friends with a hot-tempered man, do not associate with one easily angered, or you may learn his ways and get yourself ensnared."

Although the Hebrew text in **19:19** is obscure, it probably means that an easily angered man must suffer the consequences of his offensive and harmful actions. Rescue is futile. A hothead will repeat his mistakes and stir up more trouble for himself. For "hot-tempered," see the comment on "wrath" in 15:1.

Irritable, easily angered men are to be excluded from your friends and associates (**22:24**). The most effective way to avoid the dangerous tendency to become like them is to have nothing to do with them (**22:25**).

g. Disputes May Be Settled by Lot. 18:18 "Casting the lot settles disputes and keeps strong opponents apart."

The lot was an efficient way in ancient Israel to resolve arguments without resorting to bitter disputes, lengthy litigation, or violence. Both disputants trusted God to control the lots on these occasions to provide justice. See the comment about 16:33. For "disputes," see the comment about "quarrelsome" in 19:13.

22. *Intolerable Jealousy*

27:4 "Anger is cruel and fury overwhelming, but who can stand before jealousy?"

Jealousy is even more destructive than cruel anger or torrential fury (see 6:32–35; 14:30). An intense emotion that distorts our perspective, it is even more likely to sever close relationships and to produce violence. For "anger" and "fury," see the comments about "wrath" in 15:1 and "anger" in 29:8.

I. For Further Study

1. What causes you to forget your moral values when faced with sexual temptation? How can you most effectively avoid sexual temptation?

2. How does one avoid nagging and being quarrelsome?

3. Examine the classic description of the wealthy prudent wife (31:10–31). Is this exhaustive? See 5:18–19 and Ephesians 5:25. Is this picture realistic or idealistic? Is it reasonable for a woman to strive to measure up to this standard? Is she enthusiastically admired and appreciated by her husband if she does?

4. How do you train a child in the way that he/she should go (22:6)? What conclusion should you draw if he/she should go astray from your teaching?

5. How does your attitude affect your performance? What good does a cheerful, positive attitude do? What harm does a depressing, negative attitude do? To the person who has it? To the people affected by that person? How do you develop and maintain a cheerful, positive attitude?

6. Contrast the qualities of wise conversation with those of foolish conversation. What specific qualities of conversation do you want to develop? How can you do it?

7. What do you think of the principle that "What you get in this life reflects what you speak" (12:14)? How should this principle affect what you say? Does it?

8. What are the healing effects of wise, encouraging conversation (16:24)? What implications does this have for a church's healing ministry through the conversations of its people? How can you develop such a ministry in your church?

9. What is wrong with the sins of lying, perjury, gossip, and slander? What damage do they do? How can you most effectively avoid them? How can you and others in your church eliminate them?

Chapter 8

Business Principles

This group of proverbs presents principles for handling business affairs, both professional and personal. They commend working hard, being generous and honest. They warn against being lazy, stingy, dishonest, and participating in foolish practices, such as excessive eating and drinking and guaranteeing another's loan. Also included are some observations about how things are, without any moral evaluation.

A. Working Hard Contrasted with Being Lazy

1. Work in Season Produces Food and Income; Excessive Sleep Produces Inadequate Work, Food, and Income.

10:5 "He who gathers crops in summer is a wise son, but he who sleeps during harvest is a disgraceful son."

20:4 "A sluggard does not plow in season; so at harvest time he looks but finds nothing."

20:13 "Do not love sleep or you will grow poor; stay awake and you will have food to spare."

These proverbs present different facets of the same principle: Hard work at the right times is essential to success in agriculture. Being mentally and physically alert and psyched to work effectively will produce food in abundance (**20:13**). See the comment about "content" in 19:23 with its resulting income.

The lazy man (**20:4**; see "sluggard" in VF) who irresponsibly sleeps through these important work periods will find himself critically short of food, income, and headed for poverty (**20:13**; see 6:9-11). Failure to plow, plant, and harvest at the proper times results in having no food or income (**20:4**). Even looking (literally, asking or begging) for food at harvest (**20:4**) yields nothing. For the lazy man has made the basic error of expecting to achieve his goal without doing the necessary work. The wise and foolish alternatives are obvious (**10:5**).

2. The Sluggard Is Rebuked for His Disastrous Excessive Sleep.

6:9-11 "How long will you lie there, you sluggard? When will you get up from your sleep? A little sleep, a little slumber, a little folding of the hands to rest—and poverty will come on you like a bandit and scarcity like an armed man."

19:15 "Laziness brings on deep sleep, and the shiftless man goes hungry."

24:30-34 "I went past the field of the sluggard, past the vineyard of the man who lacks judgment; thorns had come up everywhere; the ground was covered with weeds, and the stone wall was in ruins. I applied my heart to what I observed and learned a lesson from what I saw: A little sleep, a little slumber, a little folding of the hands to rest—and poverty will come on you like a bandit and scarcity like an armed man."

26:14 "As a door turns on its hinges, so a sluggard turns on his bed."

These proverbs vividly portray the sluggard's (see VF) inevitable poverty. Comic hyperbole pictures the lazy man's limited movement in his bed as if he were attached to hinges on a door (**26:14**). He falls into a deep sleep (**19:15**) that makes him sluggish after too much of it, thereby stifling any productive activity. Synonymous rhetorical questions (**6:9**) ask how long the sluggard will maintain his inertia.

A mini-morality story or parable (**24:30-34**) pictures a sluggard who lacked the judgment (see the comment about "heart" in 4:23) and initiative to work his vineyard (**24:30**). His neglected field was overrun by nasty thorns and weeds (**24:31**), and the stone wall to keep stray animals from the crops had fallen down. The wise teacher (**24:32**) applied his heart (see the comments about "apply" in 22:17 and "heart" in 4:23) and learned a lesson, which was stated in **24:33–34** and is almost identical to **6:10–11**. The sluggard's lethargy leaves him vulnerable to the poverty that springs upon him like a sudden ambush by an armed robber.

3. *The Sluggard Is Too Lazy to Eat.*

19:24 "The sluggard buries his hand in the dish; he will not even bring it back to his mouth!"

26:15 "The sluggard buries his hand in the dish; he is too lazy to bring it back to his mouth."

Almost identical are **19:24** and **26:15**. Sarcastic comic hyperbole pictures the sluggard, who is usually tired when there is work to be done, as lacking the energy to eat his dinner.

4. *The Sluggard Has Wild Excuses.*

22:13 "The sluggard says, 'There is a lion outside!' or, 'I will be murdered in the streets!' "

26:13 "The sluggard says, 'There is a lion in the road, a fierce lion roaming the streets!' "

More sarcastic comic hyperbole ridicules the sluggard (see VF). The frequency of encounters with lions and murderers in ancient Israel, like automobile accidents today, was not sufficiently great to prevent people from working. Such an excuse was probably the wise teacher's caricature of the sluggard.

5. *Working the Land Produces Food; Chasing Fantasies Leads to Poverty.*

12:11 "He who works his land will have abundant food, but he who chases fantasies lacks judgment."

28:19 "He who works his land will have abundant food, but the one who chases fantasies will have his fill of poverty."

Except for the last two words of the Hebrew text, **12:11** and **28:19** are identical. Producing abundant food or a good income involves hard, intelligent work. Pouring mental energies into fantasies that involve unproductive, worthless thinking and activity is foolish and leads to poverty. It is not only hard work, but wisely productive and profitable work that is needed to produce good income. For "abundant" and "have his fill of," see the comment about "content" in 19:23.

6. Diligent, Productive Work Produces Profit, Wealth, and Authority; Laziness Breeds Poverty and Slavery.

10:4 "Lazy hands make a man poor, but diligent hands bring wealth."

12:24 "Diligent hands will rule, but laziness ends in slave labor."

12:27 "The lazy man does not roast his game, but the diligent man prizes his possessions."

13:4 "The sluggard craves and gets nothing, but the desires of the diligent are fully satisfied."

14:23 "All hard work brings a profit, but mere talk leads only to poverty."

These proverbs use the imagery of business (including farming), hunting, and administration to portray the contrasting results of diligent work and laziness. They present the general principle (not necessarily without exceptions) that working hard and intelligently brings substantial profits and wealth, while lethargy breeds poverty (e.g., **10:4**).

Mere talk (**14:23**), not supported by appropriate action, is unproductive and incapable of producing desired results, especially if the conversation distracts from work and wastes time. Hard work may involve pain and effort to the point of exhaustion. The sluggard's cravings (see "sluggard" in VF and "longing" in 13:19) are frustrated by his inactivity (**13:4**). But the diligent man's desires (see "zeal" in 19:2), as a result of his productive labor, are fully satisfied (see "prosper" in 28:25). The diligent obtain authority as government leaders, business executives, and entrepreneurs, while the lazy are reduced to compulsory labor or slavery (**12:24**).

Hunting imagery may best explain **12:27**. The word rendered "game," a cognate of a verb that means "hunt," refers to the meat obtained from the hunt. A man too lazy to hunt will have no game to roast. The "possessions" of the diligent may refer to "the wealth of the steppe," that is, the animals being hunted and eaten.[1]

7. The Sluggard Brings Misery to Those Who Send Him.

10:26 "As vinegar to the teeth and smoke to the eyes, so is a sluggard to those who send him."

The sour taste of vinegar on our teeth and smarting eyes irritated by smoke are familiar images of what is unpleasant. Similarly irritating and frustrating is the experience of one who depends upon an irresponsible and unreliable sluggard to run an errand or deliver a message.

8. Laziness Is Destructive.

18:9 "One who is slack in his work is brother to one who destroys."

Being lazy and being destructive are closely related. "Slack" pictures a half-hearted, lazy, negligent attitude, which produces shoddy work that may involve potential danger to the consumer.

9. Slackening Under Pressure Displays Weakness.

24:10 "If you falter in times of trouble, how small is your strength!"

The exact connotation of 24:10 is unclear. The Hebrew text contains a pun based upon the cognate words, ṣārâ (trouble) and ṣār (small). Strength neutralized by pressure is weakness. For one who cannot show strength to cope, endure, or produce while under pressure and in difficulty is a mental, and perhaps physical, weakling.

10. The Ant Works.

6:6-8 "Go to the ant, you sluggard; consider its ways and be wise! It has no commander, no overseer or ruler, yet it stores its provisions in summer and gathers its food at harvest."

30:24-28 "'Four things on earth are small, yet they are

---

[1] This interpretation follows the suggestive analysis by Mitchell Dahood, "The Hapax ḥārak in Proverbs 12:27," *Biblica* 63, no. 1 (Rome, Italy: Biblical Institute Press, 1982): 60-62.

extremely wise: Ants are creatures of little strength, yet they store up their food in the summer; coneys are creatures of little power, yet they make their homes in the crags; locusts have no king, yet they advance together in ranks; a lizard can be caught with the hand, yet it is found in kings' palaces.'"

The description of the ant in **6:6–8** reminds us of a fable because human qualities are ascribed to it. The industrious ways of ants[2] display their wisdom in working consistently and planning ahead, even though they lack rational thought. Without supervision, a community of ants works effectively together to store enough food during the harvest to meet their needs during the winter.

In **30:24**, there are certain compensating qualities associated with wisdom that may enable us to do some remarkable things in spite of our lack of size and strength.[3] This is illustrated by four small creatures. For "ants" (**30:25**), see the comment about 6:6–8. Coneys (rock badgers), about the size of small rabbits, are easily frightened and quick to hide (**30:26**). Yet they live safely in the virtually inaccessible rocky crags high on the mountainous cliffs. Without discernible leadership, locusts display amazingly efficient discipline and organization, as does an advancing army in its ranks (**30:27**). Their irresistible hordes can be immensely destructive (Exod. 10:4–15). The small lizard, able to climb walls and sneak into high cracks and openings otherwise inaccessible, audaciously finds its way into prestigious locations like kings' palaces (**30:28**).

11. The Worker Is Motivated by His Appetite.

16:26 "The laborer's appetite works for him; his hunger drives him on."

The cognate words rendered "laborer" and "works" picture the drudgery and unfulfilling aspects of work. The worker's "appetite" (see "zeal" in 19:2) or "hunger" (literally, "mouth") pictures in physical imagery the totality of desires that motivate him. These desires drive (literally, "press") him, by exerting

---

[2] For additional insights concerning ants in relation to this text, see S. P. Toperoff, "The Ant in the Bible and Midrash," *Dor Le Dor* 13 (1985): 179–83.

[3] For additional details, see D. Daube, "A Quartet of Beasties in the Book of Proverbs," *Journal of Theological Studies* 36 (1985): 380–86.

pressure from within. Both lines emphasize that what a person wants and how strongly he wants it will determine how hard, how long, and even how effectively he will work to fulfill his desire or to achieve his goal. His burning desire actually helps him by motivating him to do what he needs to do.

12. There Are Priorities in Work.

24:27 "Finish your outdoor work and get your fields ready; after that, build your house."

This text uses agricultural imagery to stress the importance of arranging your priorities to do the essential jobs first. In this scene the agricultural tasks appropriate for the season have a higher priority than building a house (which may include getting married).

13. The Worker's Equipment Is Essential.

14:4 "Where there are no oxen, the manger is empty, but from the strength of an ox comes an abundant harvest."

Since the meanings of the key words rendered "manger" and "empty" are unclear, the meaning of **14:4a** is obscure. The "empty manger" may reflect the absence of cattle, and thus no need to fill the feeding trough. Or, more likely, these words may indicate that there is no grain without oxen. In ancient times oxen were essential equipment for major agricultural endeavors (Deut. 22:10; 25:4). The broader meaning is that we must obtain and use the right equipment to get the best results.

14. Good Stewardship Is Important.

27:23–27 "Be sure you know the condition of your flocks, give careful attention to your herds; for riches do not endure forever, and a crown is not secure for all generations. When the hay is removed and new growth appears and the grass from the hills is gathered in, the lambs will provide you with clothing, and the goats with the price of a field. You will have plenty of goats' milk to feed you and your family and to nourish your servant girls."

This section presents in agricultural imagery guidelines for a man's handling of his resources to gain maximum productivity. It was clearly essential for a man to feed, care for, and know the condition of his flocks (**27:23**), which were an indicator of his financial status. For neither material wealth nor prestige (pictured by the "crown") will last indefinitely (**27:24**), rather they are temporary and not to be taken for granted. "Hay," "new growth," and "grass" (**27:25**) are various kinds of greenery on which the flocks grazed. The three verbs pictured the greenery as ready for grazing or harvesting and storage. Plantings were timed to produce harvests at different times as needed for the flocks to be fed. Benefits from the flocks included clothes made from the lambs' wool (**27:26**), money to expand the farm (by selling some goats), and enough nutritious goats' milk to nourish the entire household (**27:27**).

15. There Are Benefits in Hard, Effective Work.

22:29 "Do you see a man skilled in his work? He will serve before kings; he will not serve before obscure men."

27:18 "He who tends a fig tree will eat its fruit, and he who looks after his master will be honored."

In **27:18**, the words rendered "tends" and "looks after" (see "guards" and "protects" in 2:8) picture here the thorough, careful attention needed to bring maximum benefits to the object or person involved. Such conscientious, skilled care of the fig tree helps to produce delicious figs to eat and sell. Similar work for a man's employer brings him honor and advancement.

The "skilled" (literally, "quick") worker (**22:29**) fulfills his responsibilities promptly and efficiently. His competence and productivity will bring him to the top of his profession (pictured by his service to kings). He will not labor in obscurity.

B. Administration

1. A King Needs Many Subjects.

14:28 " 'A large population is a king's glory, but without subjects a prince is ruined.' "

30:29–31 " 'There are three things that are stately in their stride, four that move with stately bearing: a lion, mighty among beasts, who retreats before nothing; a strutting rooster, a he-goat, and a king with his army around him.' "

In order for a king to have honor and power, he needs to

have many people (14:28) to provide political, financial, and military support.

This numerical proverb (see introduction) mentions four examples of "stately" ("looking good") walking (30:29). The virtually fearless lion moves smoothly and confidently, constantly advancing (30:30). The identity of the second animal is uncertain because of the obscure Hebrew text in 30:31a. It may mean "girded of loins," perhaps picturing strength and readiness for action. Other suggestions include "greyhound" (KJV), "rooster" (NIV), and "war horse" (Beck). A he-goat walks with dignity. The Hebrew text is obscure concerning the king's situation (30:31b). It may picture him as "secure against revolt" (NIV footnote) or, more likely, as "with his army around him" (NIV text) or "striding before his people" (RSV). Nevertheless, we should observe the sense of confidence and superiority with which each creature walks.

2. The King's Mind Is Unsearchable.

25:3 "As the heavens are high and the earth is deep, so the hearts of kings are unsearchable."

The heights of the heavens and the depths of the earth were proverbial images of what was inaccessible and impenetrable. No one can figure out or anticipate the unpredictable and resourceful diplomatic maneuvers of a king's mind. For he may have superior intelligence, more information, or inexplicable whims that prompt his decisions.

3. An Understanding King Maintains Order.

28:2 "When a country is rebellious, it has many rulers, but a man of understanding and knowledge maintains order."

It is not clear whether the rebellion (see "transgression" in VWs) involved spiritual, moral, political, or economic issues. Whatever the cause, the "many rulers" suggest political instability, a rapid succession of one replacing another, perhaps by assassination. In contrast, a wise ruler establishes a competent, durable administration that stifles rebellious ideas by benefiting the people through policies of justice and equity.

4. A Wise King Eliminates Evil and Destroys the Wicked.

16:10 "The lips of a king speak as an oracle, and his mouth should not betray justice."

20:8 "When a king sits on his throne to judge, he winnows out all evil with his eyes."

20:26 "A wise king winnows out the wicked; he drives the threshing wheel over them."

The word rendered "oracle" (**16:10**) usually referred to pagan divination, which was prohibited (Deut. 18:10). Here, its positive, commended meaning is a rare exception. It may picture God's making the king wise to administer justice by ascertaining the truth accurately (8:15; 2 Sam. 14:17, 20). Or, it may indicate the king's use of the lot to discern the Lord's guidance when the evidence is inconclusive (16:33; 18:18; see Ezek. 21:21 where the Hebrew word rendered here as "oracle" refers to casting lots by arrows).

In winnowing evil (**20:8, 26**), the king scatters the wicked, driving them from his court and eliminating their influence. His "eyes" (i.e., the whole person) pictures his uncanny ability to discern the wicked by his penetrating scrutiny (**20:8**). The iron wheels of a threshing cart driven over the wicked (**20:26**) would cut them to pieces in a brutal form of capital punishment. This vicious agricultural image stresses their inevitable destruction.

5. The King's Favor Brings Benefits and Life; His Wrath Brings Danger and Death.

16:15 "When a king's face brightens, it means life; his favor is like a rain cloud in spring."

19:12 "A king's rage is like the roar of a lion, but his favor is like dew on the grass."

20:2 "A king's wrath is like the roar of a lion; he who angers him forfeits his life."

A king's favor is important, since he can determine life or death, prosperity or poverty. Two similes describe the beauty of a king's brightened face (**16:15**), which expresses his favorable attitude. Rain clouds in the spring (**16:15**) that bring the rain essential to the life-sustaining crops, were a beautiful sight, especially in a land with limited rainfall. Morning dew (**19:12b**) that kept plants alive during the hot, dry summers, was considered pleasant and refreshing.

The simile of a lion's roar that projects danger and instills fear (**28:15**; Amos 3:8) pictures the king's anger in both **19:12a** and **20:2a**. An enraged (**19:12a**), intensely angry (**20:2a**) king posed a dangerous threat that also instilled terror. To forfeit life (**20:2b**) is to lose it by foolishly enraging the king enough for him to terminate it. See **16:14**.

6. A King Can Have Destructive Tendencies.

28:3 "A ruler who oppresses the poor is like a driving rain that leaves no crops."

29:12 "If a ruler listens to lies, all his officials become wicked."

Translations of the word rendered "ruler" (**28:3**) include "ruler" (NIV, TEV), "wicked" (JB, Beck), and "poor" (RSV, KJV). For any of these to oppress the poor for greedy enrichment at their expense is as destructive as a torrential rain that destroys the crops, thereby leaving no food for the farmers. These analogous malfunctions turn what should be and usually is beneficial (ruler or people, and rain) into something horribly disastrous.

A ruler who acts on the basis of unverified information from liars (**29:12**) is manipulated by those who would benefit from his naiveté and irresponsibility. His vulnerability encourages more and more of his officials to take advantage of him and others by unethical means. By not insisting upon integrity as a working principle, he allows wickedness to characterize his administration.

C. Rich and Poor

1. The Bitter Tastes Sweet to the Hungry.

27:7 "He who is full loathes honey, but to the hungry even what is bitter tastes sweet."

This contrast of the full with the hungry is a perceptive observation of reality. When a person feels stuffed with food, he rejects even an exquisite delicacy like honey. However when a person is starved, mediocre or even apparently inedible food seems delicious.

2. The Rich Are Popular; The Poor Are Shunned.

14:20 "The poor are shunned even by their neighbors, but the rich have many friends."

19:4 "Wealth brings many friends, but a poor man's friend deserts him."

19:6 "Many curry favor with a ruler, and everyone is the friend of a man who gives gifts."

19:7 "A poor man is shunned by all his relatives—how much more do his friends avoid him! Though he pursues them with pleading, they are nowhere to be found."

These proverbs are observations of familiar realities without evaluation or explanation. The affluent are often popular (14:20; 19:4), especially when influential or generous with gifts (19:6). The obvious benefits of a friend in high places motivate many to "curry" (aggressively "court") a high official's favor. We are not told how many of these friends are genuine and how many are interested only in favors and gifts they hope to obtain. Perhaps, in some cases, one factor in their popularity was their development of skills in relating to people, which helped them to be successful enough to get rich!

In contrast, a poor man is shunned (literally, "hated") by his neighbors and relatives (14:20; 19:7), deserted and avoided by his friends (19:4, 7). His pursuing with pleading (19:7), probably a vigorous, persistent, aggressive effort to obtain and maintain friends, produces nothing. For they are an unwanted burden—neighbors whom no one wants to love as a friend. Their tragic desperation is well expressed in the folk song "Nobody Loves You When You're Down and Out." Perhaps, in some cases, one factor in their unpopularity was their lack of skills in relating to people, which contributed to their poverty.

3. The Poor Are Ripped Off by Injustice and by Harsh Responses.

13:23 "A poor man's field may produce abundant food, but injustice sweeps it away."

18:23 "A poor man pleads for mercy, but a rich man answers harshly."

These proverbs describe some tragic frustrations of the poor and are observations of how things are, without any evaluation. Even when a poor man worked hard to produce a bountiful crop (**13:23**), which should have been profitable, his minimal income was inadequate. The unjustly rigged economy, controlled by the large landowners, was designed to keep the poor in poverty by diverting from them much of the earnings from their work. This harsh, rough, unsympathetic response by the rich to the urgent appeals of the poor conveyed their apathy to the difficulties of the poor (**18:23**).

4. The Rights of the Poor Are to Be Defended, Not Ignored.

21:13 "If a man shuts his ears to the cry of the poor, he too will cry out and not be answered."

28:27 "He who gives to the poor will lack nothing, but he who closes his eyes to them receives many curses."

31:8–9 "'Speak up for those who cannot speak for themselves, for the rights of all who are destitute. Speak up and judge fairly; defend the rights of the poor and needy.'"

The "cry of the poor" (**21:13**) was a desperate appeal for help from the distressed. For a man to "shut his ears" (**21:13**) or close "his eyes" (**28:27**) to the needs of the poor is to refuse to listen to or observe any information concerning their needs. Such a callous attitude arouses the antagonism of the poor who curse him (**28:27**), perhaps hoping for him to experience it! (**21:13b**) Placed in a similar situation, his urgent cries will fall upon deliberately deaf ears (**21:13b**), unheard and unanswered. See James 2:12–13. In contrast, for a man to be generous to the poor builds up good will that makes people open to helping him when he has needs (**28:27**; see Matt. 5:7).

The exhortations in 31:8–9 are for King Lemuel to provide genuine justice to the poor and needy, who are otherwise legally dumb, unable to get a fair hearing, and thus defenseless in court. The obscure expression rendered "destitute" (literally, "sons of passing on") evidently pictures people as being financially wiped out or even executed because of their inability to hire a good lawyer to help them obtain justice in court.

5. The Rich Dominate the Poor.

22:7 "The rich rule over the poor, and the borrower is servant to the lender."

The word rendered "servant" (**22:7**) pictures a person with an obligation to another, for example, slave, employee, a king's subjects, or a polite reference to oneself when speaking to another. The words rendered "lender" and "borrower" are cognate forms of the same Hebrew root. A lender is one who enables another to borrow. To borrow is to bind oneself to another by means of a financial obligation. The "servant" terminology is thus appropriate.

This proverb is another observation about an economic reality, without any moral evaluation.

6. The Rich Consider Themselves Wise; The Discerning Poor Know Better.

28:11 "A rich man may be wise in his own eyes, but a poor man who has discernment sees through him."

A financial success who considers himself wise (**28:11**) may be deluding himself. Not all rich are wise and not all wise are rich. A discerning poor man may carefully examine the successful man and accurately conclude otherwise.

7. Wealth Is Considered a Fortress; Poverty, Ruin.

10:15 "The wealth of the rich is their fortified city, but poverty is the ruin of the poor."

18:11 "The wealth of the rich is their fortified city; they imagine it an unscalable wall."

Poverty exerts immense pressures upon the poor (**10:15b**), often saturating their minds with their financial burdens and material needs, posing moral temptations (30:9), and inducing social decline (14:20; 19:4). It leaves them vulnerable to disasters that might be avoided by a higher income. Poverty is a nasty, undesirable condition.

Although the rich can use their money to solve some problems, they are unrealistic if they rely upon it to be a "fortified city" (**10:15a**; **18:11a**) or "unscalable wall" (**18:11b**), which provides an impenetrable defense against all threats. For even the amassing of great wealth cannot prevent illness, injury, accidents, unhappiness, death, and even financial reverses leading to bankruptcy and poverty.

Both of these proverbs are observations of reality, without moral evaluation.

8. *Riches May Be Temporary and Are Easily Lost.*

20:21 "An inheritance quickly gained at the beginning will not be blessed at the end."

21:17 "He who loves pleasure will become poor; whoever loves wine and oil will never be rich."

23:4-5 "Do not wear yourself out to get rich; have the wisdom to show restraint. Cast but a glance at riches, and they are gone, for they will surely sprout wings and fly off to the sky like an eagle."

28:22 "A stingy man is eager to get rich and is unaware that poverty awaits him."

The word rendered "stingy" (**28:22a**) means literally "has an evil eye." It pictures a person as stingy, greedy, covetous, hostile. Such a person has an intense desire to get rich, which consumes everything else. Eager (in a rush) to get rich, he is vulnerable to unethical or ineffective shortcuts, which may plunge him into poverty. In his headlong rush toward elusive wealth, he is unaware of the hazards that may impoverish him (**28:22b**).

Or, in his rush to get rich, he works so long and so hard that he "wears himself out" (**23:4**), becoming exhausted and even "burned out," without necessarily acquiring the wealth he sought. Even if he should attain his goal, his burnout would prevent him from appreciating it or benefiting from it. A literal rendering of **23:4**, "Cease from thine own wisdom" (KJV), does not make sense. However, the idea is accurately conveyed by NIV and Beck, "Be smart enough to stop." The exhortations in **23:4** are to avoid mental exhaustion by developing a balanced perspective rather than a "tunnel vision," which limits a person to a wearying, and perhaps futile, effort to acquire material wealth.

The poetic imagery in **23:5** and the direct statement in **20:21** picture the elusiveness of wealth, which slips away as soon as it is within sight. They are the biblical equivalent of the "easy-come, easy-go" syndrome. The person who gains wealth quickly (**20:21**) may dissipate it, especially as he develops extravagant tastes for exquisite material goods and expensive pleasures that consume his income (**21:17**). In ancient Israel, wine and (olive) oil were examples of such luxuries that would destroy the budget of many (**21:17**).

9. Those Who Get Rich by Wronging the Poor Will Become Poor.

22:16 "He who oppresses the poor to increase his wealth and he who gives gifts to the rich—both come to poverty."

28:8 "He who increases his wealth by exorbitant interest amasses it for another, who will be kind to the poor."

Oppressing (defrauding and impoverishing) the poor and giving to the rich (probably as bribes) are illegitimate methods of acquiring wealth (**22:16**). The person who uses such strategies will only impoverish himself. An example was lending to the poor at exorbitant interest rates. The word rendered "interest" (**28:8**) was derived from a verb meaning "bite." The "bite" occurred when the loan was made, since the interest was deducted first. Thus, if someone borrowed 100 shekels, he would only receive perhaps 80 shekels. The "exorbitant" interest may also have included charging additional interest when a debtor defaulted and was taken into bondage.[4] This practice could keep him in debt permanently. In **28:8**, such unethical practices were condemned and also were evidently the ones prohibited by the Law (Exod. 22:25; Lev. 25:35–54; Deut. 23:19–20; see also Ezek. 18:8; 22:12). No lasting profit will accrue from this "exorbitant interest." The irony is that a generous person will acquire these illegitimate profits and redistribute them to the poor. Will the unethical lose even more than the profits of their greed?

---

[4]See M. C. Fisher, "(*nāshak*) bite," TWOT II: 604–05, for details about interest in the ancient Orient.

10. A Rich Man Ransoms His Life; a Poor Man Is Not Threatened.

13:8 "A man's riches may ransom his life, but a poor man hears no threat."

This proverb notes a rare advantage of poverty over wealth! A rich man has the financial resources to pay off the kidnapper or robber who threatens him; however, a poor man is unlikely to face such a threat.

11. Some Are Not As They Seem.

13:7 "One man pretends to be rich, yet has nothing; another pretends to be poor, yet has great wealth."

People do not always present themselves accurately. There may be hyperbole in the extreme contrasts in each of the two lines, perhaps to make it obvious how ridiculous such strategies are. Is it not better to be honest and natural about our financial status?

12. Better to Be Poor with Something Than Pretend to Be Rich with Nothing.

12:9 "Better to be a nobody and yet have a servant than pretend to be somebody and have no food."

It is satisfactory to live as an obscure person who, although lightly regarded, still has enough to function moderately well. It is not good to handle the pressure of hypocrisy and the expenses of an extravagant lifestyle to pose as an important person with honor, stature, and affluence, while not having enough food to stave off hunger.

D. Generous and Stingy

1. Gifts Open Doors.

18:16 "A gift opens the way for the giver and ushers him into the presence of the great."

This proverb is another observation of how things work, without any moral evaluation. It notes that a gift to the proper person develops an important contact's good will, which may help to achieve a goal more easily. Both positive (17:8; 21:14) and negative aspects (15:27; 17:23) of gifts are mentioned elsewhere in the Book of Proverbs. These texts do not contradict each other, but observe different facets of the complex issue of gifts and bribes.

2. The Generous Prosper; the Stingy Become Poor.

11:24 "One man gives freely, yet gains even more; another withholds unduly, but comes to poverty."

11:25 "A generous man will prosper; he who refreshes others will himself be refreshed."

11:26 "People curse the man who hoards grain, but blessing crowns him who is willing to sell."

22:9 "A generous man will himself be blessed, for he shares his food with the poor."

These proverbs describe the benefits of giving. They contain several images of generosity that include "giving freely" ("scatters") in **11:24**, "generous" ("blessed") in **11:25**, "generous" (literally, "good eye"; see 23:6; 28:22), and "sharing" ("gives") with the poor in **22:9**. The generous businessman sells his grain when needed (**11:26**), even when he expects the price to rise later.

These proverbs teach an important principle that God has evidently built into His creation: The one who gives, gets even more than he gives (**11:24**; see Luke 6:38). Stated in agricultural imagery (**11:25**), the one "who refreshes" (literally, "rains," "waters," which were immensely refreshing and necessary in a dry climate) will be refreshed. This remarkable principle evidently does not work if we give for the purpose of getting. Although it is not specified in **11:24** what the generous one gets, he evidently winds up better overall, if not financially. He who attaches more importance to meeting human needs (by selling needed grain) than to maximizing his profits (by holding it until its price rises) earns a good reputation and approval expressed by blessings (**11:26; 22:9**). The generous (**11:25**) do prosper (see the comment about 28:25).

In contrast, the stingy man withholds what he should give (**11:24**), only to have it cost him much more in the long run (see 2 Cor. 9:6). For example, a stingy man hoards his grain (**11:26**), perhaps hoping to sell it later at a higher price. His unethical effort to manipulate prices at the expense of meeting basic human needs arouses hostility expressed by curses. His resulting degraded reputation and status may ruin his business and reduce him to poverty (**11:24**).

3. *Avoid a Stingy Man.*

23:6–8 "Do not eat the food of a stingy man, do not crave his delicacies; for he is the kind of man who is always thinking about the cost. 'Eat and drink,' he says to you, but his heart is not with you. You will vomit up the little you have eaten and will have wasted your compliments."

The exhortations in **23:6** are to avoid the hospitality of a stingy (literally "evil eye"; see the comment about 28:22) man who is reluctant to share. Do not even eat his most delicious servings. Excessively cost-conscious, his invitations to eat and drink are hypocritical (**23:7**) because of his reluctance to share. The unpleasantness of a stingy host is aggravating enough to be nauseating (**23:8**). It is clearly futile to express the usual appreciative courtesies to a host whose food you have just vomited! What may be hyperbole is designed to emphasize the point.

E. Honest and Dishonest

1. *Gains from Fraud Produce Misery.*

20:17 "Food gained by fraud tastes sweet to a man, but he ends up with a mouth full of gravel."

Acquiring easy money by deceptive, fraudulent transactions may bring immediate pleasure to a con man, but such gains have no permanent value (10:2). This text may include illicit sex, which is described in the Book of Proverbs by the imagery of food (9:17; 30:20), but it is not to be limited to that. A mouth full of gravel is a repulsive image of the unpleasant results of doing business dishonestly.

2. *Dishonestly Acquired Money Dwindles, but Gradual Financial Growth Works.*

13:11 "Dishonest money dwindles away, but he who gathers money little by little makes it grow."

The word rendered "dishonest" means "vapor," "emptiness." It pictures what is futile, unsatisfying, and worthless. It may portray here an apparently legitimate business transaction that turns out to be a swindle. Someone may get rich quick that way, but not remain wealthy. The "easy-come, easy-go" syndrome dissipates his new wealth, which he was unprepared to handle wisely or responsibly. In contrast, a gradual building up of income is more likely to produce financial stability.

3. Bribes Contribute to Success and Avert Anger.

17:8 "A bribe is a charm to the one who gives it; wherever he turns, he succeeds."

21:14 "A gift given in secret soothes anger, and a bribe concealed in the cloak pacifies great wrath."

These proverbs are pragmatic observations about the effectiveness of bribes, without any moral evaluation. Bribes do motivate the recipient to help the giver succeed in his endeavor (**17:8**). They also soothe (literally, "subdue") the recipient's intense wrath (see the comment about "wrath" in 15:1), thereby functioning as an effective adult pacifier (**21:14**). Other proverbs mention both advantages (18:16; 19:6) and disadvantages of giving bribes (15:27; 17:23), which were, nevertheless, prohibited by the Law (Exod. 23:8; Deut. 16:19).

4. Kings Appreciate Honesty and Truth.

16:13 "Kings take pleasure in honest lips; they value a man who speaks the truth."

Kings, leaders, and administrators place high value upon people with integrity, whose words are reliable.

5. A Good Reputation Is More Desirable Than Wealth.

22:1 "A good name is more desirable than great riches; to be esteemed is better than silver or gold."

27:21 "The crucible for silver and the furnace for gold, but man is tested by the praise he receives."

The crucible and smelting furnace (**27:21**) were equipment used in the smelting or refining process designed to produce metals of high quality by removing impurities. Throughout his life, a wise person is removing his undesirable elements and qualities. The effectiveness of that human refining process is measured by the praise he receives. That praise is an important indicator of his reputation. A good name (i.e., reputation) is to be treasured even more (**22:1**) than the most exquisite material wealth.

F. Physical Excesses: Gluttony and Drinking

1. Too Much Honey Is Bad.

25:16 "If you find honey, eat just enough—too much of it, and you will vomit."

25:27 "It is not good to eat too much honey, nor is it honorable to seek one's own honor."

Raw honey is delicious and nutritious, but what is good becomes bad if a person indulges excessively (**25:27a**). Overeating even nutritious food, like raw honey, can be a sickening pleasure (**25:16**) as well as a sin (gluttony). Commentators rightly complain about the obscurity of the Hebrew text in **25:27b** and about the difficulty of ascertaining the relationship between **25:27a** and **25:27b**. The text is literally rendered, "the searching for one's honor [is] honor." The "nor" in **25:27b** is implied by the parallel "not" in **25:27a**. Perhaps what is dishonorable is a selfish obsession to obtain top honors based upon achievements or status that lie beyond one's capabilities.[5] Thus, eating too much raw honey and seeking too much honor for ourselves are analogous examples of good things that overindulgence turns into bad results.

2. Drunkenness and Gluttony Breed Poverty.

23:19–21 "Listen, my son, and be wise, and keep your heart on the right path. Do not join those who drink too much wine or gorge themselves on meat, for drunkards and gluttons become poor, and drowsiness clothes them in rags."

The reason for this exhortation to avoid the similar sins of drunkenness and gluttony (**23:20**) is given in **23:21**. A ravenous appetite for both food and drink is not only expensive, but also makes a man sleepy, lazy, and deprives him of self-control, sound judgment, motivation, and effective functioning. His

---

[5] See the technical and suggestive article by Raymond C. Van Leeuwen, "Proverbs 25:27 Once Again," *Vetus Testamentum* 36, 1 (New York: E. J. Brill, Inc., 1986): 105–14.

disinclination and even inability to work leave him vulnerable to declining income, bankruptcy, and poverty. His constant "drowsiness" refers here to the excessive slumber associated with laziness and inactivity (6:10; 24:33). The word rendered "rags" is derived from a verb that means to "tear in pieces." Torn clothes or rags are an obvious sign of poverty.

3. Drinking and Forgetting Go Together.

31:4–7 " 'It is not for kings, O Lemuel—not for kings to drink wine, not for rulers to crave beer, lest they drink and forget what the law decrees, and deprive all the oppressed of their rights. Give beer to those who are perishing, wine to those who are in anguish; let them drink and forget their poverty and remember their misery no more.' "

Two terms designating alcoholic beverages are mentioned in 31:4—"wine" and "beer." With water availability and quality erratic and grape vines abundant, wine[6] was a standard beverage in ancient Israel. Its abundance was a symbol of affluence (1 Chron. 12:40; Ezek. 27:18) and a source of pleasure (Ps. 104:15). Since distillation processes were not developed until the medieval period, all wine in ancient times was light wine, that is, not fortified with extra alcohol. With approximately 7–10% alcohol, ancient wine was still an intoxicating drink. That is why the prophets emphatically condemned overindulgence (e.g., Isa. 28:7–8).

The word rendered "beer" means "strong drink." A cognate verb and noun picture being drunk. It is a general term for any alcoholic beverage prepared from grain or fruit. The "beer," or the better rendering, "strong drink," was more potent than wine in ancient times. The law of Moses allowed it for the people (Deut. 14:26), but prohibited priests from drinking it when officiating in the tabernacle (Lev. 10:9). A. Cohen observes the interesting point that the Hebrew word for "beer" or "strong drink," *shekar*, developed through a cognate Arabic word to become "sugar" in English.[7] In view of the capability of sugar to

---

[6] See the informative discussion by R. Laird Harris, "(*yayin*) wine," TWOT I: 375–76.

[7] A. Cohen, *Proverbs* (New York: Soncino Press, 1952), 131.

be addictive and to make people high, this is an intriguing and perhaps significant linguistic development.

The reason why kings are not to drink "wine" and "beer" (**31:4**) is stated in **31:5**. Excessive drinking causes a man to forget his circumstances, responsibilities, and moral standards. Any leader with important responsibilities should avoid alcoholic beverages that cloud his thinking and relax his sense of responsibility. An intoxicated king may ignore the national laws and oppress the poor in court by miscarriages of justice. He will lose the respect of his subjects as a result of reduced competence and inappropriate behavior.

The closest approach to a positive contribution of strong drink is its ability to distract people who are hopelessly entangled and trapped by poverty, pain, misery, impending death, or intense physical, mental, or emotional distress (**31:6–7**). The anesthetic effect of intoxication gives such people temporary relief by enabling them to forget their misery and anguish, but drinking contributes nothing toward the solution of their problems. It only makes them more incapable of handling their problems for a short time.

4. The Dangers of Drinking Are Great.

20:1 "Wine is a mocker and beer a brawler; whoever is led astray by them is not wise."

23:29–35 "Who has woe? Who has sorrow? Who has strife? Who has complaints? Who has needless bruises? Who has bloodshot eyes? Those who linger over wine, who go to sample bowls of mixed wine. Do not gaze at wine when it is red, when it sparkles in the cup, when it goes down smoothly! In the end it bites like a snake and poisons like a viper. Your eyes will see strange sights and your mind imagine confusing things. You will be like one sleeping on the high seas, lying on top of the rigging. 'They hit me,' you will say, 'but I'm not hurt! They beat me, but I don't feel it! When will I wake up so I can find another drink?'"

Intoxication weakens self-control and releases insolent words, aggressiveness, and inclinations to fight that provoke hostilities and conflicts. These effects are so familiar that "wine" and "beer" (see the comments about 31:4) are personified as possessing them (**20:1**). It is clearly foolish and harmful to permit ourselves to be captivated by these "spirits." Why should we suffer their unnecessary, tragic, and destructive consequences?

Six rhetorical questions (**23:29**) vividly portray some unpleasant consequences of excessive drinking. These include despair, misery, quarrels, complaints, and unnecessary bruises. The "bloodshot eyes" were either red after extended drinking or dull from an alcoholic stupor. These questions would paint a comical picture if it were not so tragic. Those who display these qualities spend much time drinking wine and searching diligently for new and fresh tastes from various combinations of mixed drinks (**23:30**).

In **23:31**, there is a warning against a fascinated gaze upon the enticing red color of the sparkling wine (see 31:4) when it goes down smoothly, since these are danger signals. In spite of its initial impression, its impact is like being bitten by a poisonous snake (**23:32**).

The vivid imagery in **23:33–35** is designed to make the reader feel as if he were experiencing the strange effects of being drunk. The text (**23:33**) pictures hallucinations induced by the effects of being intoxicated.

In **23:34**, the imagery pictures the unsettling instability of being seasick, a condition aggravated by the tossing and rolling of a ship on the sea. The details of the imagery are obscure. "Lying on top of the rigging" does not make sense. Does it picture a drunkard's imaginings? Or, is it a deliberately absurd image of a drunkard's distorted perspective presented as a comical insult? Or, does it picture a drunkard's feeling so unstable that it seems as if he is being tossed around as wildly as if he were on top of a ship's rigging during a storm? To his disoriented perspective, it probably does seem as if the ground were moving up and down like a ship on the waves of a stormy sea.

The intoxicated man feels no pain from beatings (**23:35**). In his confusion he wonders vaguely when he will be awake. Even after all the misery induced by his overindulgence, his only goal is to search diligently for more drinks, to recycle the whole wretched process.

Although the Book of Proverbs contains no explicit prohibition against drinking, it vividly pictures the stupidity and tragedy of overindulgence, including its dangers, sickening effects, and distortion of the senses. Such clear warnings are virtually equivalent to a prohibition. No one who is wise will get drunk. The one who refuses the first drink is in no danger of drinking too much.

G. Buying

20:14 " 'It's no good, it's no good!' says the buyer; then off he goes and boasts about his purchase."

This is a general observation about standard bartering procedure. The purpose of saying "It's no good!" is to deprecate the merchandise in an obvious effort to lower the price. After the purchase, the buyer brags about his good deal, especially after persuading the merchant to substantially lower his price. The wise observer wryly notes this humorous change in the buyer's attitude without any moral evaluation. He does not take seriously anything said during bartering.

H. Putting Up Security for Another

1. Its Undesirable Implications

11:15 "He who puts up security for another will surely suffer, but whoever refuses to strike hands in pledge is safe."

17:18 "A man lacking in judgment strikes hands in pledge and puts up security for his neighbor."

20:16 "Take the garment of one who puts up security for a stranger; hold it in pledge if he does it for a wayward woman."

27:13 "Take the garment of one who puts up security for a stranger; hold it in pledge if he does it for a wayward woman."

"To put up security for another" (**11:15; 17:18; 20:16; 27:13**) is to be a "pledge" or "surety" to guarantee his loan. "Striking hands in pledge" (**11:15; 17:18**), similar in significance to a modern handshake, and "taking a garment in pledge" (**20:16; 27:13**) were ways of validating the transaction as part of the legal procedure. The expressions were thus equivalent to the transaction itself.

If the borrower should default, the man who guaranteed the

loan would be responsible to assume its obligations. If he should lack the financial resources to cover it, he could be ruined. For he would be required to pay it off when due, even if it should cost him all of his financial resources and selling himself into slavery to do it. That is why this transaction was so risky. For in ancient times there was no systematic way to investigate thoroughly a person's credit, especially a stranger.

The wise teacher warns against guaranteeing another's loan. To do it for a neighbor (**17:18**) is foolish, showing a lack of judgment (see "heart" in 4:23). For a man to do it for a stranger (note the Hebrew word for "stranger" was used in **11:15; 20:16; 27:13**) or a wayward woman (**20:16; 27:13**; see the comment about 2:16) was considered such incredibly stupid business judgment that the businessman was then considered a very poor risk. In modern terms, he thereby ruins his credit rating. The only safe policy is to avoid such transactions. Virtually identical are **20:16** and **27:13**.

2. *Exhortations to Avoid or to Escape from Putting Up Security for Another*

6:1–5 "My son, if you have put up security for your neighbor, if you have struck hands in pledge for another, if you have been trapped by what you said, ensnared by the words of your mouth, then do this, my son, to free yourself, since you have fallen into your neighbor's hands: Go and humble yourself; press your plea with your neighbor! Allow no sleep to your eyes, no slumber to your eyelids. Free yourself, like a gazelle from the hand of the hunter, like a bird from the snare of the fowler."

22:26–27 "Do not be a man who strikes hands in pledge or puts up security for debts; if you lack the means to pay, your very bed will be snatched from under you."

In both passages for "strike hands in pledge" and "put up security for," see the comments about 11:15. Both passages stress the urgency of avoiding any transaction involving your providing security for another's debt. If the borrower defaults and the man who is surety cannot pay it off, the lender will aggressively go after all of the latter's material possessions, including his home and land, in an effort to retrieve his investment. Snatching his bed from under him (**22:27**) emphasizes his merciless policy of sparing nothing. In addition to that, he will sell the man into slavery to reduce the debt further.

If a man has foolishly agreed to be surety for another (**6:1**), he has fallen into a dangerous trap (**6:2**) from which he should let nothing prevent his extricating himself (**6:3–5**). His financial future is controlled by his unpredictable neighbor (**6:3**). He is to humble himself and press, that is, aggressively persuade his neighbor to release him from his pledge (**6:3**). The matter was so urgent that not even sleep was to deter his unrelenting desperate effort to cancel the contract (**6:4**). The imagery of trapping animals (**6:5**) stresses the danger of the arrangement and makes clear the urgency of escaping from this ominous threat.

I. For Further Study

1. What is wrong with being extremely lazy? What are its consequences? How do you overcome your lazy inclinations?

2. What are the benefits of working hard and intelligently when the work needs to be done? How do you motivate yourself to do that?

3. What attitude should you have toward the poor? Why? What should you endeavor to do for them? To what extent? How many different ways can you effectively encourage and help them?

4. What attitude should you have toward material wealth? Why? What are its benefits? What are its dangers? What implications does it have for service?

5. Why is it desirable to be generous? What are its benefits? How do you develop generosity?

6. Why is it desirable to be honest? What are its benefits? How do you develop honesty?

7. What is wrong with gluttony? How is it similar to drunkenness? What damage does it do? How do you overcome it? Why are warnings against it so rarely heard?

8. What is your attitude toward alcoholic beverages? Why? What damages result from excessive drinking and drunkenness? How do you overcome such tendencies? What should the Christian's policy be with regard to drinking and drunkenness? Why?

Subject Index

Abbreviations, 15
Acrostic, 14
Administration, 634, 144, 150–151, 210–213
Adulteress, 154–165, 227–228
Advice, 38, 88, 92, 111
Arrogance. See Pride
Attitude, 180–181
Authorship, 8–9

Bartering, 227
Boasting, 193–194
Bribes, 130, 172, 214, 219–220, 222

Cheerfulness, 182
Children, 173–175
Command, 40
Conversation, 115, 182–201

Death, 58, 75, 100, 142–145
Deceit, 43–44, 192–193, 221
Discernment. See Understanding
Discipline, 38–39, 70, 100, 118–119, 174–175
Discouragement, 179–182
Discretion, 37–38
Dishonesty, 73, 221–222
Drunkenness, 223–227

Encouragement, 179–182
Envy, 71, 181

Evil, 47–48

Family, 171–175
Fear of the Lord, 51–59
Foolish, 40–42, 52, 72, 100–121, 184–187
Friend, 92, 175–177

Generosity, 178, 219–221
Gluttony, 88–89, 121, 223–224
God, 60–81
Good, 46
Gossip, 198–199
Greed, 71, 129, 132–133, 172

Hatred, 177
Heart. See Mind
Honesty, 73, 221–223
Hope, 56, 142
Humility, 55–56, 111–113
Husband, 167, 169–170, 171–172

Inconsiderate, 193
Integrity, 45

Justice, 44–45, 130–131, 150–151, 212, 215–216

Kindness, 79, 178–179
Knowledge, 36–37

Lazy. See Sluggard
Life, 56, 58, 95, 97–98
Lots, 61–62, 201

Love, 172–173, 177
Lying, 191, 194–198

Mind, 96–98
Mocker, 42, 103, 104, 107, 118–119

Neighbor, 176–177, 178
Numerical Sayings, 13

Oppressed, 182

Parallelism, 11–13
  Antithetic, 12
  Basic qualities, 11–12
  Emblematic, 13
  Step, 12–13
  Synonymous, 12
  Synthetic, 12
Parents, 98, 108, 143
Perverse, 49–50, 141
Poor, 58, 78–80, 129, 136–137, 151, 214–217
Pride, 111–113, 133
Prosperity, 67, 72–73, 80–81, 95
Proverb, 11
Prudence, 38, 111, 114
Putting up security for another, 227–229

Quarrelsome, 114, 199–201

Rebuke, 39
Redeemer, 79–80
Revenge, 77–78, 196–197
Riddle, 11
Rich, 78–80, 136–137, 171–172, 205–207, 214–219
Righteous
  Evaluation of, 135–138
  God's attitude toward, 68–69, 72
  Meaning and usage, 44
  Qualities of, 89–90, 123–135, 186–187, 189, 190

  Results of being, 138–152
Security, 57–58, 68–69, 141–142
Self-control, 88–89, 90, 113–115
Simple, 42
Sin, 48–49, 152
Slander, See Gossip
Sluggard, 43, 110, 123–124, 132, 203–207
Stewardship, 209–210
Stinginess, 215, 217, 221

Teaching, 39–40
Testimony. See Witness
Transgression, 49
Truth, 73, 195–196, 197

Understanding, 35–36
Unfriendliness, 175–176
Upright, 145–146

Vengeance. See Revenge

Wealth, 58–59, 80–81, 140, 147–148, 210, 213–219
Weights, 73
Wicked, 69, 46–47, 70–73, 123–152
Wife, 62–63, 162–164, 167–171
Wisdom
  Ancient, 9–10
  Benefits of, 57–59, 95–98, 116–121
  Meanings and usage, 34–35
  Obtaining, 57, 66–68, 83–87
  Qualities of, 52–53, 87–95, 108–116, 184–187
  Results of rejecting, 53–54, 67, 98–100
Witness (in court), 130–131, 196–198
Word of God, 63–64
Work, 203, 205–210

Scripture Index

1:1–5 85–86	4:7 94	9:1–6 84
1:6 ....10–11, 85–86	4:8–13 92–93	9:7–9 ......117, 118, 119
1:7 51–52	4:14–17 ....125, 126	
1:8–9 92	4:18–19 126	9:10–11 55
1:10–19 128–29	4:20–23 96–97	9:12 116
1:20–21 84	4:24 186	9:13–18 161
1:22–28 99–100	4:25–27 125	10:1 121
1:29–31 54	5:1–2 88	10:2 140
1:32–33 100	5:3–6 155–156	10:3 69
2:1–5 57	5:7–20 75	10:4 206
2:6–8 66	5:21 75	10:5 204
2:9–15 91	5:22–23 149	10:6–7 146–147
2:16–19 155	6:1–5 228–229	10:8 115
2:20–22 89–90	6:6–8 208	10:9 141
3:1–2 95	6:9–11 203–204	10:10 108
3:3–4 66–67	6:12–15 141	10:11 145
3:5–6 69	6:16–19 74	10:12 177
3:7–8 55	6:20–23 96–97	10:13 116
3:9–10 80–81	6:24–29 156–157	10:14 115
3:11–12 70	6:30–35 157–158	10:15 216–217
3:13–18 94–95	7:1–4 87	10:16 145
3:19–20 65	7:5–18 159	10:17 118
3:21–24 92–93	7:19–27 160	10:18 105
3:25–26 ..68–69, 93	8:1–7 84	10:19 184
3:27–28 178	8:8–9 90	10:20 186–187
3:29–30 196	8:10–11 94	10:21 115
3:31–32 ....71, 72	8:12–13 53	10:22 81
3:33–35 72	8:14–21 94–95	10:23 109
4:1–4 86	8:22–31 65	10:24 146
4:5 ....85, 86	8:32–34 87	10:25 ....141, 142
4:6 91	8:35–36 67	10:26 207

233

10:27 55	12:13 ....189, 190	14:6 109
10:28 149	12:14 188	14:7 101
10:29 68–69	12:15 111	14:8 111
10:30 ....141, 142	12:16 114	14:9 ....113, 115
10:31 ....185, 186	12:17 197	14:10 179
10:32 186	12:18 191	14:11 ....141, 142
11:1 73	12:19 ....195, 196	14:12 143–144
11:2 ....112, 113	12:20 149	14:13 179
11:3 124	12:21 138–139	14:14 147
11:4 140	12:22 73	14:15 111
11:5 124–125	12:23 ....110, 111	14:16 52
11:6 139–140	12:24 206	14:17 103
11:7 142	12:25 181	14:18 ....110, 111
11:8 138–139	12:26 133	14:19 151
11:9 189	12:27 206–207	14:20 214
11:10 137	12:28 145	14:21 179
11:11 189	13:1 ....118, 119	14:22 ....145, 146
11:12 184	13:2 188	14:23 206
11:13 198–199	13:3 190	14:24 120
11:14 88	13:4 206	14:25 197
11:15 227–228	13:5 134	14:26 57–58
11:16 179	13:6 125	14:27 58
11:17 179	13:6 125	14:28 210–211
11:18 147	13:7 219	14:29 114
11:19 145	13:8 219	14:30 180–181
11:20 ....71, 72	13:9 126	14:31 79
11:21 138	13:10 111	14:32 ....141, 142
11:22 164–165	13:11 221–222	14:33 109
11:24–26 ...220–221	13:12 181	14:34 ....150, 151
11:27 ....145, 146	13:13 ....118, 119	14:35 114
11:28 148	13:14 97	15:1 187
11:29 172	13:15 116	15:2 ....185, 186
11:30 ....97, 98	13:16 ....110, 111	15:3 75
11:31 147	13:17 138–139	15:4 191
12:1 118	13:18 ....118, 119	15:5 118
12:2 72	13:19 102–103	15:6 148
12:3 ....141, 142	13:20 116	15:7 ....185, 186
12:4 ....167, 168	13:21–22 148	15:8–9 ....71, 72
12:5 126	13:23 215	15:10 100
12:6 ....189, 190	13:24 ....174, 175	15:11 75
12:7 141	13:25 148	15:12 119
12:8 119–120	14:1 115	15:13 180
12:9 219	14:2 52	15:14 110
12:10 132	14:3 190	15:15 182
12:11 205–206	14:4 209	15:16 58
12:12 148	14:5 197	15:17 172–173

Scripture Index

15:18 199–200	16:31 144	18:16 ....219, 220
15:19 124	16:32 90	18:17 130
15:20 121	16:33 61–62	18:18 201
15:21 ....110, 111	17:1 172–173	18:19 200–201
15:22 88	17:2 172	18:20 188
15:23 187	17:3 75	18:21 188
15:24 97	17:4 195	18:22 62–63
15:25 ....79, 80	17:5 79	18:23 215
15:26 ....71, 72	17:6 175	18:24 176
15:27 172	17:7 104–105	19:1 136–137
15:28 ....185, 186	17:8 222	19:2 100–101
15:29 72	17:9 177	19:3 67
15:30 182	17:10 ....118, 119	19:4 214
15:31 88	17:11 125	19:5 198
15:32 118	17:12 103	19:6 214
15:33 55–56	17:13 ....145, 146	19:7 214
16:1 61	17:14 200	19:8 95–96
16:2 75–76	17:15 74	19:9 198
16:3 68	17:16 106	19:10 106
16:4 61	17:17 176	19:11 89
16:5 76–77	17:18 227–228	19:12 213
16:6 53	17:19 200	19:13 108,
16:7 69	17:20 195	166–167
16:8 136	17:21 108	19:14 62–63
16:9 61	17:22 180–181	19:15 204
16:10 212	17:23 130	19:16 ....118, 119
16:11 73	17:24 109	19:17 79
16:12 ....150, 151	17:25 108	19:18 ....174, 175
16:13 222	17:26 131	19:19 201
16:14 89	17:27 184	19:20 86
16:15 212–213	17:28 184–185	19:21 61
16:16 94	18:1 175–176	19:22 195
16:17 125	18:2 101	19:23 56
16:18 ....112, 113	18:3 134	19:24 205
16:19 136	18:4 183–184	19:25 ....118, 119
16:20 67	18:5 131	19:26 134
16:21 87	18:6 190	19:27 99
16:22 116	18:7 189	19:28 130–131
16:23 186	18:8 198	19:29 107
16:24 191	18:9 207	20:1 225
16:25 143–144	18:10 68–69	20:2 213
16:26 208–209	18:11 216–217	20:3 114
16:27 128	18:12 112–113	20:4 203–204
16:28 199	18:13 185	20:5 183–184
16:29 128	18:14 180–181	20:6 176
16:30 128	18:15 85	20:7 125

20:8 212	21:24 104	24:1–2 139
20:9 152	21:25–26 132	24:3–4 84–85
20:10 73	21:27 138	24:5 90
20:11 135–136	21:28 198	24:6 88
20:12 62	21:29 133	24:7 109
20:13 203–204	21:30 62	24:8–9 103
20:14 227	21:31 62	24:10 207
20:15 94	22:1 223	24:11–12 76
20:16 227–228	22:2 78	24:13–14 92
20:17 221	22:3 116	24:15–16 135
20:18 88	22:4 55–56	24:17–18 77
20:19 198	22:5 138–139	24:19–20 142
20:20 143	22:6 173–174	24:21–22 54
20:21 218	22:7 216	24:23–26 ... 131–132
20:22 77	22:8 139	24:27 209
20:23 73	22:9 220	24:28–29 ... 196–197
20:24 161	22:10 104	24:30–34 ... 204–205
20:25 190	22:11 187	25:1 8
20:26 212	22:12 72	25:2 63
20:27 76	22:13 205	25:3 221
20:28 151	22:14 165	25:4–5 ...... 150, 151
20:29 173	22:15 174	25:6–7 ...... 112, 113
20:30 107	22:16 218	25:8–10 197
21:1 61	22:17–21 67–68	25:11 187
21:2 76	22:22–23 79–80	25:12 88
21:3 74–75	22:24–25 201	25:13 182
21:4 133	22:26–27 ... 228–229	25:14 193
21:5 170	22:28 79	25:15 187–188
21:6 195	22:29 210	25:16 223
21:7 129	23:1–3 89	25:17 178
21:8 124	23:4–5 217–218	25:18 196
21:9 166–167	23:6–8 221	25:19 124
21:10 125	23:9 .... 101, 102	25:20 193
21:11 .... 117, 119	23:10–11 79	25:21–22 77–78
21:12 77	23:12 87	25:23 192
21:13 215	23:13–14 174	25:24 166–167
21:14 222	23:15–16 98	25:25 182
21:15 149	23:17–18 56	25:26 136
21:16 100	23:19 87	25:27 223
21:17 218	23:20–21 ... 223–224	25:28 89
21:18 151	23:22 86	26:1 106
21:19 166–167	23:23 85	26:2 190
21:20 120	23:24–25 98	26:3 107
21:21 145	23:26 87	26:4–5 101–102
21:22 90	23:27–28 165	26:6 105
21:23 190	23:29–35 227	26:7–9 106–107

26:10 105–106	28:1 135	29:11 114
26:11 100	28:2 211	29:12 213
26:12 105	28:3 213	29:13 78
26:13 205	28:4 135	29:14 151
26:14 204	28:5 ....71, 72	29:15 ....174, 175
26:15 205	28:6 136–137	29:16 151
26:16 110	28:7 121	29:17 174
26:17 200	28:8 218	29:18 133–134
26:18–19 196	28:9 138	29:19 175
26:20 199	28:10 148	29:20 185
26:21 199	28:11 216	29:21 175
26:22 198	28:12 137	29:22 199
26:23–26 ...192–193	28:13 152	29:23 ....112, 113
26:27 149	28:14 54	29:24 150
26:28 194	28:15–16 144	29:25 69–70
27:1 193–194	28:17 150	29:26 77
27:2 194	28:18 141	29:27 134
27:3 103–104	28:19 205–206	30:1 9
27:4 201	28:20 146–147	30:2–6 63–64
27:5 177	28:21 131	30:7–9 81
27:6 176	28:22 217	30:10 199
27:7 213–214	28:23 194	30:11–14 ...127–128
27:8 171	28:24 143	30:15–16 ...132–133
27:9 92	28:25 ......71, 72–73	30:17 143
27:10 176	28:26 110	30:18–19 171
27:11 98	28:27 215	30:20 165
27:12 116	28:28 137	30:21–23 166
27:13 227–228	29:1 ....118, 119	30:24–28 208
27:14 193	29:2 137	30:29–31 211
27:15–16 ...166–167	29:3 ....121, 165	30:32–33 104
27:17 178	29:4 ....150, 151	31:1 9
27:18 210	29:5 194	31:2–3 164
27:19 180	29:6 149	31:4–7 224–225
27:20 132	29:7 ....129, 130	31:8–9 215–216
27:21 222–223	29:8 114	31:10–31 ...169–171
27:22 107–108	29:9 113	
27:23–27 ...209–210	29:10 134–135	

www.ingramcontent.com/pod-product-compliance
Lightning Source LLC
Chambersburg PA
CBHW070312230426
43663CB00011B/2095